EXPLOSION

THE OUTBREAK OF WORLD WAR I

FRANK B. WHELAN III

Copyright © 2012 by Frank B. Whelan III

ISBN 978-0-7414-7949-5 Paperback
ISBN 978-0-7414-7950-1 eBook
Library of Congress Control Number: 2012948221

Printed in the United States of America

Published November 2012

INFINITY PUBLISHING

Toll-free (877) BUY BOOK
Local Phone (610) 941-9999
Fax (610) 941-9959
Info@buybooksontheweb.com
www.buybooksontheweb.com

TABLE OF CONTENTS

PREFACE

KEY FIGURES IN THE STORY OF JULY 1914

XII. NIGHTMARE

PREFACE

Over nine million soldiers died in World War I. It seemed as though everybody in the combatant countries knew someone whose father, son, brother, uncle, nephew, cousin, or friend had been killed or wounded. Other than the one that followed a quarter-century later, it was history's deadliest war.

Aside from the horrible human toll, the Great War reshaped the world map forever by destroying four empires. It helped facilitate the rise of the communists, whose conflict with the West was the defining international event between 1946 and 1989. And the Ottoman Empire's collapse created, to some degree, a power vacuum in the Middle East that helped lead to the Arab-Israeli struggle that still exists today.

This book is the first in a four-part series designed to give the general reader a summary of the Great War. While many histories of the war focus on the Western Front, this series will address the conflict on a global scale. The Eastern, Italian, Balkan, and Middle Eastern theaters will therefore be covered at some length. Also, much greater emphasis will be placed on the war's strategic and diplomatic aspects than on individual battles and what life was like for soldiers in the trenches. Most people already know that the conditions the troops faced were less than pleasant.

The present volume covers the period from the late 1800s to the outbreak of hostilities in early August 1914. The first chapter addresses Germany's growing pre-war isolation, the second chapter deals with Austria-Hungary's internal and external difficulties, and the remaining chapters concentrate on the five weeks following Archduke Franz Ferdinand's assassination on June 28, 1914.

I hope this book and series helps readers obtain a better understanding of, appreciation for, and interest in this terrible but fascinating world event. Such compensation would be much greater than any amount of effort I could have put into this endeavor.

Concerning the sources used:

1. In the footnotes, "B.D." and "G.D." stand for "British Document" and "German Document," respectively. The British documents are from Volume XI of *British Documents on the Origins of the War*; the German documents are from *Outbreak of the World War: German Documents Collected by Karl Kautsky.*

2. Quotations in the British Blue Book, French Yellow Book, Russian Orange Book, Serbian Blue Book, German White Book, and Austro-Hungarian Red Book are from *Collected Diplomatic Documents Relating to the Outbreak of the European War* (published by the British government) and the Carnegie Endowment for International Peace's *Diplomatic Documents Relating to the Outbreak of the European War*. These six books are referenced in the footnotes as, respectively, "B.B.B.", "F.Y.B.", "R.O.B.", "S.B.B.", "G.W.B.", and "A.R.B.", and the specific volume of the Austro-Hungarian Red Book is noted (e.g., "A.R.B. II"). The collection from which the quote is taken is identified as "C.D.D." (the British government version) or "D.D." (the Carnegie version).

Unless indicated otherwise, all parentheses in the quotations in this book are my own and were not part of the original quote.

I must express my heartfelt thanks to my wonderful and beautiful wife, Christy, for her support and patience during the years I spent writing this book. This work is dedicated to her.

KEY FIGURES IN THE STORY OF JULY 1914

<u>Germany</u>

Wilhelm II	Kaiser
Theobald von Bethmann-Hollweg	Chancellor
Gottlieb von Jagow	Secretary of State for Foreign Affairs
Arthur Zimmermann	Undersecretary of State for Foreign Affairs
Friedrich von Pourtales	Ambassador to Russia
Karl Max Lichnowsky	Ambassador to England
Heinrich Leopold von Tschirschky und Bogendorff	Ambassador to Austria-Hungary
Wilhelm von Schoen	Ambassador to France
Hans von Flotow	Ambassador to Italy
General Helmuth von Moltke	Chief of the General Staff
General Erich von Falkenhayn	Prussian Minister of War
Admiral Alfred von Tirpitz	State Secretary of the Navy

<u>Austria-Hungary</u>

Franz Josef I	Emperor of Austria and King of Hungary
Leopold von Berchtold	Foreign Minister
Stephen Tisza	Prime Minister of Hungary
Alexander von Krobatin	Minister of War
Ladislaus Szogyeny	Ambassador to Germany
Friedrich Szapary	Ambassador to Russia
Albert von Mensdorff-Pouilly-Dietrichstein	Ambassador to England
Kajetan Merey von Kapos-Mere	Ambassador to Italy
Wladimar Giesl von Gieslingen	Ambassador to Serbia
General Franz Conrad von Hotzendorf	Chief of the General Staff

England

George V	King
Herbert Asquith	Prime Minister
Edward Grey	Foreign Secretary
Arthur Nicolson	Undersecretary of State for Foreign Affairs
Eyre Crowe	Assistant Undersecretary of State for Foreign Affairs
Maurice de Bunsen	Ambassador to Austria-Hungary
Edward Goschen	Ambassador to Germany
George Buchanan	Ambassador to Russia
Francis Bertie	Ambassador to France
Rennell Rodd	Ambassador to Italy
Horace Rumbold	*Charge d'Affaires* at Berlin
Dayrell Crackanthorpe	*Charge d'Affaires* at Belgrade

Russia

Nicholas II	Tsar
Sergei Sazonov	Foreign Minister
Nikolai Schebeko	Ambassador to Austria-Hungary
Sergei Sverbeyev	Ambassador to Germany
Alexander Izvolsky	Ambassador to France
Alexander Benckendorff	Ambassador to England
General Nicholas Janushkevich	Chief of the General Staff
Adjutant-General Vladimir Sukhomlinov	Minister of War

France

Raymond Poincare	President
Rene Viviani	Prime Minister
Jean-Baptiste Bienvenu-Martin	Acting Foreign Minister
Maurice Paleologue	Ambassador to Russia
Jules Cambon	Ambassador to Germany
Paul Cambon	Ambassador to England

Italy

Marquis Antonio di San Giuliano	Foreign Minister
Duke of Avarna	Ambassador to Austria-Hungary

"The interests of our own existence demanded the unmutilated survival of Austria."

Former German Chancellor Theobald
von Bethmann-Hollweg in 1920

I

ISOLATION

A. A New European Powerhouse

During the mid-to-late 1800s, Britain, France, Russia, Prussia, Italy, Austria (the Habsburg Empire, or Austria-Hungary), and Turkey (the Ottoman Empire) competed for power and influence in Europe and, in some cases, overseas. This naturally caused friction between them. The tension increased when Prussia unified with other German states and principalities to create the new German Empire (Germany). One of the wars that facilitated this unification was the Franco-Prussian War of 1870-71, in which Prussia beat France badly and captured her provinces of Alsace and Lorraine. Within France, the humiliating defeat fostered a deep hatred of Germany and a longing for both revenge and the two lost territories. The attitude of many Frenchmen towards the disaster was, "Never speak of it; think of it always." [1]

Europe looked warily at this powerful new nation. But German Chancellor Otto von Bismarck was not looking to dominate the continent by force. Bismarck recognized that Germany's geographic position left her vulnerable to assault from the east, south, and west; indeed, he suspected that the embittered French might attempt to attack Germany to retake Alsace and Lorraine. [2] He knew that Germany needed secure borders so she could focus on economic and industrial growth. The best way to

---

[1] Barbara Tuchman, *The Guns of August* (1962; reprint, New York: Ballantine Books, 1994), 29.
[2] Sidney Fay, *The Origins of the World War*, 2 vols., 2nd ed. (New York: The Free Press, 1966), 1:53.

achieve this, he reasoned, was to establish close ties with one or more European Great Powers. Treaties, rather than wars of conquest, would be used to safeguard Germany.

So Bismarck went to work. In 1873, the so-called League of the Three Emperors - consisting of Germany, Austria, and Russia - came into being. [3] More an informal understanding than an iron-clad pact, the three nations agreed to work together to preserve the monarchial principle and to combat the rising influence of socialism. [4] Souring German-Russian relations effectively ended the League in 1878, but Bismarck quickly bolstered Berlin's position by forging a formal alliance with Austria in 1879. [5] He essentially compensated for the departure of one League member by tightening Germany's bonds with the other. The Austro-German pact (the "Central Powers") was buttressed in 1882 when Italy joined it to form the Triple Alliance; the following year, Romania secretly allied herself with Berlin and Vienna. [6]

The German-Russian relationship having improved, the Three Emperors' League was reborn in 1881. [7] Six years later it again collapsed, this time due largely to Austro-Russian tensions. [8] Similar to what he did in 1879, Bismarck shored up Germany's eastern flank. He signed a "Reinsurance Treaty" with Russia in 1887 whereby Berlin and St. Petersburg agreed to remain neutral if the other fought another Great Power. [9] While it did not apply if Germany attacked France or Russia attacked Austria, the treaty – like the Leagues – gave the Germans some protection in the East. [10] Meanwhile, though Britain had no major allies, she had closer relations with Berlin than with Paris and St. Petersburg; her

---

[3] Ibid., 1:57.
[4] Ibid., 1:56; Laurence Lafore, *The Long Fuse: An Interpretation of the Origins of World War I* (Philadelphia: J.B. Lippincott Company, 1965), 87.
[5] Fay, *Origins*, 1:67-68.
[6] Historically, the term "Central Powers" refers to the pact between Germany, Austria, and their allies during the Great War. In this book, it will also refer to the *pre-war* Berlin-Vienna alliance.
[7] Fay, *Origins*, 1:74-76.
[8] Ibid., 1:77.
[9] Ibid., 1:78.
[10] Ibid.

centuries-old rivalry with France still simmered, and she was suspicious of Russia's intentions in Asia. [11]

By the late 1880s, Germany's diplomatic position was impressive. She was allied with two Great Powers (Austria and Italy) and on decent terms with two others (Russia and Britain). Conversely, her foremost adversary, France, was diplomatically isolated with no Great Power allies; as such, the threat she posed to Germany was reduced. Bismarck's diplomacy in the two decades following the Franco-Prussian War had given Germany the security she needed.

Times were good.

B. Wilhelm Arrives, Bismarck Exits, and Germany's Diplomatic Situation Deteriorates

In 1888, Wilhelm II became Germany's Kaiser (emperor) after the death of his father, Frederick III. Wilhelm was by no means inherently evil or malicious - certainly not the monster that Germany's wartime enemies later portrayed him as. He was not unintelligent and was very capable of charming behavior. Nevertheless, he was arrogant and erratic and often displayed limited skill in dealing with other countries. He also had a penchant for making outrageous and irresponsible statements. Grand Duke Nicholas Nikolaevich of Russia, an uncle of Tsar Nicholas II, furnished his opinion of Wilhelm years later to France's ambassador to Russia, Maurice Paleologue:

> What a miserable figure to cut! What a low comedian! I've always said so; he's nothing but a pompous puppet. And even more of a coward than a braggart!..................If he hadn't been born on the steps of a throne, he'd have had no rival as the clown at a fair! [12]

Frederick III himself wrote in 1886: "In view of the immaturity and inexperience of my eldest son, as shown by his tendency to

---

[11] Winston Churchill, *The World Crisis: 1911-1918* (1931; reprint, New York: Free Press, 2005), 7, 9.
[12] Quoted in Maurice Paleologue, *An Ambassador's Memoirs: 1914-1917* (1923; reprint, London: Hutchinson & Co., 1973), 587.

overestimate himself, I cannot but call it dangerous to introduce him this early to foreign policy questions." [13]

Frederick's concerns proved warranted. One of his son's first significant acts as Kaiser was to effectively remove Bismarck as chancellor in 1890, in part because Wilhelm resented Bismarck's power and wanted to exercise more control over German foreign policy. [14] Another ill-advised move was Wilhelm's refusal that same year to renew the Reinsurance Treaty with Russia. He and his advisors concluded that maintaining the treaty would be incompatible with Berlin's alliance obligations towards Austria. [15] Wilhelm still desired good relations with Russia and, in fairness, seemed inclined to renew the treaty before being convinced otherwise. [16] But it appeared that he had sided with Austria and thrown the far more powerful (and for Germany, the far more dangerous) Tsarist Empire overboard.

Now isolated, Russia signed several accords with France, culminating in an alliance between them in 1894 whereby each agreed to lend support if the other were attacked by Germany. [17] Bismarck had long feared a Franco-Russian pact and strove mightily to prevent it. Yet it was now a reality, and he blasted Berlin for its failure to renew the Reinsurance Treaty, alleging that this led to the Paris-St. Petersburg alliance. [18] There were, in fact, additional reasons for the 1894 pact, such as the two countries' close financial ties. [19] Still, Russia's diplomatic seclusion after Berlin's 1890 decision was a big factor in her gravitation towards France.

Thanks largely to her dubious statesmanship, Germany - within a five-year period - went from a powerful diplomatic and strategic position to the prospect of a two-front war with France and Russia. It represented a partial unraveling of Bismarck's wise strategy of ensuring Germany's safety through treaties. Though her alliances with Austria and Italy - and her solid relationship

---

[13] Quoted in Erich Eyck, *Bismarck and the German Empire* (1950; reprint, New York: W.W. Norton and Company, 1968), 306.

[14] Lafore, *Long Fuse*, 102.

[15] Ibid.

[16] Fay, *Origins*, 1:92-93.

[17] Ibid., 1:117-19.

[18] Eyck, *Bismarck*, 290.

[19] Ibid., 294-95.

with Britain - remained intact, Germany was now less secure than she had been before Wilhelm became Kaiser.

Berlin's new dilemma did not induce Wilhelm to always act tactfully on the public stage. Indeed, he frequently spoke in aggressive tones. In an 1897 speech, he exhorted his brother, Prince Henry - who was to command the East Asia Naval Squadron assigned to guard German commercial interests in China - to abide by the following: "If anyone should undertake to insult us in our rights or to wish to harm us, then drive in with the mailed fist." [20] Two years later, in comparing Germany to a beautiful yet still-growing tree, he publicly promised to protect it by "exterminating the animals which would gnaw at its roots." [21] A particularly damaging pronouncement – one picked up by the international press - came in 1900 when he urged German forces en route to China to act like the monstrous Huns:

> You must know, my men, that you are about to meet a crafty, well-armed, cruel foe! Meet him, and beat him! Give no quarter! Take no prisoners! Kill him, when he falls into your hands! Even as, a thousand years ago, the Huns under their King Attila made such a name for themselves as still resounds in terror through legend and fable, so may the name of German resound through Chinese history a thousand years from now, and may you so conduct yourselves that no Chinaman will ever again so much as dare to look crooked at a German! [22]

Such idiotic statements, when viewed today, seem like mere tough-talk from a pompous blowhard. True, the Kaiser was more interested in boasting about war than engaging in it. And other countries, recognizing Wilhelm's pretentious nature, often dismissed his bluster for what it was. Still, when the supreme commander of arguably the world's finest military machine

---

[20] Quoted in Christian Gauss, *The German Emperor as Shown in His Public Utterances* (New York: Charles Scribner's Sons, 1915), 121.
[21] Quoted in ibid., 140.
[22] Quoted in Emil Ludwig, *Wilhelm Hohenzollern: The Last of the Kaisers* (New York: G.P. Putnam's Sons, 1927), 272.

encourages his troops to act like medieval thugs, some Europeans had to question the stability and intentions of Wilhelm and his nation.

C. An Increasingly Strained German-British Relationship

Having helped drive Russia into France's arms, Berlin proceeded to gradually steer England into the camp of Germany's potential adversaries.

Up through the late 1890s, German-British relations had generally been good. The Kaiser, after all, was Queen Victoria's grandson, the British and German peoples were of similar ethnic stock, and the two countries had tight economic ties. [23] Naturally, they did not agree on everything. But there was genuine mutual respect. Even the notorious Kruger Telegram episode of 1896 – in which Wilhelm needlessly antagonized London by congratulating Paul Kruger, the president of the Transvaal Republic (in southern Africa), for halting an incursion into the Transvaal by British colonial raiders - failed to seriously derail German-English relations. [24]

Yet things began to change when Germany enacted "Navy Laws" in 1898 and 1900 that were designed to bolster her naval strength. [25] An island nation, England relied upon her fleet to protect her from invasion and blockade and to ensure her continued access to her colonies. It was the shield of the British Empire, and England always made certain that her navy was the world's foremost. Now many Britons wondered, "We are no threat to Germany from the sea, much less from land; so why does she want this huge fleet?" Some drew only one conclusion: Germany was attempting to build a navy that would overtake England's – something that could endanger Britain.

Actually, Germany's reasons for her naval expansion were less sinister than that. Like England, she wanted a strong fleet to

---

[23] Imanuel Geiss, ed., *July 1914, The Outbreak of the First World War: Selected Documents* (New York: Charles Scribner's Sons, 1967), 22; Churchill, *World Crisis*, 9-10.

[24] Churchill, *World Crisis*, 10.

[25] Additional laws were enacted over the next 12 years that called for further increases in German naval strength.

guard her colonies, maintain her access to overseas trade, and protect her coastline if war erupted. [26] She also desired a navy befitting a country of her enormous economic strength. [27] In his memoirs, German Admiral Reinhard Scheer recalled Berlin's mindset at the time:

> The conduct of a Great Power which left its sea interests without protection would have been as unworthy and contemptible as dishonorable cowardice in an individual; but it would have been most highly impolitic also, because it would have it dependent on States more powerful at sea. The best army we could create would lose in value if Germany remained with the Achilles-heel of unprotected foreign trade amounting to thousands of millions. [28]

Germany's fleet buildup was never intended to threaten England. [29] And though some militant German groups desired it, there were no serious plans to even achieve parity with Britain's navy. [30] Berlin generally viewed the naval expansion as a defensive measure. But many Britons saw it differently. Even those British officials who recognized Berlin's real motivations feared a naval arms race that would force England to spend enormous sums of money to maintain her decisive edge over Germany. [31]

Despite this, Britain still desired close relations with Berlin. For decades, she had maintained a policy of relative isolationism. She declined to ally herself with other Powers lest she be drawn into a conflict in which she had no interest. [32] By the mid-1890s, this isolationist sentiment started to weaken slightly. True, standing alone would give London freedom of action in a crisis. But what if the Franco-Russian pact or another coalition

---

[26] Reinhard Scheer, *Germany's High Seas Fleet in the World War* (1920; reprint, Nashville, TN: Battery Press, 2002), xi-xiv.
[27] Lafore, *Long Fuse*, 119.
[28] Scheer, *High Seas Fleet*, xii.
[29] Ibid., xi.
[30] Lafore, *Long Fuse*, 131.
[31] David Lloyd George, *War Memoirs of David Lloyd George,* vol. 1, 2nd ed. (London: Odhams Press, 1938), 6-7.
[32] Churchill, *World Crisis*, 10.

threatened Britain's European or overseas interests? [33] With territories around the world, England frequently quarreled with France and Russia in areas where they, too, had colonial considerations. [34] It was not inconceivable that a particular dispute would escalate to an armed conflict in which Britain had no allies. She needed a friend, and British Colonial Secretary Joseph Chamberlain thought that Germany would make a good one. He approached Berlin several times between 1898 and 1901 about a possible alliance. [35]

The Germans were unenthusiastic for several reasons. First, they questioned the military value of a Berlin-London pact; in a European war, Britain's navy would be of little use to Germany on the battlefield. [36] Second, they were reluctant to commit themselves to fight for Britain's interests. [37] Third, there was growing anti-British sentiment among the German people. [38] The two countries' commercial rivalry and even some latent envy of Britain's massive empire were possible factors. Yet much of it stemmed from England's war against the Boers of southern Africa, with whom the Germans sympathized. [39] Berlin recognized that public feeling could not be ignored.

Since much of Europe shared Germany's dismay at England over the Boer War, Berlin believed that London's international standing was weak. [40] Convinced that Britain needed Germany more than Germany needed her, Berlin elected to hold out for more concessions; if Britain desired an alliance, she would have to pay heavily for it. [41] In particular, Berlin wanted England to link herself with the Triple Alliance; a separate German-British pact

---

[33] See Fay, *Origins*, 1:125-26.

[34] Ibid., 1:126.

[35] See ibid., 1:130-38; Churchill, *World Crisis*, 10. Some British Cabinet members did not share Chamberlain's desire for an alliance with Germany. Fay, *Origins*, 1:130, 138.

[36] Fay, *Origins*, 1:130-31, 140.

[37] Lafore, *Long Fuse*, 123.

[38] Fay, *Origins*, 1:136-37.

[39] Ibid., 1:136, 139; Virginia Cowles, *The Kaiser* (New York: Harper and Row, 1963), 179.

[40] Cowles, *Kaiser*, 179.

[41] Fay, *Origins*, 1:140.

was unacceptable. [42] England refused. She did not want to get involved in Austrian quarrels in the Balkans or Eastern Europe. [43] With no deal in sight, Britain ended the negotiations in December 1901. [44]

Germany believed that her reasons for resisting an alliance with London were entirely rational. Yet they were based on a false premise: that her action would have few negative consequences. Chamberlain had indicated to Berlin that England might turn elsewhere if a British-German deal failed to materialize. [45] Berlin seemed to doubt this, considering it unlikely that England would ally with France or Russia because of her difficult relationships with them. [46] But England did look for other partners. While her alliance with far-away Japan (signed in 1902) may not have unnerved Berlin, the diplomatic strides she was about to make in Europe certainly would.

Though France and Britain had long been rivals, circumstances by 1904 were bringing them closer together. Paris was concerned about St. Petersburg's poor performance to date in the Russo-Japanese War, which erupted in early 1904; with her ally weakened, France felt isolated in the face of Germany's power and wanted any support she could get. [47] She also believed it would be easier to achieve her colonial ambitions by working *with* England rather than against her. [48] Britain, meanwhile, was tired of the constant friction with France over colonial matters. King Edward VII, who succeeded Victoria in 1901, admired France and was more well-disposed towards her than towards Germany, whom he did not entirely trust. [49] Moreover, London feared that the fighting between Russia and Japan could bring in their respective French and British allies – and England did not

---

[42] Lafore, *Long Fuse*, 123; Cowles, *Kaiser*, 191.

[43] Lafore, *Long Fuse*, 123; Cowles, *Kaiser*, 192.

[44] Fay, *Origins,* 1:137.

[45] Ibid., 1:130; Cowles, *Kaiser*, 187.

[46] Fay, *Origins,* 1:139; V.R. Berghahn, *Germany and the Approach of War in 1914* (New York: St. Martin's Press, 1973), 45.

[47] Churchill, *World Crisis*, 11.

[48] Fay, *Origins,* 1:152.

[49] Ibid., 1:153-54; Lafore, *Long Fuse*, 125. Though Edward was Wilhelm's uncle, the two were not on especially warm terms.

want war with France. [50] Simply put, there was no reason for Britain not to improve her relations with Paris, particularly since France desired better relations, too.

So despite their long-standing tensions, Britain and France signed an agreement in the spring of 1904 that, among other things, settled several of their African colonial disputes. [51] It was not an alliance. England refused to go that far with France. Yet it signified a vast improvement in Franco-British relations, and that was the key. To some extent, the agreement marked the beginning of a second realignment of Great Powers against Germany (the first being the Franco-Russian pact). [52] Although German Chancellor Bernhard von Bulow said publicly that he welcomed any agreement that reduced Franco-British friction, the Germans were worried about it. [53] The calculation they had made during the Chamberlain discussions that London and Paris would remain at odds proved wrong.

The 1904 accord was not Germany's only diplomatic dilemma. There was also the matter of Italy.

Following her gradual unification in the late 1850s and 1860s, Italy desperately sought security. By 1880, she concluded that joining Europe's most formidable alliance – the Berlin-Vienna pact - could provide it. With Great Power allies, Italy also hoped to gain support for her colonial ambitions. [54] Germany and Austria, meanwhile, favored aligning with Rome because if they went to war with Russia, Austria would not have to assign forces to guard her border with Italy; she could instead throw them against Russia. [55] And in a Franco-German war, France - who had poor relations with Rome at the time - would have to man her Italian border, leaving fewer French troops available to fight the

---

[50] Fay, *Origins,* 1:166.

[51] Churchill, *World Crisis,* 11.

[52] Winston Churchill later went so far as to say: "England and all that she stood for had left her isolation, and had reappeared in Europe on the opposite side to Germany." Ibid., 12.

[53] Fay, *Origins,* 1:179.

[54] Ibid., 1:81, 86.

[55] Gordon Martel, *The Origins of the First World War* (New York: Longman, 1987), 18.

Germans. [56] These and other considerations were behind the Triple Alliance's creation in 1882.

Berlin and Vienna knew that Italy's adherence to their alliance was based solely on her self-interest, and neither of them ever completely trusted her. In fact, tensions developed between Rome and the Central Powers in the late 1880s. Italy felt that Berlin was not sufficiently supporting her colonial goals; Bismarck countered that the Triple Alliance, as a defensive pact, was never intended to advance a member's overseas ambitions. [57] Furthermore, the Habsburg Empire contained several territories that Italy herself desired. They included (1) the Adriatic port city of Trieste and (2) the Trentino, a mountainous region bordering northern Italy. As both territories contained many ethnic Italians, Rome wanted to incorporate them into Italy – much to Austria's resentment.

Also disturbing to the Central Powers was the improving Franco-Italian relationship. In 1900, Rome and Paris reached an accord on certain colonial questions. [58] Of greater significance was their secret 1902 understanding, in which each agreed to remain neutral if the other were (1) attacked by one or more Great Powers or (2) compelled to declare war on another Power because of a "direct provocation." [59] This agreement did not verbatim violate the Triple Alliance treaty, but it seemed inconsistent with its spirit. [60] Though the Central Powers were unfamiliar with the 1902

---

[56] Fay, *Origins,* 1:85.

[57] Ibid., 1:86-87, 144.

[58] Ibid., 1:145.

[59] Ibid., 1:147-48.

[60] Ibid. Article II of the Triple Alliance treaty (December 1912 version) called for Italy to aid Germany if France attacked the latter without direct provocation. Carnegie Endowment for International Peace, *Outbreak of the World War: German Documents Collected by Karl Kautsky* (New York: Oxford University Press, 1924), 607. Article III stated: "If one or two of the high contracting parties should be attacked, without direct provocation on their own part, and should find themselves involved in a war with two or more Great Powers who are not signatories to the present treaty, the *casus foederis* shall be deemed to exist simultaneously for all the high contracting parties." Quoted in ibid., 608. The proviso in the 1902 agreement calling for Italy's neutrality if a Great Power (e.g., Germany) attacked France did not explicitly contradict Articles II and III, for neither article required Italy to participate in such an attack.

agreement's exact terms and though Italy continued to proclaim her loyalty to the Triple Alliance, Berlin and Vienna sensed her drift from them. [61]

In sum, the decade following the Franco-Russian pact's formation saw a further deterioration in Germany's diplomatic position. Relations with Britain and Italy, though still not bad, were increasingly strained, while France - in contrast to her isolation in the 1880s - remained allied to Russia and was becoming friendlier with England.

The diplomatic stars were lining up against Germany. And she wanted to halt this.

D. Bulow's Gamble - The 1905-06 Moroccan Crisis

Morocco was of interest to several Great Powers. Under the 1904 Franco-British agreement, Paris received more of a free hand in Morocco and Britain the same in Egypt; France thereupon began exercising greater control over Moroccan affairs. [62] In Berlin, Bulow was irked that Paris and London had apparently determined the fate of Morocco (where the Germans had commercial interests) without any consideration for Germany. [63] While he did not publicly rip the two countries, he secretly encouraged the Sultan (Morocco's nominal ruler) to resist France's creeping influence. [64] And in March 1905, Bulow began to implement a somewhat bizarre scheme. [65]

At the time, the Kaiser was on a sea voyage to the Mediterranean. [66] Bulow intended to plant a story in a German newspaper that Wilhelm was scheduled to stop in Morocco along the way, believing this would obligate him to do so. [67] The Kaiser's presence in Morocco, Bulow surmised, would show Germany's support for the Sultan and her displeasure with

---

[61] Lafore, *Long Fuse*, 127.

[62] Ibid., 126; Churchill, *World Crisis*, 11, 18.

[63] Fay, *Origins*, 1:178-80.

[64] Ibid., 1:182.

[65] Cowles, *Kaiser*, 211.

[66] Lafore, *Long Fuse*, 129.

[67] Fay, *Origins*, 1:183.

France's plans. [68] He wanted Paris to effectively admit that it could not decide matters affecting German interests without consulting her. A broader aim, however, was to orchestrate events such that Britain would fail to support France, thus breaking their increasingly amicable ties.

Wilhelm questioned the wisdom of visiting Morocco. For all of his big talk, he did not want trouble with France; in fact, he sought closer ties with her. [69] He also believed it would *benefit* Germany to have Paris deeply engaged in Morocco, which was a sea of instability. [70] The more bogged down France became in Morocco, he reasoned, the less she would focus on European matters (like Alsace and Lorraine!) and, hence, the fewer problems she would cause Germany. [71] But Bulow stressed to him that his visit had already been announced; backing out now might give the impression that France had forced Berlin to cancel it, thus making Germany look weak. [72] Wilhelm relented.

Upon arriving in the Moroccan port city of Tangier on March 31, the Kaiser publicly announced:

> It is to the Sultan in his position as an independent sovereign that I am paying my visit today. I hope that under the sovereignty of the Sultan, a free Morocco will remain open to the peaceful rivalry of all nations, without monopoly or annexation, on the basis of absolute equality. The object of my visit to Tangier is to make it known that I am determined to do all in my power to safeguard efficaciously the interests of Germany in Morocco, for I look upon the Sultan as an absolutely independent sovereign. [73]

Talk about a provocation! Berlin's desire to protect its Moroccan interests was one thing. But referring to the Sultan as an

---

[68] Lafore, *Long Fuse*, 128.
[69] Ludwig, *Wilhelm Hohenzollern*, 283.
[70] Cowles, *Kaiser*, 208.
[71] Ibid.
[72] Fay, *Origins*, 1:183.
[73] Quoted in Frank Maloy Anderson and Amos Shartle Hershey, *Handbook for the Diplomatic History of Europe, Asia, and Africa: 1870-1914* (Washington, DC: United States Government Printing Office, 1918), 332.

"independent" sovereign sounded like a direct challenge to France's predominant role in Morocco.

None of this bothered Bulow. He followed up Wilhelm's pronouncement with a demand for an international conference to settle the Moroccan issue; Berlin even intimated to France that her refusal of the conference could lead to war! [74] Though he did not, of course, want war, Bulow was playing a very dangerous game. Yes, a humiliating French cave-in would be a huge triumph for Berlin. But what if Paris declined the conference? Germany would either have to take up arms for a questionable cause (her Moroccan interests) or back down in the face of France's determination.

The following weeks were tension-filled. Wilhelm's visit, the conference demand, and Berlin's sudden intransigence about Morocco had caused a sensation. [75] Few in Europe understood what Germany was up to. The bigger question was this: how would France respond? Her notoriously anti-German foreign minister, Theophile Delcasse, whom Bulow detested, suspected that Berlin's hints of war were hot air. [76] Even if Germany were serious, he would rather stand up and defend France's honor than submit to Germany's threats. [77] Delcasse therefore urged the French Cabinet not to fold.

Yet many of Delcasse's colleagues, including Premier Maurice Rouvier, desperately wanted to avoid war. [78] Militarily impotent and saddled with domestic turmoil after losing her war with Japan, Russia could not effectively assist France against Germany. [79] Nor could England necessarily be counted on. While she had not abandoned France during this tense period, she had not encouraged Paris to decline the conference, either. [80] Furthermore, Rouvier felt that even if England aided the French militarily, her navy and small army could do little to help stop Germany's

---

[74] Fay, *Origins*, 1:184, 188; Churchill, *World Crisis*, 18; Cowles, *Kaiser*, 211.

[75] Martel, *Origins*, 48.

[76] Fay, *Origins*, 1:187-88.

[77] Ibid., 1:188.

[78] Ibid., 1:186-89; Cowles, *Kaiser*, 211.

[79] Cowles, *Kaiser*, 211.

[80] Churchill, *World Crisis*, 19.

powerful land forces. [81] Ultimately, the French Cabinet seemed less fearful of a diplomatic humiliation than a cataclysmic military defeat. [82] Paris therefore agreed to the conference. Delcasse resigned.

Bulow's gamble appeared to have worked beautifully. France had been humiliated. The despised Delcasse was gone. And Paris was compelled to consider Germany's views regarding Morocco. Few countries in recent memory had scored such a resounding diplomatic success. But Berlin now sought higher stakes: the damaging of Franco-British relations. This soon became the heart of the Moroccan affair. German officials cared much less about Morocco *per se* than about the tightening diplomatic vice around Germany. The Franco-Russian alliance was bad enough. Yet if the British-French partnership evolved into a formal pact, an anti-German, Paris-London-St. Petersburg coalition could follow. Believing that it could not let things get that far, Berlin wanted to break the Paris-London link *now*.

In fact, Berlin hoped to completely reverse the European diplomatic landscape in Germany's favor. If Britain abandoned France, the latter - now without Delcasse around and weakened by her Moroccan capitulation - might be lured into aligning with Germany. This, in turn, could bring Germany and Russia closer together. The Kaiser himself had visions of a German-Franco-Russian coalition. [83] If such a grouping could be tied to the Triple Alliance, five of Europe's six Powers would be diplomatically united, with Germany – the strongest of them – at the head of this "Continental League." [84] Meanwhile, Germany's main commercial and naval rival, Britain, would stand alone. The peace of Europe would be secured, Germany's prospect of a two-front war ended, and her diplomatic glory days of the 1880s revisited. Her growing isolation over the previous 15 years would be entirely erased. And

---

[81] Cowles, *Kaiser*, 211.

[82] Fay, *Origins*, 1:186-89.

[83] Ibid., 1:132, 170-71.

[84] Ibid. France's inclusion in this coalition, Wilhelm reasoned, might make her forget about Alsace and Lorraine and quench her desire for revenge against Germany. Ibid., 1:132.

with France diplomatically and Russia militarily weakened in late 1905, Berlin believed it was in a powerful bargaining position. [85]

After months of planning, the Moroccan conference began in Algeciras, Spain, in January 1906. If Berlin thought that France could be pushed around, it was in for a surprise. Determined to avoid another humiliation, France held firm in Algeciras. London, which did not want to see France again succumb to German pressure, staunchly backed Paris. Even Berlin's Italian ally sided with France's position! [86] In the end, although the Germans received minor concessions and limits were placed on Paris's influence over Morocco, they were essentially compelled to recognize France's special interests there. [87]

Embarrassing as this was for Germany, there were two far worse outcomes. First, she acquired a reputation as a bully. Rather than quietly approach France about their concerns over Morocco, the Germans tried to publicly steamroll her. [88] They succeeded at first, but it was Germany who ultimately suffered the diplomatic defeat. Her actions so alienated Britain that she now considered Germany her primary adversary. This led to the second bad outcome for Berlin: a stronger Franco-British relationship. In fact, the two countries eventually began secret discussions to coordinate their efforts in the event of war with Germany! [89] They were still not allies. England remained unwilling to formally commit to fight alongside France. But they were more intimate than ever in the face of what they believed was an increasingly aggressive Germany.

---

[85] The Kaiser certainly thought so. While the Powers were organizing the Moroccan summit, he arranged to meet Tsar Nicholas II on their yachts in the Bay of Bjorko. Surmising that (1) Russia's weakness, (2) Germany's sympathetic attitude towards her during the Japan war, and (3) Nicholas's indecisive nature would make him susceptible to German advances, the Kaiser offered him an alliance. Cowles, *Kaiser*, 213. Nicholas accepted. But his foreign minister told him that a pact with Germany would be inconsistent with the spirit of Russia's alliance with France. Nicholas thus notified Wilhelm that the Bjorko treaty was on hold. It was never consummated. Fay, *Origins*, 1:176-77.
[86] Fay, *Origins*, 1:151.
[87] Lafore, *Long Fuse*, 130; Cowles, *Kaiser*, 222.
[88] Fay, *Origins*, 1:180.
[89] Churchill, *World Crisis*, 19.

The Moroccan affair, in short, was disastrous for Berlin. Instead of splitting France from England and creating a German-dominated Quintuple Alliance of sorts, Berlin's actions tightened British-French ties, further damaged Franco-German relations, and left Germany more isolated than before. While Delcasse's exit was a gain for Berlin, the price paid for it was much too great. Bulow's risky, borderline harebrained scheme to reverse Germany's slow diplomatic descent had completely backfired.

E. The 1907 British-Russian Agreement

Things would get no better for Berlin.

One of France's foremost goals was to bring St. Petersburg and London closer together, for a Franco-British-Russian coalition might deter Germany from undertaking any aggressive ventures. Russia and England were not on particularly good terms. Each was suspicious of the other's territorial ambitions in Asia. And Nicholas distrusted Edward VII; according to Wilhelm, the Tsar labeled Edward as "the greatest 'mischief-maker' and the most dangerous and deceptive intriguer in the world." [90] Britain, meanwhile, despised Russia's autocratic government. She also had been infuriated over the 1904 Dogger Bank incident, in which Russian ships en route to East Asia to fight Japan mistakenly fired on several British fishing vessels (sinking one of them) in the North Sea. [91] And some Britons may have had unrealistic but nevertheless frightening visions of millions of Russian troops one day sweeping westward across Europe.

Yet as Paris had hoped, events were pushing Russia and England towards one another. Still militarily fragile, Russia needed peaceful relations with Tokyo to give her time to recuperate. [92] Being allied with Japan, London was well-positioned to facilitate a Russian-Japanese rapprochement. [93] For their part, the British wanted to end the ongoing tension with

---

[90] Quoted in Cowles, *Kaiser*, 214.
[91] Berghahn, *Germany and the Approach*, 46.
[92] Fay, *Origins*, 1:215.
[93] Ibid.

Russia over colonial affairs. [94] They also felt it would be difficult to further strengthen their relationship with France if they remained hostile to her chief ally. [95]

To that end, Russia and England signed an agreement in 1907 that settled various colonial issues. There was, of course, too much distrust between them for an alliance. The British-Russian link was much weaker than France's links with Russia and England. But to Paris, it only mattered that the London-St. Petersburg link had been established.

Some in Europe believed that a Paris-London-St. Petersburg "Triple Entente" now existed. The only actual alliance among the trio, to be sure, was between France and Russia. Yet it did appear that three of Europe's six Powers were positioning themselves against Germany. Bismarck would have been disgusted to learn that his success in isolating France had been undone and that it was Germany who faced isolation.

F. Germany's Fears of Encirclement

What were the emotions of Germany's leaders in light of this new diplomatic order? Paranoia and bewilderment were among them. In mid-1908, future British Prime Minister David Lloyd George and several colleagues spoke with Germany's vice-chancellor, Theobald von Bethmann-Hollweg. The latter seemed convinced that France, Britain, and Russia were ganging up on Germany. Lloyd George recalled:

> The impression he (Bethmann-Hollweg) left on my mind was that official Germany was generally apprehensive of the rapprochement between France and England, and England and Russia. They were quite convinced that King Edward was organizing a Confederacy with a hostile purport against Germany. The King was regarded as an inveterate enemy of German might.

---

[94] Edward Grey, *Twenty-Five Years: 1892-1916,* 2 vols. (New York: Frederick A. Stokes Company, 1925), 1:147-48, 154, 160.
[95] Ibid., 1:147-48.

This led to one extraordinary outburst in the course of (our) conversation, when (Bethmann-Hollweg) reverted to the theme of the growing hostility of England, France and Russia against Germany, and the 'iron ring' they were pressing round her. 'An iron ring!' he repeated violently, shouting out the statement, and waving his arm to the whole assembled company. 'England is embracing France. She is making friends with Russia. But it is not that you love each other; it is that you hate Germany!' And he repeated and literally shouted the word 'hate' thrice. He became very excited, and his discretion was certainly not under control. [96]

That autumn, the contents of an informal interview the Kaiser gave to a British acquaintance were published in the *Daily Telegraph,* a London newspaper. Wilhelm had expressed astonishment over England's attitude towards Germany:

You English are like mad bulls – you see red everywhere! What on earth has come over you that you should heap on us such suspicion as is unworthy of a great nation? What can I do more? I have always stood forth as the friend of England............Have I ever once broken my word?...............I regard this misapprehension as a personal insult!...............You make it uncommonly difficult for a man to remain friendly to England. [97]

For all of their whining, Bethmann-Hollweg (who became chancellor in 1909), the Kaiser, and others in Berlin seemed unable to grasp that it was their own actions that fostered this distrust of Germany. Consider the *Daily Telegraph* affair. Wilhelm's comment regarding the difficulty of remaining friendly to England was irresponsible enough. Yet he also claimed that when Britain was struggling in the Boer War, Russia and France had secretly suggested to Germany that the three of them humiliate England by helping the Boers, but he had refused; the implication was that Germany had saved Britain from a potentially disastrous

---

[96] Lloyd George, *War Memoirs,* 17-18.
[97] Quoted in Ludwig, *Wilhelm Hohenzollern,* 385-86.

situation. [98] He further asserted that to assist England during the Boer conflict, he had devised a military plan of campaign for her and forwarded it to London. [99] Since the ultimately victorious battle strategy Britain used was similar to his own plan, he hinted that she must have adopted it. [100] His generosity had bailed her out.

There was a slight problem, though. Wilhelm's claims were gross exaggerations. And Europe knew it. France and Russia were furious at his accusations, while many Britons became increasingly convinced that Wilhelm was a galoot of the first order. Even average Germans were aghast at his comments. [101] The matter died down, and Wilhelm wisely kept his mouth shut for a while thereafter. But it represented another German self-inflicted wound.

More would follow.

After the 1906 Algeciras conference, France's influence over Moroccan affairs increased. [102] In the spring of 1911, unrest erupted in Morocco, whereupon Paris sent troops to the city of Fez to stabilize things. While the Germans did not immediately protest the Fez operation, they believed that it overstepped the terms of the 1906 understanding; they therefore hinted that if Paris planned to keep these forces in Fez long-term, Germany was entitled to compensation. [103] France did not dispute this but seemed to stall in making a concrete offer. [104]

The Germans could have continued using relatively quiet diplomacy to get France to act. Similar to 1905, however, they opted for provocative action. They took the totally unnecessary step of dispatching a warship (the *Panther*) to the Moroccan coastal city of Agadir. Their stated reason was to protect German interests in the Agadir area; the real motivation, though, was to

---

[98] Cowles, *Kaiser*, 258.

[99] Ibid., 258-59.

[100] Ibid.

[101] Ludwig, *Wilhelm Hohenzollern*, 387-89.

[102] Fay, *Origins*, 1:280.

[103] Grey, *Twenty-Five Years*, 1:211. Wilhelm did not oppose France's action. As he saw it, the more troops France had in Morocco, the fewer she would have in Europe to face Germany. Fay, *Origins*, 1:279.

[104] Fay, *Origins*, 1:284.

pressure Paris into offering concessions. [105] France, naturally, was surprised and alarmed by Berlin's move but the British even more so. It appeared to them that Germany was trying to not only intimidate Paris but also to establish a naval base in Morocco, something London had long feared. [106] In early July 1911, British Foreign Secretary Edward Grey conveyed England's concerns to Berlin through Germany's ambassador to London, Paul von Wolff Metternich. Berlin did not respond. [107] Offended and puzzled by Germany's apparent disregard for England's views, the British government authorized Lloyd George, then serving as chancellor of the exchequer, to warn in a July 21 speech:

> If a situation were to be forced upon us in which peace could only be preserved by the surrender of the great and beneficent position Britain has won by centuries of heroism and achievement, by allowing Britain to be treated, where her interests were vitally affected, as if she were of no account in the Cabinet of nations, then I say emphatically that peace at that price would be a humiliation intolerable for a great country like ours to endure. [108]

Shocked by this threat, Berlin told London that it was not looking to establish a Moroccan base. [109] Tensions gradually eased, and Paris and Berlin struck a deal in November whereby Germany received part of the Congo. [110] Like the first Moroccan crisis, however, the second one enhanced London's and Paris's

---

[105] Ibid., 1:284-85. In his memoirs, Bethmann-Hollweg explained Germany's action as follows: "(Berlin) came to the conclusion eventually that France could not even be brought to negotiate except by drastic means. This is how the much-debated dispatch of the *Panther* to Agadir came about. It was no more than a notification that France would not be allowed to ignore our desire for a thorough discussion, forced upon us by the dilatory procedure of the Cabinet at Paris. It was a defensive rejoinder to an aggressive action on the part of France." Theobald von Bethmann-Hollweg, *Reflections on the World War, Part I* (London: Thornton Butterworth, 1920), 32.

[106] Fay, *Origins,* 1:286.

[107] Ibid., 1:286-88; Grey, *Twenty-Five Years,* 1:215.

[108] Quoted in Grey, *Twenty-Five Years,* 1:216.

[109] Fay, *Origins,* 1:289-90.

[110] Ibid., 1:290.

suspicions of Berlin and strengthened the British-French relationship. [111] Germany's strong-arm tactics had won her some territory, but the ill-will she brought upon herself more than offset this. Too frequently, Berlin chose a brutish style of diplomacy when there was no reason to.

By 1914, Germany's only true Great Power ally was Austria. Italy was an ally on paper only, France effectively remained an antagonist, and Britain and Russia were wary of Berlin. The previous quarter-century had seen a dramatic change in Germany's diplomatic fortunes. The security she enjoyed during Bismarck's era had deteriorated into near-isolation. Her diplomatic descent had not been along a perfectly straight line, of course. There were periods when Berlin had decent relations with England, Russia, and even France. Indeed, Wilhelm and Nicholas were cousins and in their correspondence often affectionately addressed each other as, respectively, "Willy" and "Nicky." And German-British tensions eased significantly in the 18 months prior to July 1914. Despite these occasional upswings of good feelings, however, the overall downward trend for Germany was unmistakable.

In all of the aforementioned affairs – the Moroccan crises, the naval buildup, etc. - Berlin was not looking to start a war. But other countries often saw Germany's actions as those of an aggressive and reckless nation. Leery of Germany's military might and concerned about her ambitions, the "Triple Entente" nations drew closer together. This, in turn, generated fears within Germany that London, Paris, and St. Petersburg were conspiring against her. Bulow later recounted a strange conversation he had with Wilhelm (shortly after the war erupted) in which the Kaiser spoke of the evil intentions of his cousins Nicholas and King George V (who had succeeded Edward in 1910):

> (Wilhelm) gave me his views on the real origin of the war. In May of 1913, at the celebration festivities for the marriage of Princess Victoria Louise to the Duke of Brunswick, the King of England, his cousin, and his other cousin, the Tsar of Russia, had conspired together to

---

[111] Ibid., 1:290-91.

betray him!..................Together they had plotted his betrayal, for which God would punish them some day! His Majesty told how, on the eve of the wedding, he had entered unawares, in Berlin Castle, the apartment of his cousin, the King of England, whom he had surprised in close conference with the Tsar. Both had started to their feet. He could see now that this had been the moment when the two were putting their final touches to a plot for falling upon Germany. [112]

Bulow surely gave little credence to Wilhelm's ridiculous theory. Still, many in Germany viewed the Entente as a real threat. It was irrelevant that both Germany and the Paris-London-St. Petersburg trio overrated the danger posed by (and mistook the intentions of) the other side. All that mattered was that they sincerely held such views. In 1914, perception was more important than reality.

The Germans, of course, had only themselves to blame for their predicament. Their oafish statesmanship between 1890 and 1914 put Germany in a position whereby in a European war, she would likely have to fight not one but two – and perhaps even three - Great Powers. The Kaiser may seem like a convenient scapegoat for Germany's pre-war diplomatic blunders. While his verbal belligerence did not help Berlin, the actions of other top German officials were no less harmful. In fact, Wilhelm sometimes frowned upon provocative proposals from his subordinates, fearing the negative diplomatic consequences; the 1905 Tangier visit, for instance, was not his idea and he undertook it reluctantly.

Germany's self-isolation, in the end, had been a group effort.

---

[112] Bernhard von Bulow, *Memoirs of Prince von Bulow,* vol. 3 (Boston: Little, Brown and Company, 1932), 228-29.

II

PARANOIA

A. The Fragile Habsburg Empire

Another source of tension in Europe involved the composition – indeed, the very existence - of the Habsburg Empire, or Austria-Hungary. The kingdom contained many nationalities. These included, obviously, the ruling Austrians (who were of German descent) and Hungarians (or Magyars) but also Poles in the northern part of the Empire, Italians in the extreme southwest, Czechs in the north-northwest, Romanians in the southeast, Slovaks in the north-central region, Serbs and Croats in the far south and along the Adriatic coast, and Ruthenes in the northeast. [113] The Empire's complex ethnic makeup and unusual political system made her, as we will see, susceptible to internal dissension and to efforts by neighboring countries to destabilize her.

Situated in the middle of Europe, the Habsburg realm had been around for centuries. As of 1855, her breadth was impressive, extending from the central region of modern-day Germany south to Venice. Yet her situation deteriorated over the next 15 years. Her defeats in the Franco-Austrian War of 1859 and the Austro-Prussian War of 1866 cost her much of northern Italy and central Germany, respectively. [114] Just as cataclysmic were the political repercussions of the 1866 disaster. Seizing upon the Empire's military weakness and domestic difficulties, her sizable and

---

[113] Lafore, *Long Fuse*, 66-67.
[114] Ibid., 58; Martel, *Origins*, 16-18.

powerful Hungarian population sought greater autonomy. With the Austrians in no position to crush the Magyars, the Compromise of 1867 (or *Ausgleich*) came about. It effectively established two separate, practically independent countries (Austria and Hungary) within one empire – and within each country resided several sub-nationalities.

Austria and Hungary shared a common monarchy, foreign ministry, and army (though each had a separate, militia-type force); they also shared a finance ministry to handle the funding of these common functions. [115] In virtually all other areas, however, the two states governed themselves; each, for example, had its own prime minister and parliament. [116] Hungary was fiercely protective of her rights and interests, even establishing her own industries so she could remain as economically independent from Austria as possible. [117] Since the Empire's survival depended largely on the Magyars' continued support, Budapest could blackmail Austria – and the Empire in general - into granting Hungary more concessions.

Both states agreed, of course, on the need to preserve Austro-Hungarian control of the Empire. Yet they were divided on many other things. For instance, Austria-Hungary had a smaller military budget than other Great Powers because Vienna and Budapest frequently disagreed on the appropriate level of funding. [118] And the Empire never reached her full economic potential because the two states failed to sufficiently integrate their respective economies and resources. [119] Tensions between Austria and Hungary even extended to the Monarchy's highest levels; the heir to the Habsburg throne, Archduke Franz Ferdinand, thoroughly despised the Magyars.

But the friction within the Habsburg realm was not only between Vienna and Budapest.

---

[115] Gary Shanafelt, *The Secret Enemy: Austria-Hungary and the German Alliance, 1914-1918* (Boulder, CO: East European Monographs, 1985), 1. The two states also had a treaty (renewable every 10 years) governing their financial and commercial relations. Lafore, *Long Fuse*, 60.

[116] Shanafelt, *Secret Enemy*, 1; Lafore, *Long Fuse*, 61.

[117] Shanafelt, *Secret Enemy*, 3.

[118] Ibid., 2.

[119] Ibid., 3.

Many of the Empire's non-Austrian and non-Hungarian minorities were at least modestly loyal to the Empire as a whole and to Emperor Franz Josef I in particular. [120] In his eighties in 1914 and having been emperor for over 60 years, Franz Josef was greatly respected. Indeed, some of his non-Austrian, non-Magyar subjects may have felt pride in being part of one of the world's oldest, greatest empires. And they were hardly living impoverished existences under a monstrous, Nazi-like police regime. People seemed fairly content in their everyday lives. While these minorities desired more autonomy, they were not violently pushing to secede from the Empire. [121] That said, some of them had serious problems with the Austrian or Hungarian state in which they resided. This was in large part because the ruling Austrians, for instance, represented only about one-third of Austria's total population; the rest of Austria consisted mostly of Ruthenes, Poles, Czechs, Slovenes, and Italians. [122] The figure was somewhat higher for the Magyars, who constituted roughly 40 percent of Hungary's population; yet this was coupled with the Hungarian government's efforts to force Magyar culture and traditions onto the non-Magyar groups, which the latter resented. [123]

So while the Habsburg realm's non-Austrian and non-Hungarian groups were not openly rebelling against the Empire, they were irritated at being ruled by two nationalities that were themselves minorities in their own state! This tension, combined with that between Austria and Hungary, made the Empire's delicate political and ethnic framework even more precarious. It also raised questions as to how long the Empire could withstand this internal pressure before she began to crack.

B. Austria and Serbia – A Hate-Filled Quarrel

To many Habsburg officials, however, the Empire's biggest threats came from the outside. Several neighboring countries believed that the Empire's patchwork cultural makeup symbolized her weakness and foretold her eventual collapse, after which they

---

[120] Officially, Franz Josef was Emperor of Austria and King of Hungary.
[121] Lafore, *Long Fuse*, 71, 81.
[122] Ibid., 63-70.
[123] Ibid., 61.

could seize those former Habsburg lands containing their ethnic kin. Two such countries, Italy and Romania, were, we know, allied with Austria. As such, they were not overly aggressive in trying to detach Franz Josef's Italian and Romanian subjects from the Empire.

Serbia was another matter altogether.

All of Europe knew that Serbia pined for the Serbs of southern Austria-Hungary, most of whom lived in Bosnia, a province that (per agreement with the other Powers) Austria had occupied and administered since 1878. [124] A small country, Serbia was not in Austria's league militarily; a unilateral Serbian invasion and conquest of Bosnia was not an option. However, virulent anti-Austrian propaganda and secret (even terrorist) groups intent on uniting all the Serb peoples *were* feasible options. And Serbian elements used them to destabilize Austria. Fifth-column agitators from Serbia, for instance, would cross into Bosnia to clandestinely stir up the Serb population against their Habsburg rulers. Serbia's efforts to foment turmoil within the Empire far exceeded anything that Rome or Bucharest did. She was easily Austria's most problematic neighbor. Accentuating Vienna's angst was that Serbia's ally and fellow Slav state, Russia, did little to stop Belgrade's troublemaking.

Predictably, Austro-Serbian tensions escalated after 1900, resulting in several crises. One was the so-called "Pig War," which began in 1906 and lasted off-and-on for about five years. [125] To weaken Serbia by ensuring her economic dependence on the Empire, Vienna stopped importing from Serbia her principal export - livestock. [126] The move backfired, for Serbia developed markets for her livestock in other countries. [127] Far from breaking Serbia's economy, the Pig War emboldened Belgrade and frustrated Vienna.

A more serious confrontation arose in 1908-09. Seeking a diplomatic coup, Russia's foreign minister, Alexander Izvolsky, secretly reached a preliminary understanding with his Austrian

---

[124] Arthur May, *The Passing of the Habsburg Monarchy: 1914-1918* (Philadelphia: University of Pennsylvania Press, 1966), 20.
[125] Lafore, *Long Fuse*, 147.
[126] Ibid.
[127] Ibid., 148.

counterpart, Alois von Aehrenthal. Under the apparent agreement, Vienna would support Russia's longstanding ambition of free passage for her warships through Turkey's Bosporus and Dardanelles Straits; in exchange, St. Petersburg would approve Austria's formal annexation of Bosnia. [128] In October 1908, Austria announced the annexation. This did not trouble Izvolsky – until he learned that Britain opposed the opening of the Straits only to Russian warships! [129] Now realizing that he might lose on the Straits question and believing that Aehrenthal - in getting Bosnia for nothing – had somehow double-crossed him, Izvolsky went ballistic. [130] Compounding his rage was the knowledge that Aehrenthal could blackmail him (and Russia) by threatening to disclose their secret negotiations. [131] Serbia, we know, badly wanted Bosnia and considered St. Petersburg her chief supporter. If she learned the details of what Izvolsky had done behind her back, it could seriously damage Serbian-Russian relations.

Of course, Belgrade was already furious over Vienna's stunning annexation. The Serbian army mobilized. [132] War was not impossible.

Over the winter of 1908-09, Russia pushed for a conference to settle the annexation dispute. [133] Vienna, with Berlin's backing, declined. [134] In March 1909, the Austrians played their trump card: unless Russia accepted the annexation, they would reveal the clandestine Straits-Bosnia discussions. [135] Furthermore, if Serbia continued her war-like attitude, Vienna would take action against her. [136] The underlying message to Russia seemingly was, "Get Serbia in line - or else." Anxious to avoid the threatened revelations and having not yet recovered from her 1904-05 defeat, Russia folded. Without St. Petersburg's armed support, Serbia, too, had to cave in. In a March 31, 1909 statement, Belgrade

---

[128] Ibid., 151-54.
[129] Ibid., 155-56.
[130] Ibid., 156.
[131] Ibid.
[132] Churchill, *World Crisis*, 21.
[133] Lafore, *Long Fuse*, 159.
[134] Churchill, *World Crisis*, 21.
[135] Lafore, *Long Fuse*, 159.
[136] See Fay, *Origins*, 1:391.

acceded to the annexation and promised to live on good terms with Austria. [137]

The Bosnian crisis was a humiliating defeat for Russia and Serbia. Some Serbians felt that Russia had abandoned them. This stung St. Petersburg - and fearful of losing influence in the Balkans, the Russians resolved to never capitulate like that again. [138] Not surprisingly, the Serbian population's hatred of Austria became almost pathological. The vehemence of Serbian anti-Habsburg rhetoric reached new heights. [139]

Vienna and Berlin may have privately gloated over their success. But they, too, paid a price though they may not have realized it. For Austria, the annexation guaranteed more trouble from the outraged Serbians. And her blackmailing behavior further damaged Habsburg-Russian relations. Meanwhile, the diplomatic ring around Germany tightened as Russia and France – dismayed by what they believed was Berlin's encouragement of Austrian belligerence - enhanced their ties. [140] Russia, in fact, initiated a military rearmament program soon after the crisis. [141] Even the Austro-German relationship became temporarily strained. Vienna had not forewarned Berlin of the secret Izvolsky-Aehrenthal understanding. [142] The Germans were therefore surprised and displeased over the annexation because Vienna had triggered an international crisis on its own volition, placing Germany in a tough spot. [143] They backed Austria during the affair, but some in Berlin remained miffed at her.

The next serious Austro-Serbian dispute occurred in 1913. In the fall of 1912, the First Balkan War erupted, in which a coalition of Serbia, Greece, Bulgaria, and Montenegro seized upon the Ottoman Empire's tremendous weakness and drove the Turks – who controlled part of the southern Balkans - almost completely out of southeastern Europe. [144] Vienna had rooted for Turkey during the war, viewing her as a buffer against Serbian

---

[137] Ibid., 1:392-93.
[138] Lafore, *Long Fuse*, 163.
[139] Ibid.
[140] See Churchill, *World Crisis*, 22.
[141] Fay, *Origins*, 1:397.
[142] Ibid., 1:385-87; Lafore, *Long Fuse*, 158.
[143] Fay, *Origins*, 1:385-87; Lafore, *Long Fuse*, 158.
[144] Lafore, *Long Fuse*, 169.

expansion. The Ottoman defeat, with Serbia's subsequent enlargement at Turkey's expense, thus badly unnerved Austria. [145] The only positive for Vienna occurred at the post-war peace conference when the Great Powers agreed to the establishment of the new nation of Albania. Austria had wanted this because Albania's geographic position would continue to block landlocked Serbia from the Adriatic. [146] This would prevent her from becoming a naval or economic threat to Austria - something of great importance to Vienna in light of Serbia's enlarged status. [147]

Naturally, this infuriated Serbia. But her mood improved with the Second Balkan War, which erupted in mid-1913 from disputes between Bulgaria and her Serbian and Greek allies over the division of spoils from the first war. Again, Serbia (along with Greece, Montenegro, and Romania) was victorious. Her territory expanded even further per the August 1913 Treaty of Bucharest, which officially ended the Balkan Wars. Emboldened by her success and determined to gain access to the Adriatic, Serbia refused to withdraw her forces from northern Albania. [148]

Already aghast at her foremost enemy's explosive growth, Austria had seen enough. She had declined to intervene in the Balkan Wars to stop Serbia, deeming such an adventure too risky and one that her German ally – nervous that Austrian intervention could draw in other Powers - did not want to see. [149] Yet Serbia's occupation of northern Albania was too much. She had to be reined in. Austria therefore demanded in October 1913 that Serbian forces evacuate Albania. [150] Serbia had to comply, for her action went against the wishes of the Great Powers – including Russia, who had no desire for war over Belgrade's occupation of territory that she and others had agreed would be part of Albania. [151] Serbia's ambitions were again thwarted and Austria, as always, was the target of her venom.

---

[145] Ibid., 170.

[146] Ibid., 175.

[147] Ibid.; Fay, *Origins,* 1:440-41.

[148] Lafore, *Long Fuse,* 177.

[149] Ibid., 171-72; Fay, *Origins,* 1:452. Austrian military officials had actually pushed for intervention, but the civilians overruled them. Lafore, *Long Fuse,* 172.

[150] Fay, *Origins,* 1:473.

[151] Ibid., 1:474.

For Vienna and Belgrade, there were three main effects of the aforementioned crises. First, notwithstanding her diplomatic defeats in the Bosnian and Albanian affairs, Serbia had grown much larger. With enhanced feelings of power and prestige, she was more determined than ever to unify all Serbs. Second, Serbia's fury over Vienna's efforts to obstruct her territorial and ethnic aspirations approached the boiling point. Serbian elements therefore intensified their verbal attacks on Austria and their subversive activities in Bosnia. Third, the mindset of some Habsburg officials was increasingly paranoiac. To them, Austria-Hungary was an empire under siege. Her neighbors were eyeing her territories and, particularly in Serbia's case, getting bigger. Vienna also believed that Russia fully supported Serbia's agitation. If Serbia had no Great Power patron to protect her, Austria could have ended Belgrade's troublemaking through armed force. But since a Habsburg assault on Serbia could mean war with Russia, Austria's military options seemed limited. Indeed, St. Petersburg's backing of Serbia helped fuel Austria's insecurity. She viewed Serbia as the sledgehammer with which Russia was trying to break the Habsburg realm apart. Somewhat apocalyptically, she saw a huge Slavic tidal wave roaring in from the east and southeast that could engulf and destroy the Empire if it were not checked.

The Habsburg realm's fragile internal structure worsened Vienna's anxiety. Austria-Hungary, as we saw, consisted solely of minorities - unlike Germany and France, which were more ethnically homogenous - and had a very limited central government. Old Franz Josef, to be sure, was a revered figure. As Bismarck said: "Only let the Emperor (Franz Josef) mount into the saddle, and the sons of all the peoples of his empire will gladly follow his leadership." [152] But he was unlikely to rule much longer. What would happen when he passed? Would his peoples' loyalty to the Empire – which was, in general, more moderate than intense - die with him? Would some other event encourage a particular minority group to seek independence, which could spur other groups to do likewise and thus bring the whole Empire

---

[152] Quoted in Edmund von Glaise-Horstenau, *The Collapse of the Austro-Hungarian Empire* (New York: E.P. Dutton and Co., 1930), 2.

31

crashing down? Between Austria-Hungary's domestic weakness and her fear of the Slavic, Serbian-Russian threat, Habsburg officials looked towards the future with grimness and foreboding.

C. The European Situation in Mid-June 1914

There were several diplomatic danger points in Europe as the summer of 1914 approached: (1) the mistrust between Germany and the Triple Entente, (2) Austro-Serbian tensions, and (3) Vienna's strained relations with Russia. Europe's Great Powers were divided into two competing factions, whose respective members (other than Italy) were strengthening the bonds between them largely in response to the perceived threats posed by the other faction.

Each side in the Germany-Entente relationship misunderstood the other's intentions. Many German officials could not see that the Franco-British-Russian grouping was *defensive* in nature and that Berlin's own actions had helped tighten the Entente's links. And contrary to what some in the Entente countries suspected, Germany was not looking to militarily dominate Europe.

This overestimation of threats also existed in the Balkans. St. Petersburg believed that Austria was attempting to increase her power in the region at Russia's expense. Yet Austria's Balkan mindset was generally defensive. She was more focused on retaining her existing territories (e.g., Bosnia) than on expanding her influence into others. Meanwhile, Vienna arguably exaggerated the Serbian menace. Yes, Belgrade's agitation was real. And many Serbs in Bosnia increasingly sympathized with the Pan-Serb ideal. [153] However, Serbia was no military threat to Austria; and while Serbian propaganda might eventually harm the Empire's stability, the danger was not necessarily imminent. Even the Kaiser felt that Vienna was overly nervous about Serbia. [154] As with the mutual Berlin-Entente mistrust, however, it mattered little that Austria's views of her external threats might have been overly dire. It only mattered that she held them.

---

[153] Fay, *Origins,* 1:183.
[154] Ibid., 1:207.

None of this meant that a European war loomed in mid-June 1914. To the contrary, things were quieter than they had been in some time. Europe had settled down after the Balkan Wars. Even British-German relations had improved. The continent was at peace. Nevertheless, with deep suspicion lingering beneath this calm surface, it was possible that the next Moroccan, Bosnian, or Albanian crisis would not end peacefully. It did not help that Germany and Russia were allied with two countries – Austria and Serbia, respectively – who detested each other. This increased the chances that Berlin and St. Petersburg would get sucked into any Austro-Serbian conflict, which could then bring in Russia's French ally and, ultimately, much of the rest of Europe.

III

MURDER

A. The Assassination of Franz Ferdinand

On June 28, 1914, Franz Ferdinand and his wife, Sophie, visited the city of Sarajevo in Bosnia. While riding in an open car, they were shot and killed by Gavrilo Princip, a Bosnian Serb and a Habsburg subject. He was associated with the Black Hand, a terrorist group that aimed to unify all Serbs.

The assassination shocked Europe. British newspapers ripped Serbia for her ongoing harassment of Austria; one newspaper proclaimed: "If it were physically possible for Serbia to be towed out to sea and sunk there, the air of Europe would at once seem cleaner." [155] In Germany, naturally, there was much outrage; the Kaiser, who had been friendly with Franz Ferdinand, was particularly saddened. Even Tsar Nicholas, no friend of Austria, seemed shaken. He ordered that a memorial service be held in St. Petersburg and that Russian court and government officials attend. [156] That said, there was no initial, widespread belief across Europe that the assassination would lead to war - not even between Austria and Serbia. [157]

The first reactions in Austria-Hungary, strangely enough, were mixed. While some people were genuinely distressed, others were not. Franz Ferdinand, truth be told, had not been a popular figure. His prickly, hot-tempered personality had endeared him to

---

[155] Quoted in May, *Passing*, 52.
[156] Lafore, *Long Fuse*, 208-09.
[157] See Geiss, *July 1914*, 54.

few. His morganatic marriage to Sophie, whom Habsburg court circles deemed of lower social rank, had greatly offended Franz Josef. [158] The Habsburg army chief, General Franz Conrad von Hotzendorf, had also had differences with the Archduke. Conrad had long advocated a preemptive attack against Serbia. [159] To his frustration, he was repeatedly thwarted by Franz Ferdinand, who thought that Conrad's idea was insane. [160] Aside from his view that Austria should avoid Balkan quarrels, the Archduke believed that any assault on Serbia would likely mean a war with Russia that could destroy the Habsburg realm. [161] Even if St. Petersburg did not intervene and Austria defeated Serbia, he felt that the likely need to occupy Serbian territory would (1) add more troublesome Serbs to the Empire, (2) fail to end the Pan-Serb movement, and (3) force Austria to, in his words, "spend millions on keeping these people down." [162] As he tactlessly exclaimed at a dinner in 1913: "What would we get out of war with Serbia? We'd lose the lives of young men and we'd spend money better used elsewhere. And what would we gain, for heaven's sake? Some plum trees and goat pastures full of droppings, and a bunch of rebellious killers. Long live restraint!" [163]

Most controversial, however, had been Franz Ferdinand's suggestion of a tripartite Habsburg Empire, in which Austria and Hungary would be joined by a new "South Slav" state that would include Bosnia. He reasoned that if the Serbs here had their own state within the Empire, they might lose interest in uniting with Serbia. [164] In his memoirs, future Habsburg Foreign Minister Ottokar von Czernin indicated that the Archduke's designs might have even gone beyond the tripartite stage. Specifically, separate South Slav, Czech, Polish, and possibly other ethnically-based states would be established to "convert the Monarchy into

---

[158] Lafore, *Long Fuse*, 208. The Archduke had been Franz Josef's nephew.

[159] Conrad even favored a preemptive attack on Austria's Italian ally! See Fay, *Origins*, 1:344-45.

[160] Frederic Morton, *Thunder at Twilight: Vienna 1913/1914* (New York: Collier Books, 1989), 36-38.

[161] Richard Hamilton and Holger Herwig, *Decisions for War: 1914-1917* (Cambridge: Cambridge University Press, 2004), 55.

[162] Quoted in Morton, *Thunder*, 38.

[163] Quoted in ibid., 37.

[164] Geiss, *July 1914*, 51.

numerous more or less independent national states, having in Vienna a common central organization for all important and absolutely necessary affairs – in other words, to substitute Federalization for Dualism." [165] Franz Ferdinand believed that the Empire could survive long-term only if certain minorities had more autonomy and the Hungarians' power was curbed. [166] Such ideas infuriated the Magyars, for their influence would be diluted if additional states were created. Small wonder that the Archduke's hatred of them was fully reciprocated. In fact, Hungary's prime minister, Stephen Tisza, was somewhat relieved at his death because it appeared to diminish the prospect of federalism. [167]

Nevertheless, no matter what people thought of him, Franz Ferdinand had been the heir to the Habsburg throne. If nothing else, his assassination was seen as a crime against the monarchy and the Empire. And Serbia was almost immediately deemed the prime suspect.

There is no conclusive evidence that the Serbian government *as a whole* actively backed or nurtured the murder plot. The assassination was certainly not something that Serbia's leaders wanted, for they realized it could push Austro-Serbian tensions to the breaking point. Still, they knew of the conspiracy beforehand but made only a half-hearted effort to stop it. [168] Moreover, the plot had been organized in Belgrade by the Black Hand with the collusion of several army officers and low-level government officials. [169] One might have thought that Serbia would be partial to Franz Ferdinand because of his suggestion that her Serb brethren in Bosnia have more autonomy. This was not so. Belgrade feared that if the Empire became tripartite, the Habsburg Serbs would (as the Archduke had hoped) grow disinterested in linking with Serbia, thus destroying the Greater Serbian dream. [170]

---

[165] Ottokar von Czernin, *In the World War* (1919; reprint, Charleston, SC: BiblioBazaar, 2007), 50. Czernin stressed, however, that the Archduke's thoughts on federalism were general and never evolved into an official, concrete blueprint. Ibid., 57-58.

[166] See ibid., 46-47.

[167] May, *Passing*, 47.

[168] Ibid., 32-35.

[169] Lafore, *Long Fuse*, 204.

[170] May, *Passing*, 29.

Even those in Vienna who may have doubted that top Serbian officials participated in the conspiracy concluded that the murder resulted from years of Pan-Serb agitation that the Belgrade government had failed to stop. Serbian leaders might not have pulled the trigger at Sarajevo. But Vienna believed that they had fostered an environment that encouraged the gun to be fired. Indeed, soon after the assassination almost all of the Empire's ethnic groups raged at Serbia. [171] Fueling their indignation was the vitriol of many Serbian newspapers. They not only attacked Austria, but they also cheered the assassination! [172] As Maurice de Bunsen, London's ambassador to Vienna, told Arthur Nicolson, Britain's undersecretary of state for foreign affairs:

> I must say that I think the Serbian press is behaving shamefully. Long extracts are published here (in Vienna) from the Serbian newspapers, which seem inclined to regard the assassins as martyrs, sacrificed in a holy cause. Insulting expressions are used against this country (Austria) – 'worm-eaten' is the favorite epithet. Ordinary decency would have at least postponed such expressions for a time, and would have made some pretense of offering sympathy and disclaiming the murderers. [173]

---

[171] Ibid., 48; Lafore, *Long Fuse*, 208. Even the Hungarians, who had loathed Franz Ferdinand, were incensed at Belgrade. Britain's consul-general in Budapest, Max Muller, informed Grey: "The Hungarian nation, so far as it is mourning at all, mourns not the person, but the dignity and office, of the victim of the tragedy of Sarajevo, and is willing to go to any lengths in its desire to revenge itself on the despised and hated enemy who is looked on as the author and inspirer of this outrage against the prospective wearer of the Crown of St. Stephen." B.D. 70, July 14. Bosnian Serbs were targeted, too. Maurice de Bunsen, England's ambassador to Vienna, reported that in Sarajevo on June 28 and 29: "The Roman Catholic Croat population, with a strong admixture of Mussulman Slavs, proceeded to demolish all the property of the Orthodox Serbs they could lay their hands on. Serb hotels, shops, and private homes were ransacked, and their contents thrown into the street. The marauding bands were in some cases preceded by Austrian banners and portraits of the Emperor." B.D. 28, Bunsen to Grey, July 2.

[172] May, *Passing*, 49.

[173] B.D. 29, July 3. Germany's secretary of state for foreign affairs, Gottlieb von Jagow, warned Britain's *charge d'affaires* at Berlin, Horace Rumbold,

The reaction of many average Serbians to the assassination was equally disgraceful. Austria's *charge d'affaires* at Belgrade, Wilhelm Ritter von Storck, reported to Leopold von Berchtold, the Habsburg foreign minister: "According to eyewitnesses, people (in Belgrade) embraced each other in delight, and jubilant remarks were heard, such as 'Serves them right!' 'We expected it for a long time!' 'That's the revenge for the annexation!'" [174] Similarly, Vienna's consul-general in Serbia informed Berchtold: "When..............the news of the horrible crime...............was circulated, the feeling which animated the fanatical (Serbian) crowd was, to judge by the numerous expressions of applause reported to me by authorities in whom I have absolute confidence, one that I can only describe as inhuman." [175]

Serbia's prime minister, Nikola Pashitch, and other government leaders were embarrassed by this behavior. [176] But

---

that "if the Serbian press continued to use the language it did, matters would become serious." B.D. 44, Rumbold to Grey, July 11.

[174] D.D., A.R.B. I, Document No. 1, June 29.

[175] C.D.D., A.R.B. I, Document No. 3, July 1.

[176] Dayrell Crackanthorpe, England's *charge d'affaires* at Belgrade, informed London: "(On the 29th), the (Serbian) Government organ *Samouprava* published a leading article expressing deep regret for the sad event, condemning the murder of the Archduke and stating that it could only be the act of some irresponsible maniac." B.D. 27, Crackanthorpe to Grey, July 2. But Crackanthorpe also noted Belgrade's insistence that it was not responsible for the murder. Ibid. He reported a nasty encounter between Storck and the secretary-general of Serbia's foreign office: "I am informed in confidence by my Italian colleague that an interview of considerable violence took place between M. Grouitch and (Storck)............It appears that (Storck) asked the secretary-general unofficially whether the Serbian Government did not consider it advisable to hold an investigation into the circumstances of the crime in view of the fact that both prisoners had recently been in Belgrade. This was apparently much resented by M. Grouitch as implying responsibility for the crime on the part of the Serbian Government. High words ensued, and for the moment relations between the Austrian Legation and the Serbian Ministry for Foreign Affairs are very strained." Ibid. In a separate *Samouprava* article, Belgrade denounced the accusatory tone of Austro-Hungarian newspapers. Crackanthorpe related to Grey: "The article concluded by emphasizing the fact that the Austro-Hungarian press has seized the opportunity to open a campaign of slander and menace against (Serbia), and to incite the (Austro-Hungarian) populace

they were also in a fix. Elections in Serbia were coming up, and no party wanted to appear overly friendly towards Austria. [177] Serbian leaders also probably recalled the gruesome events of June 1903, when Serbian army officers attacked Serbia's pro-Austrian King Alexander and his wife in their palace, shot them to death, chopped up their bodies with sabers and, as a finishing touch, threw their remains out the window. [178] Europe collectively vomited over the incident's brutality; several countries even temporarily recalled their ambassadors from Belgrade. [179] Loath to share Alexander's fate, Pashitch and his colleagues likely concluded that if they tried to suppress the Black Hand and other Pan-Serb goon squads, they risked not only their official positions but also their very lives.

Habsburg officials, however, cared nothing about Pashitch's difficulties. And they were not at all (1) mollified by the Serbian government's condolences, (2) swayed by Pashitch's lame "freedom of the press" excuse for the tone of Serbia's newspapers, or (3) willing to exonerate Belgrade simply because Princip had been a Habsburg (rather than a Serbian) subject. [180] By July 3, after receiving reports that Princip and his cohorts had obtained the murder weapons in Belgrade, Berchtold tentatively concluded that tough measures against Serbia were warranted. [181]

Yet Austria first needed Germany's support. She could not act unilaterally against Serbia because of Russia's potential response. Vienna thus dispatched Alexander von Hoyos, a top Habsburg foreign ministry official, to Germany to discuss things with Berlin.

---

to outrages on innocent and peaceful citizens, thereby incurring the blame of every civilized State." B.D. 45, July 10.

[177] See May, *Passing*, 49.

[178] Morton, *Thunder*, 191; Fay, *Origins*, 1:357.

[179] Fay, *Origins*, 1:357.

[180] May, *Passing*, 49.

[181] See Hamilton and Herwig, *Decisions*, 61. Berchtold met with Franz Josef on June 30. They agreed to wait until more information arrived about the assassins before choosing a course of action. See ibid.

B. Austria and Germany - A Close but Uneasy Partnership

The Austro-German alliance was tight. Both countries felt increasingly threatened by their neighbors. With Italy only a nominal ally and with no one else to turn to, Berlin and Vienna clung to each other. In some ways, Germany was the guardian of the Habsburg Empire. The realization that war with Austria would also mean war with Berlin helped deter other Powers from attacking her. Moreover, it was not inconceivable that Berlin would militarily aid Vienna if some of the Empire's minority groups revolted; indeed, should the Empire disintegrate, Germany would stand alone against the Entente and have new and potentially hostile states near her southeastern flank. Germany therefore shielded Austria from certain dangers; the Empire, in turn, gave Germany diplomatic and, if need be, military support.

But their relationship was not tension-free. Germany was far more militarily and economically powerful than Austria. Despite Vienna's efforts to assert its equality within the alliance, Berlin remained the dominant partner. Each country needed the other, but Austria needed Germany more. While the pact gave Germany some security, it was a matter of life and death for Vienna; without Germany's protection and support, the Empire would have difficulty surviving. Austria was Berlin's weak, ugly stepsister - something she realized and resented but could do little about.

Another issue was that each became embroiled in diplomatic quarrels that threatened to negatively affect the other. Germany's belligerent actions risked giving Austria a bad name since Vienna frequently had to take Germany's side regarding them. [182] Berlin, meanwhile, was frustrated with Austria's constant Balkan disputes. Bismarck had believed that Germany should distance herself from these catfights or at least try to restrain Austria lest Vienna draw Berlin into a Balkan war. [183] In fact, Berlin - ostensibly to keep the Central Powers out of trouble in the

---

[182] See Shanafelt, *Secret Enemy*, 8.

[183] Erich Brandenburg, "Conclusion: The Causes of the War," in *The Outbreak of the First World War: Who Was Responsible?* ed. Dwight Lee (Boston: D.C. Heath, 1963),11.

Balkans – had advised Austria to seek a rapprochement with Serbia, a suggestion that Vienna believed was unrealistic. [184]

In short, the Austro-German marriage was very stable yet laced with feelings of inequality and irritation. Recognizing Austria's internal fragility and overall weakness *vis-a-vis* other Great Powers, Germany perhaps wished that she had wedded someone better.

C. Germany Offers Vienna Her Support and Some Risky Advice

Still, Berlin was determined to back Vienna after Sarajevo. Bethmann-Hollweg outlined Austria's importance to Berlin to a German commission of inquiry after the war:

> The necessity for a powerful Austria has been so often and so earnestly asserted by German statesmen that it must be recognized as a firm basis of our foreign policy. Prince Bismarck, even at the time when, at the conclusion of the Reinsurance Agreement, he met halfway the Russian wishes concerning the Balkans, did not depart from the opinion that 'the existence of Austria-Hungary as a strong and independent Great Power' was 'for Germany a necessity,' yes, 'a necessity of the very highest order,' which would compel us to act, even by force of arms, for the preservation of this condition............Any threat to the independence of Austria endangered our own position in the world, and forced our political course upon us. [185]

In his memoirs, Bethmann-Hollweg wrote that if Austria had collapsed:

---

[184] Berchtold felt that Berlin did not appreciate the seriousness of Vienna's problems concerning Pan-Serb agitation in Bosnia. Samuel Williamson, Jr., "Aggressive and Defensive Aims of Political Elites? Austro-Hungarian Policy in 1914," in *An Improbable War? The Outbreak of World War I and European Political Culture before 1914*, ed. Holger Afflerbach, et al. (New York: Berghahn Books, 2007), 62.

[185] Quoted in Carnegie Endowment for International Peace, *Official German Documents Relating to the World War,* vol. 1 (New York: Oxford University Press, 1923), 12-13.

Germany would (have been) completely isolated. (She) would (have been) choked to death by a ring of enemies, banded together in a common campaign for world dominion by jealous dislike for a growing commercial rival, by Slav race hatred against Teutons, and by lowering ill-will against the victor of 1870.............If Austria had fallen, the Slav world would have secured the success of centuries. Such an uncontested conquest by Moscow would have inaugurated an epoch in which Russia would have pressed heavily on the West. Germany would only have survived the fall of Austria as a vassal to the Eastern potentate...............The oppressors of Germany could then have determined the day at their ease on which Germany should cease to exist as a Great Power [186]

Germany's secretary of state for foreign affairs in 1914, Gottlieb von Jagow, similarly told the post-war commission:

A permanently weakened and finally crumbling Austria could no longer have remained for us – as it is expressed in our White Book of 1914 – an ally with whom we could reckon and on whom we could depend. Germany's isolation would then have been complete. We should have been delivered to the mercy of the Entente's political play: Russia's urge for expansion, France's passion for revenge, and the jealousy of England's rivalry. Thus were we, too, face-to-face with a question of vital interest...........In this case (the Sarajevo matter), we could not refuse our help to Austria.............Germany had no choice; not merely because of romantic loyalty, but out of consideration for her own position, she could not let Austria fall. [187]

And Sarajevo was not a situation where Austria had gotten into trouble through irresponsible behavior. No, this was different. Berlin believed that Austria had been the victim of an unprovoked

---

[186] Bethmann-Hollweg, *Reflections*, 113, 117.
[187] Quoted in Carnegie Endowment, *Official German Documents*, 27.

attack. Such Serbian aggression had to be stopped. Jagow later explained:

> We had always advised our Vienna ally to pave the way for a more friendly relationship with Serbia and to strive for a community of interest. But the murder at Sarajevo – the fruit of the Greater Serbia propaganda – which threw a brilliant side-light on the intentions of the neighboring States, proved even to us the impossibility of such a rapprochement...........
>
> The alliance with Austria-Hungary had been from the time of Bismarck the main-spring of our policy. To be sure, it did not extend to entering the field on behalf of every Austro-Hungarian special interest in the Balkans. But in this case (Sarajevo), it was not a matter of some special Balkan problem of Austria's, not a matter of the extension of her power and sphere of influence there, but a matter of the status as a World Power of our ally herself, and of her defense against an aggressive Serbian policy that threatened the state of the realm and the security of her southern borders. It was an act of self-preservation to quench the fire that continuously threatened the home of a neighbor and all Europe with a conflagration; and for Austria it was a question of life itself. Security could only be attained when the necessary guarantees for future good behavior had been promptly and energetically extorted from Serbia, the hearth of all these firebrands. [188]

When German officials met with Hoyos on July 5-6, therefore, they promised Austria their complete support in whatever action she chose to take in response to the assassination. Furthermore, they advised Vienna to act quickly and firmly against Serbia. The Kaiser was particularly belligerent. While he, too, had previously recommended that Vienna pursue better relations with Serbia, Sarajevo altered his thinking. [189] After reviewing a June 30 telegram to Bethmann-Hollweg from Berlin's

---

[188] Quoted in ibid., 24, 26-27.
[189] Fay, *Origins,* 2:207-08.

ambassador to Austria, Heinrich Leopold von Tschirschky und Bogendorff, in which Tschirschky revealed that he had advised Vienna not to react hastily to the assassination, Wilhelm wrote: "Who authorized him (Tschirschky) to act that way? That is very stupid! It is none of his business...............Let Tschirschky be good enough to drop this nonsense!.................The Serbs must be disposed of, and that right soon!" [190]

Berlin advised quick action for two main reasons. First, Austria had to capitalize on her population's desire for revenge against Belgrade and Europe's post-assassination sympathy for her. [191] If she waited too long to act, the horror of Sarajevo would wear off. Her populace might lose interest in punishing Serbia, and other Powers might prove less willing to tolerate such punishment. Here was a golden chance for Austria to smite Serbia while European opinion was generally on her side. Circumstances so favorable might never come again. The moment therefore had to be seized. Second, Berlin felt that significant hesitation by Austria would make her look indecisive and feeble.

This apprehension about her ally's weakness also prompted Germany's recommendation of firm measures against Belgrade. If Vienna let a small country like Serbia continue to get away with her agitation (especially after Sarajevo), it would show that Austria could be pushed around at will. Her already shaky Great Power status would be destroyed and her enemies emboldened. [192] This would result in a weaker Austro-German coalition (*vis-à-vis* the Entente) and thus a more vulnerable Germany. Tough Austrian

---

[190] Marginal comment of Wilhelm on G.D. 7. Wilhelm also wrote, "Now or never," seemingly in response to Tschirschky's statement that some in Vienna wanted a final reckoning with Serbia. Marginal comment of Wilhelm on ibid. Even so, Germany's undersecretary of state for foreign affairs, Arthur Zimmermann, initially favored caution; he advised Austria to exercise restraint and to avoid making humiliating demands on Serbia. Fay, *Origins,* 2:199, 221.

[191] May, *Passing,* 58-59.

[192] As Bethmann-Hollweg later wrote: "Practically speaking, Austria could only master the Serbian danger if it handled it severely. Keeping on the gloves would only have encouraged the Greater Serbia propaganda............It would have been better not to have put up a fist at all. Only a strong decision could check the dissolution of the Austrian Monarchy." Bethmann-Hollweg, *Reflections,* 123.

action, however, would send a message to Serbia and Russia (and even to those Bosnian Serbs within Austrian-Hungary who were attracted to the Greater Serbia concept) that the Empire was strong and should not be trifled with.

The Germans stressed that the final decision on what steps to take rested with Vienna. They did not want the Entente to accuse them of egging Austria on and inciting war. [193] They also probably thought that if they *pushed* (rather than merely *advised*) Austria to take or not take certain measures, Vienna would blame them if things went awry. [194] Yet despite their willingness to step back and let Austria take the lead, the Germans worried that Vienna would show irresolution. [195]

Since harsh action against Serbia could spur Russia to intervene militarily, Berlin's advice to Vienna carried risks. In fact, Arthur Zimmermann, Germany's undersecretary of state for foreign affairs, deemed the chances that a European war would erupt to be 90 percent! [196] Others in Berlin, however, were less certain of Russian intercession. [197] In his memoirs, German Admiral Alfred von Tirpitz noted a conversation between his deputy and the Kaiser on July 6 in which Wilhelm opined that a larger war was unlikely:

> The Emperor did not consider an intervention by Russia to protect Serbia as probable because the Tsar would not support the assassination of royalty and, moreover, Russia

---

[193] Bethmann-Hollweg alluded to this in his memoirs: "We have been given to understand from other quarters that after approving the Austrian action, we should have taken over entire control of it................But we must remember that we should have at once given an international scope to the Austro-Serbian dispute if we had converted the Austrian action into an Austro-German action. We should have lost thereby every possibility of localizing the conflict or, failing that, of mediating it internationally." Bethmann-Hollweg, *Reflections*, 121. This concept of "localization," as we will see, became the cornerstone of Berlin's crisis diplomacy.

[194] Indeed, in his comments on Tschirschky's June 30 telegram, in which he criticized the ambassador for advising restraint, Wilhelm added: "Later, if plans go wrong, it will be said that Germany did not want it!" Marginal comment of Wilhelm on G.D. 7.

[195] Lafore, *Long Fuse*, 215.

[196] Hamilton and Herwig, *Decisions*, 85.

[197] Martel, *Origins*, 65; Geiss, *July 1914*, 71-72.

was at the time militarily and financially unfit for war. The Emperor proceeded to argue in somewhat sanguine fashion that France would put the brakes on Russia because of France's unfavorable financial position and her shortage of heavy artillery. The Emperor did not mention England; there was no thought of complications with this State. Thus, the Emperor himself regarded any far-reaching dangers as improbable. [198]

In a July 12 note to Berchtold, Ladislaus Szogyeny, Vienna's ambassador to Germany, indicated that Berlin felt the assassination's sheer dreadfulness would dissuade Europe from helping Serbia:

> The eyes of the whole world have been opened, and there is no nation that does not condemn the bloody deed of Sarajevo and all admit that we must make Serbia responsible for it. If Serbia's foreign friends for political reasons do not openly blame Serbia, still we cannot believe that they will stand up for it at the present moment, at least not with armed forces. [199]

Likewise, Jagow told the aforementioned post-war commission: "Should the action of Austria then follow upon the fresh impression of the murder, which had filled all the world with horror, it would be so much the more reasonable to expect that the Powers, even Russia, would scarcely deny Austria's right to take steps, and would therefore refrain from intervening." [200]

As for France, some in Berlin felt that she was too preoccupied with domestic problems to go to war and, in any event, was unlikely to fight simply to help protect Russia's Balkan interests. [201] They also shared Wilhelm's view that Russia was

---

[198] Alfred von Tirpitz, *My Memoirs,* vol. 1 (New York: Dodd, Mead and Company, 1919), 316. See also Geiss, *July 1914,* 72; Berghahn, *Germany and the Approach,* 189.

[199] Quoted in Geiss, *July 1914,* 111.

[200] Quoted in Carnegie Endowment, *Official German Documents,* 28.

[201] Martel, *Origins,* 65; note from Lichtenau to Vitzthum, July 2, in Geiss, *July 1914,* 68. (Lichtenau was the Saxon minister in Berlin; Vitzthum was the Saxon minister of state for foreign affairs.)

militarily unready for war; Russia's rearmament program, after all, would not be completed for several years. [202] In his July 12 message to Berchtold, Szogyeny further explained Berlin's position:

> Germany has recently found its conviction confirmed that Russia is preparing for a war with its western neighbors, and does not regard war as a possibility of the future, but positively includes it in the political calculations of the future. This is important: it intends on waging war, it is preparing for it with all its might, but does not propose it for the present – or, we should rather say, is not prepared for it at the present time. It is therefore anything but certain that if Serbia is engaged in a war with us, Russia would lend an armed hand; and should the Tsar's empire resolve for war, it would not be ready from a military point of view, and not by any means so strong as it will be a few years hence. [203]

And as Jagow told Berlin's ambassador to London, Karl Max Lichnowsky, on the 18th:

> The more determined Austria shows herself and the more energetically we support her, so much the more quiet will Russia remain. To be sure, there will be some agitation in St. Petersburg, but, on the whole, Russia is not ready to strike at present............(Russia is) therefore determined to have peace for a few years yet. I readily believe your cousin (Alexander) Benckendorff (Russia's ambassador to London) when he says that Russia wants no war with us at present. [204]

Berlin was extremely nervous about Russia's growing military power. Under her rearmament plan, Russia's standing

---

[202] Martel, *Origins*, 65; Geiss, *July 1914*, 71-72, 74; Fritz Fischer, *Germany's Aims in the First World War* (New York: W.W. Norton and Company, 1967), 53-54.

[203] Quoted in Geiss, *July 1914*, 110.

[204] G.D. 72. See also James Joll, *The Origins of the First World War*, 2nd ed. (Essex: Pearson Longman, 1992), 13, 16.

army was to increase in size by a whopping 40 percent by 1918. [205] Such huge forces could conceivably overwhelm the Central Powers, a point Jagow emphasized in his July 18 note to Lichnowsky: "According to all competent observation, Russia will be prepared to fight in a few years. Then she will crush us by the number of her soldiers; then she will have built her Baltic Sea fleet and her strategic railroads. Our group, in the meantime, will have become weaker right along." [206] Other German officials, too, feared that the military pendulum would soon swing in the Franco-Russian pact's favor. Furthermore, Berlin believed that Russia was attempting to organize a new league of Balkan states under her aegis. [207] If this pro-Russian (and presumably anti-Austrian) bloc materialized, Vienna would have not only Serbia and Russia as adversaries but also perhaps Greece, Bulgaria, and even Romania.

There was, hence, a feeling in Berlin that if a European war erupted from an Austro-Serbian conflict, now might be the best time for the Central Powers to fight it. Germany's military strength was at its peak, Russia's was not, and no St. Petersburg-dominated Balkan League yet existed. There was a window of opportunity for war under circumstances reasonably favorable for Germany. Once it closed, it was unlikely to reopen. To be sure, she neither wanted nor expected a European conflict to happen. [208] But if one did, she felt that her chances of success were as good as they would ever be.

The overall mindset of Germany's leadership in mid-July can be summarized as follows. Berlin believed that Austria had to act firmly against Serbia to show her strength, restore her prestige, and enhance her security. While the Germans recognized the possibility of a wider conflict, they generally felt that war with the Franco-Russian alliance was a worst-case – and not the likeliest - scenario. Still, if it happened, they believed it was better to fight it now, before Russia became too strong. And they felt that the Central Powers could win it. Victory, in turn, would end the

---

[205] Martel, *Origins*, 65.

[206] G.D. 72.

[207] Telegram from Szogyeny to Berchtold, July 6, in Geiss, *July 1914*, 79.

[208] Even Zimmermann, we shall see, began to doubt that a continental war would erupt.

Entente's threat to Germany and ensure her supremacy in Europe. Conversely, if Russia did not intervene, Austria would surely defeat Serbia, Belgrade's agitation would cease, and St. Petersburg's abandonment of Serbia would devastate its position in the Balkans.

There were dangers for Germany, of course. Berlin knew that a war with the Franco-Russian pact – unlikely though it seemed - would bring cataclysmic loss of life. Moreover, the Central Powers would enter it outmanned. In 1914, Germany and Austria had respective populations of about 65 million and 51 million; the respective figures for Russia and France were 167 million and 40 million. [209] This almost 2-to-1 advantage for St. Petersburg and Paris did not necessarily translate into a similar edge in troop numbers. But Russia's enormous population almost guaranteed that she and France would bring more men to the battlefield than the Central Powers. Defeating the Franco-Russian alliance, while perhaps doable, would not be easy. [210] Yet Berlin accepted these risks because it believed that the Habsburg Empire's existence was at stake. Austria was deemed to be that important to Germany's security.

Germany's belief that the Central Powers could defeat Russia and France was partly based on her assumption that England would remain neutral in such a conflict. German-British relations, we know, had recently improved. And Berlin recognized that while Britain had grown much closer to Paris and St. Petersburg, she was not formally allied with them. [211] We saw earlier Tirpitz's statement that Wilhelm "did not mention England; there was no thought of complications with this State." [212] Szogyeny similarly noted in his July 12 message to Berchtold:

> (T)he German government believes that it has proofs that England would not take part in a war caused by

---

[209] Kevin Stubbs, *Race to the Front: The Material Foundations of Coalition Strategy in the Great War* (Westport, CT: Praeger Publishers, 2002), 19.

[210] See Chapter VIII, Part E, for a discussion of Germany's strategic dilemma in this regard.

[211] G.D. 30, Lichnowsky to Bethmann-Hollweg, July 9.

[212] Tirpitz, *My Memoirs*, 316.

disturbances in the Balkans, even if Russia and France were involved in it. Not only have the relations between England and Germany improved so far that Germany need no longer fear direct hostilities on England's part, but England just now desires anything rather than a war, and would certainly not expose itself to danger for Serbia's or even Russia's sake. [213]

The Germans did not deem British intervention to be absolutely impossible. Yet they felt it was extremely unlikely. Berlin thus appeared to back harsh measures against Serbia without seriously considering the prospect of war with England. An incorrect assumption, however, could prove catastrophic. If England fought alongside France and Russia, the Triple Entente would be the favorite to win the war. Not only would the British Empire's population add to the Franco-Russian pact's manpower superiority, but also a British naval blockade of the Central Powers would curtail their ability to import food and materials – a crucial, perhaps decisive factor if the war dragged on for several years.

The futures of Germany and Austria could well rest upon whether Berlin guessed right as to Britain's intentions.

D. Austria Decides on a Final Showdown with Serbia

Armed with Germany's support, the Common Ministerial Council – a small group of top Habsburg officials - met in Vienna on July 7. According to the minutes:

> (Berchtold) was clear in his own mind that hostilities with Serbia would entail war with Russia. Russia, however, was now playing a far-seeing game, and was calculating on a policy of being able to unite the Balkan States, including Romania, with the eventual objective of launching them at an appropriate moment against the Monarchy. He suggested that we must reckon on the fact that in the face of such a policy our situation was bound

---

[213] Quoted in Geiss, *July 1914*, 110-11.

steadily to deteriorate, and all the more if an inactive policy of *laisser aller* were to be interpreted as a sign of weakness by our own South Slavs and Rumanians, and were to be a direct encouragement to the power of attraction of the two neighbor States (Serbia and Romania). The logical inference to be drawn from his remarks was that we must be beforehand with our enemies and, by bringing matters to a head with Serbia, must call a halt to the gathering momentum of events; later, it would no longer be possible to do so. [214]

The war minister, Alexander von Krobatin, shared Berchtold's view:

---

[214] Quoted in Charles Horne, ed., *Source Records of the Great War,* vol. 1 (1923; reprint, Indianapolis: American Legion, 1930), 277. On July 10, Russia's ambassador to Serbia, Nicholas Hartwig, dropped dead of a heart attack at the Austrian legation in Belgrade. Considered by some European statesmen to be as pleasant to deal with as a stomach virus, Hartwig harbored extreme anti-Austrian and pro-Serbian sentiments. He had visited the legation to address rumors regarding his post-Sarajevo actions. As Crackanthorpe related to Grey: "The *Reichspost* of Vienna had recently published an article attacking (Hartwig) for holding a bridge party on the evening of the Archduke's murder. It is true that M. Hartwig was having a quiet game of bridge that evening with the Romanian and Greek Ministers and the Italian *charge d'affaires*, but, under the circumstances, the article in the *Reichspost* seems to have contained some very unnecessary animadversions; (2) (Hartwig) had been accused of not hoisting the Russian flag at half-mast on the day of the funeral service of the Archduke. Though M. Hartwig himself affirmed that the flag was flying, several of my colleagues state that this was not the case. The Austrian Legation took a strong view of the matter and doubtless (Hartwig) was anxious to smooth matters over; (3) I regret to state that M. Hartwig had recently been using very inappropriate and ill-advised language in regard to the private life and character of the present heir to the Austro-Hungarian throne, in the presence, among others, of my Italian colleague." B.D. 62, July 13. While British Assistant Undersecretary of State for Foreign Affairs Eyre Crowe wrote that "in the political and diplomatic world, M. Hartwig's death will not cause much grief," preposterous rumors circulated in Belgrade that Austrian legation officials had poisoned Hartwig. Comment of Crowe on B.D. 48, Crackanthorpe to Grey, July 11; B.D. 62.

From the military point of view, he (Krobatin) must emphasize the fact that it would be better to wage the war now, rather than later, as the balance of power would move disproportionately against us later on..............We had already neglected two opportunities of solving the Serbian question and had deferred decision on both occasions. If we did this again and took no notice of this latest provocation, this would be taken as a sign of weakness in every South Slav province and we should be inducing an increase of the agitation directed against us.[215]

Tisza, however, was more cautious. Several days before this conference, he had urged Franz Josef to be wary of Habsburg officials who might demand immediate military action against Serbia.[216] He recognized that Austria had to respond to the assassination. But he did not believe that force was necessary yet. The conference minutes stated:

During the last few days, the results of our investigations and the tone of the Serbian press had put a materially new complexion on events, and emphasized the fact that he (Tisza) held the possibility of warlike action against Serbia to be more obvious than he had thought in the period immediately after the act at Sarajevo. But he would never give his consent to a surprise attack on Serbia without previous diplomatic action..............(W)ere that done, in his opinion, our position in the eyes of Europe would be an extremely bad one, and in all probability we should have to reckon with the enmity of the whole Balkans, except Bulgaria, while Bulgaria herself being at present very much weakened would not be able to give us the necessary support.

---

[215] Quoted in Horne, *Source Records*, 281-82.

[216] Fay, *Origins*, 2:189-90. In fact, before Sarajevo Tisza had devised a plan to reduce the Serbian threat through diplomacy - not war – by bringing Bulgaria into the Triple Alliance. This, he reasoned, could push Greece towards a more pro-Austrian position, isolate Serbia, and reduce Russia's Balkan influence. Ibid., 2:189-93.

It was absolutely necessary that we should formulate demands against Serbia and only send an ultimatum in case Serbia failed to satisfy them. These demands must undoubtedly be hard, but should not be impossible of fulfillment. Should Serbia accept them, we should be able to quote a dazzling diplomatic victory, and our prestige in the Balkans would be raised. Should our demands not be accepted, he himself would then be for warlike action, but even at this point he thought it essential to lay stress on the fact that the object of such action ought to be the reduction of Serbia, but not her complete annihilation; first, because this would never be allowed by Russia without a life and death struggle, and also because he, as Hungarian Premier, could never consent to the annexation of part of Serbia by the Monarchy.

(He also believed that it) was not Germany's place to judge whether we should now deal a blow at Serbia or not. Personally, he was of the opinion that it was not absolutely necessary to go to war at this moment. [217]

Krobatin countered that a purely diplomatic victory would "be of no value" and "only be interpreted as a weakness." [218] Berchtold concurred:

The history of the last years had shown that while diplomatic successes against Serbia raised the reputation of the Monarchy for the time being, the actual tension in our relations with Serbia had only increased. Neither our success during the annexation crisis, nor at the creation of Albania, nor Serbia's submission later in consequence of our ultimatum of the autumn of last year, had altered the

---

[217] Quoted in Horne, *Source Records,* 277-78. Tisza was also leery of military action because Austria lacked a strong friend in the Balkans who could support her. Carvel de Bussy, *Count Stephen Tisza, Prime Minister of Hungary: Letters (1914–1916)* (New York: Peter Lang, 1991), 1. The alliance with Romania was shaky (see Chapter XI), while Bulgaria – as Tisza indicated to the Council - was too exhausted after the Balkan Wars to be of much help.
[218] Quoted in Horne, *Source Records,* 281.

real situation in any way. (Berchtold) imagined that energetic action alone would suffice to solve once and for all the problems created by the systematic propaganda for a Greater Serbia encouraged from Belgrade. [219]

Karl Sturgkh, the premier of the Austrian half of the Empire, stressed to Tisza the need to take advantage of Germany's support:

> Unconditional loyalty (from Germany) was, as we were informed, promised to us and that, in addition, on our making inquiry, we were urged to act at once; Count Tisza ought to weigh this fact, and to consider that a hesitating, weak policy would run us into the danger of losing the certainty of this unconditional support of the German Empire on a future occasion. [220]

Conrad attended the conference's afternoon session. [221] Not surprisingly, the always-bellicose army chief was itching to attack Serbia. Franz Josef, meanwhile, was not in attendance. Initially undecided on how Austria should respond, he eventually favored tough measures against Belgrade. [222]

Even before Hoyos's mission to Germany, there seemed to be a rough consensus among Habsburg officials (excluding Tisza) that military action was necessary. With Berlin's support solidifying this sentiment, the July 7 minutes stated:

> At the end of this discussion, agreement was reached:
>
> (1) That all present wish for the speediest decision which is practicable in the conflict with Serbia, whether by means of war or peace.

---

[219] Quoted in ibid., 278-79.

[220] Quoted in ibid., 280. On July 18, Hans von Schoen, the Bavarian *charge d'affaires* at Berlin, reported to Bavaria's prime minister, Georg Hertling, that the degree of Germany's backing surprised Austria: "In Vienna, they do not seem to have expected such an unconditional support of the Danube Monarchy by Germany." Quoted in Geiss, *July 1914*, 129.

[221] Horne, *Source Records*, 283.

[222] Fay, *Origins*, 2:187-88, 198.

(2) That the Ministerial Council is prepared to adopt the point of view of the Hungarian Premier (Tisza) to the effect that mobilization shall only follow after concrete demands have been addressed to Serbia, and have been refused, and an ultimatum has further been sent.

(3) On the other hand, all present, excepting the Hungarian Premier, hold that a purely diplomatic success, even if ending in a startling humiliation for Serbia, would be without value, and that, therefore, the demands to be put to Serbia must be so far-reaching as to pre-suppose a refusal, so that the way would be prepared for a radical solution by means of military intervention. [223]

So notwithstanding Tisza's reservations, the Council decided to force a final showdown with Serbia. Several factors were involved. First, Austria had Berlin's complete support. For all she knew, she might never get it again. She thus needed to capitalize on it *now*. Second, she worried that a weak response to the assassination would damage the Austro-German relationship and make Berlin question Vienna's worth as an ally. [224] Third, Austria (like Germany) saw the balance of power tilting towards Russia and the Slavs. It was therefore, as Krobatin said, "better to wage the war now, rather than later."

Lastly, previous Austrian threats against Serbia (e.g., during the Bosnian crisis) had not halted Belgrade's troublemaking. To the contrary, as Austria's ambassador to Serbia, Wladimar Giesl von Gieslingen, noted to Berchtold on July 21, many Serbians believed that the Empire was finished:

After the annexation crisis, the relations between the Monarchy and Serbia were poisoned on the Serbian side by national chauvinism, animosity and an effective propaganda of Greater Serbian aspirations carried on in that part of our territory where there is a Serbian population; since the last two Balkan Wars, the success of

---

[223] Quoted in Horne, *Source Records*, 283.
[224] See Fischer, *Germany's Aims*, 57; Fay, *Origins*, 2:226.

Serbia has increased this chauvinism to a paroxysm, the expression of which in some cases bears the mark of insanity...........

The crime at Sarajevo has aroused among the Serbians an expectation that in the immediate future the Habsburg States will fall to pieces..............Austria-Hungary, hated as she is, now appears to the Serbians as powerless, and as scarcely worthy of waging war with; contempt is mingled with hatred; she is ripe for destruction, and she is to fall without trouble into the lap of the Greater Serbian Empire, which is to be realized in the immediate future.............

For both internal and external reasons, the Monarchy is held to be powerless and incapable of any energetic action, and it is believed that the serious words which were spoken by leading men among us are only 'bluff.' [225]

With Serbia's agitation seemingly out of control, Habsburg officials saw no option left but force. [226] They believed that her antagonistic pressure on Austria-Hungary had to stop before it broke the Empire apart. They knew that military action carried risks. In fact, Berchtold, as the July 7 minutes indicated, appeared more convinced of Russian intervention than was Berlin. Yet Austria's apparent willingness to gamble her existence on a potential European war signified how desperate she viewed her situation. She saw her enemies growing stronger and converging on her. Time, as Berchtold implied on the 7th, was running out. He and others in Vienna felt that drastic action was needed to preserve the Empire. And this might be their last, best chance to take it. It was less a question of exacting revenge against Serbia than of using the June 28 tragedy to save the Habsburg realm.

---

[225] C.D.D., A.R.B. I, Document No. 6.

[226] There may also have been a feeling that with Franz Josef – to some degree, the glue that held the heterogeneous Habsburg realm together - unlikely to live much longer, it was crucial to use this opportunity to bolster the Empire so that it did not crumble after his death.

E. Vienna's Delay in Action and Germany's Impatience

But Vienna was not yet ready to move. There were four main reasons for this. First, some Habsburg army units were on leave to assist with the harvest and were not scheduled to return for several weeks. [227] Conrad was reluctant to immediately recall them lest this disrupt the harvest and prematurely reveal Austria's planned response. [228] Military action would therefore have to wait. Second, Vienna needed time to accumulate evidence about the Serbian government's role in the murder conspiracy. [229] If government officials could be implicated, this might help keep European opinion on Austria's side. Third, Tisza's concerns had to be alleviated. Without Hungarian support, the Empire could not act. In a July 8 note to Franz Josef, Tisza again expressed reservations about going to war:

> All of the members of the Council of Ministers reached agreement yesterday on the need to provoke a war which would allow us finally to settle accounts with the Serbs, our oldest enemies. I was unable to approve this plan in its entirety. An attack against Serbia would quite probably bring about the intervention of Russia and a world war would follow............

> After having studied the political situation, if I think of the economic and financial upheaval, of the sufferings and sacrifices which the war will unavoidably bring, I cannot support, after the most painfully conscientious reflection, the thought of sharing my part of the responsibility for the military attack proposed against Serbia. It is far from my intention to recommend a policy without energy regarding our neighbors. We cannot remain the inert spectators of the agitation being carried on at Belgrade which arouses our own subjects against us and foments crime. Not only the Serbian press and the official journals, but even the representatives of Serbia abroad are showing such hatred for us and are so lacking in the observance of international

---

[227] Hamilton and Herwig, *Decisions*, 64.
[228] Ibid.
[229] Shanafelt, *Secret Enemy*, 29.

courtesy, that our prestige, on one hand, and our security, on the other, urgently require us to assume an energetic attitude towards Serbia. Indeed, I am not implying that we should tolerate all the provocations without saying a word, and I am ready to accept responsibility for any war which might be caused by a refusal of our just demands.

But we ought to give Serbia the opportunity of avoiding conflict by means of a severe humiliation. We must be able to prove to the world that when we decided on war, we were in a situation of legitimate defense. So it is my view to send a note to Belgrade in a moderate, not threatening, tone, explaining precisely our grounds for complaint and our demands. If the reply is not satisfactory, or if it were to drag matters out, we should answer by an ultimatum and, after the deadline passed, begin hostilities. But then we should find ourselves facing a war which was forced upon us, one of those wars which it is a nation's duty to prosecute without weakness to the very end if it wants to continue to be a State, and the responsibility would fall upon our adversary, who would have started it by its refusal to act as an honest neighbor, even after the frightful act at Sarajevo. By acting in this way..............perhaps even Russia would refrain from entering the conflict. In all probability, England would exercise a calming influence on the other powers of the Entente. There is also no doubt that the Tsar will reflect that it is not his role to defend anarchists and the assassins of kings.

After such (an Austro-Serbian) war................we should content ourselves with asking for the rectification of certain important points in our strategic border. Perhaps we could also demand repayment of our war costs. This would give us a guarantee of holding Serbia in our hands for a long time..............But in case Serbia accepts our demands, we should naturally accept her submission in good faith and not close the road for retreat. We ought to be satisfied with bringing down her pride and this diplomatic victory would allow us to pursue a profitable policy in the other Balkan countries..............

I have the honor of advising adoption of the golden mean indicated in this memorandum. It appears to me to have the advantage of not ruling out a peaceful solution and of improving the chances of war in many ways, if the latter becomes inevitable. I have the honor of stating with greatest respect that, in spite of my loyalty, or more exactly, because of it, it would be impossible for me to accept the solution of a war at any price. [230]

By the 14th, however, Tisza had come around to Berchtold's hard-line position. [231] Franz Josef's support for firm measures against Serbia, the promise of German backing, and the continuing vitriol of Serbia's press all seemed to factor into Tisza's shift towards war. [232] The clincher, perhaps, was Berchtold's agreement that Vienna would not annex any Serbian territory captured in the upcoming military campaign. To avoid diluting the Magyars' influence, Tisza wanted no more Serbs in the Empire. [233]

Fourth, an ultimatum to Belgrade had to be drafted. Habsburg officials recognized that attacking Serbia without warning could undo Europe's sympathy towards Austria. Tisza, we saw, initially desired strong demands that Serbia could nonetheless accept. But he eventually agreed that the ultimatum should be harsher than that. Vienna remained unconvinced that a diplomatic triumph, no matter how complete, would end Belgrade's agitation; even if it subsided at first, it was bound to

---

[230] Quoted in de Bussy, *Count Stephen Tisza*, 3-6. Tisza had expressed even stronger concerns on July 1. He told Berchtold that using the assassination "as a motive for revenge against Serbia" would be "a disastrous mistake and (I) (Tisza) should not share the responsibility under any condition. First, we have up to now insufficient basis for making Serbia responsible and for provoking a war with that country in spite of eventual satisfactory declarations by the Serbian government. We would have the worst possible position, would stand before the entire world as a disturber of the peace, and encourage a great war under the most unfavorable conditions." Letter from Tisza to Franz Josef, July 1, quoted in ibid., 1-2.

[231] Fay, *Origins,* 2:242.

[232] Ibid., 2:241-43; May, *Passing*, 60.

[233] Fay, *Origins,* 2:239-40.

pick up again. An ultimatum that Serbia could accept would therefore be of no use.

The plan was to hand the ultimatum to Serbia around July 25. [234] French President Raymond Poincare was scheduled to visit Russia on the 20th and depart for Paris several days later. [235] The Austrians wanted to wait until Poincare left St. Petersburg before presenting the note. They felt it would be an affront to France and Russia if the bombshell came while their heads of state were meeting. [236] A more cynical motivation was that once Poincare left Russia, the French and Russian leaderships would be unable to coordinate their efforts and influence each other face-to-face. [237] As Berchtold told Szogyeny on the 15th:

> We should consider it unwise to undertake the threatening step in Belgrade at the very time when the peace-loving, reserved Tsar Nicholas and undeniably cautious Herr (Sergei) Sazonov (Russia's foreign minister) are under the influence of the two who are always for war, Izvolsky (now serving as Russia's ambassador to Paris) and Poincare. [238]

Vienna regretted this delay but felt it had no choice. Berlin was getting frustrated with Austria's foot-dragging, however. Her inaction threatened to (1) make her look weak and (2) create suspicions that the Central Powers were plotting something sinister. And with the horror of Sarajevo wearing off, Berlin feared that sympathy for Austria would wither away as well. She needed to act while European opinion was on her side. Also, the longer Vienna waited, the more time Belgrade would have to launch a pre-emptive diplomatic strike by offering Austria promises of

---

[234] See G.D. 50, Tschirschky to Bethmann-Hollweg, July 14.

[235] Lafore, *Long Fuse*, 212.

[236] Fay, *Origins,* 2:240.

[237] Lafore, *Long Fuse*, 212.

[238] Quoted in Geiss, *July 1914*, 117. Similarly, Tschirschky informed Bethmann-Hollweg that Vienna felt "it was best to avoid if possible the celebration of a (Franco-Russian) fraternization at St. Petersburg under the influence of champagne..............It would be much better to have the toasts gotten over with before the delivery of the note." G.D. 50.

better behavior. [239] Much of Europe would pressure her to accept them; if she refused and war erupted, she would be held responsible.

Vienna's slowness particularly disturbed the Kaiser. When Tschirschky wired Jagow on July 10 about Franz Josef's view that Austria had "to come to some determination in order to put an end to the intolerable conditions in connection with Serbia," Wilhelm commented: "(I)t is taking a long time!" [240] And upon learning of Vienna's decision to wait until Poincare left Russia to present the ultimatum, he wrote: "What a pity!" [241] Indeed, some in Berlin perhaps started to question whether Austria really had the guts to get rough with Serbia. [242]

F. The Central Powers Finalize Their Preparations

Notwithstanding whatever concerns Berlin had about Austria's backbone, the Central Powers began laying the diplomatic groundwork for what was coming. The first step involved remaining relatively silent about Austria's plans. The quieter things were, the easier it would be for Vienna to finalize its preparations without interference from other countries. [243] While Austria told Europe that (1) Serbia's agitation must end and (2) a response to the assassination might be necessary, she revealed few specifics. [244] Likewise, Germany defended Austria and condemned

---

[239] Geiss, *July 1914*, 98.

[240] G.D. 29; marginal comment of Wilhelm on ibid. Even the Austro-Hungarian populace seemed to be getting antsy. Bunsen wrote to Nicolson on the 17th: "There is one topic in the Vienna press..........namely, when will the protest against Serbia be put in, and what will it contain?" B.D. 56.

[241] Marginal comment of Wilhelm on G.D. 50. He was relieved, however, when Tisza finally adopted Berchtold's hard-line stance, writing: "Well, a real man at last!" Marginal comment of Wilhelm on G.D. 49, Tschirschky to Bethmann-Hollweg, July 14; Geiss, *July 1914*, 95.

[242] See note from Schoen to Hertling, July 18, in Geiss, *July 1914*, 128.

[243] Geiss, *July 1914*, 89-91.

[244] Fay, *Origins,* 2:243-46. Austrian secretiveness was apparent even in early July. Bunsen reported to Grey on the 5th that Nikolai Schebeko, Russia's ambassador to Austria, lamented "the difficulty which he, in common with most of his colleagues, including myself (Bunsen), finds in extracting from

Serbia but was vague about Vienna's concrete intentions. Even the Central Powers' Italian ally was kept in the dark. Vienna feared that if it discussed its plans with Italy, the latter – in order to thwart a Habsburg advance in the western Balkans, where Rome had territorial ambitions – would reveal them to Europe. [245]

The second step (which, like the first, was meant to keep things quiet) was to give the appearance that neither Austria nor Germany viewed the situation as alarming. [246] Berchtold, for instance, had Conrad and Krobatin leave Vienna on vacation. [247] And the Kaiser proceeded with his scheduled Scandinavian voyage. [248] As Hans von Schoen, the Bavarian *charge d'affaires* at Berlin, explained on the 16th to Georg Hertling, the Bavarian prime minister:

> (The German Foreign Office) has emphasized to the representatives of the other Powers that it regards the situation without any trace of nervousness, and as evidence of this has pointed out that H.M. the Kaiser would otherwise not have left for his Scandinavian journey, that the Imperial Chancellor would not then have gone to Hohenfinow, and the Chief of the General Staff would not have gone on leave. [249]

Count Berchtold...............anything like an explicit statement of his views on international affairs." B.D. 40.

[245] Telegram from Szogyeny to Berchtold, July 6, in Geiss, *July 1914*, 79; Luigi Albertini, *The Origins of the War of 1914*, vols. 2 and 3 (1952; reprint, New York: Enigma Books, 2005), 2:220.

[246] Geiss, *July 1914*, 89-90.

[247] Fay, *Origins*, 2:243-44.

[248] Bethmann-Hollweg had warned Wilhelm that an abrupt cancellation would raise European eyebrows. Geiss, *July 1914*, 89; Bethmann-Hollweg, *Reflections*, 129.

[249] Quoted in Geiss, *July 1914*, 106. In his memoirs, Lloyd George indicated that the Central Powers' strategy initially worked: "When I first heard the news of the assassination of the Grand Duke Ferdinand, I felt that it was a grave matter, and that it might provoke serious consequences which only the firmest and most skillful handling could prevent from developing into an emergency that would involve nations. But my fears were assuaged by the complete calm with which the rulers and diplomats of the world seemed to regard the event. The Kaiser departed for his usual yachting holiday in the

Berlin also avoided making overt war preparations. Around July 5, Wilhelm asked the Prussian minister of war, General Erich von Falkenhayn, if the army was ready should hostilities erupt. [250] Falkenhayn said that it was. Yet when the general asked whether certain military measures should be initiated, Wilhelm said no. [251] The Kaiser's response may have reflected his feeling that war, though not impossible, was unlikely. However, it seems that he primarily wanted to avoid arousing suspicion.

The third step involved "localizing" the coming conflict - that is, restricting matters to Austria and Serbia and keeping other countries from intervening. As Schoen reported to Hertling on the 18th:

> The (German) administration will, immediately upon presentation of the Austrian (ultimatum) at Belgrade, initiate diplomatic action with the Powers in the interest of the localization of the war. It will claim that the Austrian action has been just as much of a surprise to it as to the other Powers, pointing out the fact that the Emperor is on his northern journey.............It will lay stress upon the fact that it is a matter of interest for all the monarchial governments that 'the Belgrade nest of anarchists' be once

---

Norwegian fjords. His Chief Minister left for his usual shooting party on his estate in Silesia. The acting head of the German Foreign Office went off on a honeymoon trip. A still more reassuring fact – the military head of the German Army, (Helmuth) von Moltke, left for his cure in a foreign spa. The President of the French Republic and its Prime Minister were on a ceremonial visit to Russia...............Our Foreign Office preserved its ordinary tranquility of demeanor and thought it unnecessary to sound an alarm even in the Cabinet Chamber. I remember that sometime in July, an influential Hungarian lady, whose name I have forgotten, called upon me at 11 Downing Street, and told me that we were taking the assassination of the Grand Duke much too quietly; that it had provoked such a storm throughout the Austrian Empire as she had never witnessed, and that unless something were done immediately to satisfy and appease resentment, it would certainly result in war with Serbia, with the incalculable consequences which such an operation might precipitate in Europe. However, such official reports as came to hand did not seem to justify the alarmist view she took of the situation." Lloyd George, *War Memoirs,* 32-33.

[250] Fay, *Origins,* 2:211-12; Geiss, *July 1914,* 71.

[251] Ibid.

and for all rooted out; and it will make use of its influence to get all the Powers to take the view *that the settlement between Austria and Serbia is a matter concerning those two nations alone.* [252]

Indeed, Jagow planted a statement in the *North German Gazette* on the 19th that read in part: "The solidarity of Europe, which made itself felt during the long Balkan crisis in maintaining peace among the Great Powers, demands and requires that the settlement of differences which may arise between Austria-Hungary and Serbia should remain localized." [253] And Britain's *charge d'affaires* at Berlin, Horace Rumbold, telegraphed Grey on the 22nd that Jagow "insisted that the question at issue between Austria and Serbia was one for discussion and settlement by those two countries alone. That being his view, (Jagow) had not considered it opportune to say anything to the Austro-Hungarian Government." [254] So while defending Austria, Berlin also tried to publicly distance itself from her. It felt that localization would be more difficult if the Central Powers appeared to be acting in cahoots. Bethmann-Hollweg later explained: "We should have at once given an international scope to the Austro-Serbian dispute if we had converted the Austrian action into an Austro-German action." [255]

While meeting in Vienna on the 19th, the Common Ministerial Council decided to issue the ultimatum sooner than previously planned. Berchtold said to the Council: "Berlin was beginning to get nervous (over the delays) and news of our intentions had already transpired in Rome, so that untoward incidents could not be guarded against if action were again postponed." [256] The note would be presented to Serbia on the 23rd even if Poincare had not yet departed Russia. [257]

---

[252] Quoted in Geiss, *July 1914*, 129-30 (emphasis added).

[253] Quoted in ibid., 142.

[254] B.D. 77.

[255] Bethmann-Hollweg, *Reflections*, 121.

[256] Quoted in Geiss, *July 1914*, 139. The ultimatum's text was agreed upon during an informal discussion immediately preceding the Council meeting. Ibid.

[257] Ibid.

Vienna also decided to (1) give Serbia only 48 hours to reply to the ultimatum and (2) require an all-or-nothing acceptance. Individual demands in the note would not be negotiated lest the crisis drag on and Austria lose the diplomatic initiative. Berchtold telegraphed Albert von Mensdorff-Pouilly-Dietrichstein, Austria's ambassador to London, on the 23rd:

> With regard to the short time-limit attached to our demand, this must be attributed to our long experience of the dilatory arts of Serbia. The requirements which we demand that Serbia should fulfill..........cannot be made the subject of negotiations and compromise...........(W)e cannot take the risk of a method of political action by which it would be open to Serbia at her pleasure to prolong the crisis which has arisen. [258]

And as we will see, these "requirements" would be severe. In fact, after reading the planned text of the ultimatum, Jagow told Szogyeny that it was "too sharp" and demanded too much of Serbia. [259] Still, he did not insist that Vienna modify it before the note was handed to Belgrade.

G. Britain, France, Russia, and Serbia Sense Trouble

To this point, many everyday Europeans seemed unconcerned about the potential fallout from Sarajevo. [260] They went on with their lives. Few believed that this was the real thing - that after a number of close calls (e.g., the Bosnian crisis), *this* would be the event that pushed Europe into a holocaust.

---

[258] C.D.D., A.R.B. I, Document No. 9.
[259] Quoted in Fay, *Origins,* 2:265. Jagow later conceded to Rumbold that Serbia "could not swallow certain of the Austro-Hungarian demands" and that the ultimatum "as a diplomatic document left much to be desired." B.D. 122, Rumbold to Grey, July 25. Bethmann-Hollweg, too, felt that the note was overly harsh. Fay, *Origins,* 2:266. He wrote in his memoirs that he had "deplored the severity of the ultimatum because it could give the impression that the Central Powers desired a world war." Bethmann-Hollweg, *Reflections,* 123.
[260] See Joll, *Origins,* 13.

The British, French, and Russian governments, however, were more worried than the average European. True, earlier in the month some Entente officials thought that hostilities would be avoided. On the 5th, Bunsen wired Grey that Nikolai Schebeko, Russia's ambassador to Vienna, believed that "to make the country in which a plot was prepared responsible for its execution was a new doctrine, and he (Schebeko) did not think the Austrian Government would be induced by a few violent articles in the press to act upon it." [261] This spurred Nicolson to comment: "I have my doubts as to whether Austria will take any action of a serious character and I expect the storm will blow over." [262] On the 9th, moreover, Lichnowsky reported to Bethmann-Hollweg that Grey "was in a thoroughly confident mood, and declared in cheerful tones that he saw no reason for taking a pessimistic view of the situation." [263]

As the days passed, however, Austria's inactivity and vagueness about her plans made the Entente suspicious. What was going on? Why had Austria not responded to the assassination? The vibes that France, Russia, and England received were disconcerting. On the 20th, French consular officials in Vienna warned Paris: "From information furnished by a person specially well-informed as to official news, it appears that the French Government would be wrong to have confidence in disseminators of optimism; much will be demanded of Serbia." [264] Likewise, St. Petersburg gathered from Italian sources that Austria was preparing something big. [265] Around the 21st, Friedrich von Pourtales, Berlin's ambassador to Russia, had the following tense conversation with Sazonov, who had long distrusted Vienna:

> Mr. Sazonov, who spent several days last week at his country estate in the Government of Grodno, has been

---

[261] B.D. 40. Bunsen added that Schebeko "cannot believe that (Austria) will allow itself to be rushed into war, for an isolated combat with Serbia would be impossible and Russia would be compelled to take up arms in defense of Serbia." Ibid.

[262] Comment of Nicolson on ibid.

[263] G.D. 30. See also footnote 249 for Lloyd George's early view of the situation.

[264] C.D.D., F.Y.B., Document No. 14.

[265] Fay, *Origins,* 2:248-49, 276.

quite anxious since his return from there on account of the relations between Austria-Hungary and Serbia. He told me (Pourtales) that he had received very alarming reports from London, Paris and Rome, and that Austria-Hungary's attitude was inspiring an increasing worry everywhere. Mr. Schebeko, too, who was in general a calm observer, reported that the feeling in Vienna against Serbia was constantly growing more bitter.

The Minister (Sazonov) took the opportunity of giving his wrath at the Austro-Hungarian policy free rein, as usual. That the Emperor Franz Josef and even Count Berchtold were friends of peace, Mr. Sazonov was, it is true, willing to admit. But he said that there were very powerful and dangerous influences at work, which were constantly gaining ground in both halves of the (Habsburg) Empire, and which did not hesitate at the idea of plunging Austria into a war, even at the risk of starting a world conflagration. One anxiously asked oneself the question whether the aged Monarch and his weak Foreign Minister (Berchtold) would always be able to oppose these influences successfully. Previously, the belligerent elements, among which clerical intrigues also played an especially important role, had set their hopes on the dead Archduke, Franz Ferdinand. The death of the Archduke had in no way discouraged them; on the other hand, they were the very ones who were inspiring the dangerous policy which Austria-Hungary was pursuing at the present moment. The actual leaders in this policy were two men, particularly, whose increasing influence appeared to the highest degree dubious – namely Count (Johann) Forgach, who is 'an intriguer of the basest sort,' and Count Tisza, who is 'half a fool.'

I replied to Mr. Sazonov that his unmeasured reproaches against Austro-Hungarian policy appeared to me to be strongly influenced by his too great sympathy for the Serbs, and to be utterly unjustified. No sensible man could refuse to recognize the complete restraint observed by the Vienna Cabinet since the assassination at Sarajevo. It seemed to me that to decide just how far Austria-Hungary was justified in holding the Serbian Government responsible for the Greater Serbia agitations, as early as this, before the result of the inquiry concerning the assassination was known, was absolutely premature. But according to everything that was already known, one could scarcely doubt that the Greater Serbia agitation was stirred up under the very eyes of the Serbian Government, and that even the shameless assassination itself had been planned in Serbia. No great nation, however, could possibly tolerate permanently the existence along its borders of a propaganda that directly threatened its own security. Should, therefore, as appearances now seemed to indicate, traces be discovered at the inquiry into the origin of the crime which pointed back to Serbia, and should it be proved that the Serbian Government had regrettably connived at the intrigues directed against Austria, then the Austro-Hungarian Government would unquestionably be justified in using strong language at Belgrade. I could not conceive that in such a case the representations of the Vienna Cabinet to the Serbian Government could meet with the objection of any Power whatsoever.

The Minister met these arguments with the assertion that the support of the Greater Serbia propaganda in Austria-Hungary by Serbia or by the Serbian Government in any way had not been proved. A whole country could not be held responsible for the acts of individuals. Furthermore, the murderer of the Archduke was not even a Serbian subject. There certainly was a Greater Serbia propaganda in Austria, but it was the result of the bad methods of government by which Austria had distinguished herself for ages back...........

I interjected here that it did not suffice for members of the Serbian Government themselves to refrain from participation in the anti-Austrian propaganda. Austria-Hungary had far more reason to require that the Serbian authorities should proceed actively against the anti-Austrian propaganda, for it was impossible that the

Government should refuse responsibility for everything that was going on in the country.

Mr. Sazonov remarked...........that those people in Austria who were advocating proceeding against Serbia would apparently not content themselves with making representations at Belgrade, but that their object was the annihilation of Serbia. I answered that I had never heard of any object but one, namely the 'clarification' of Austria-Hungary's relations with Serbia.

The Minister continued excitedly, saying that in any case Austria-Hungary, if she was absolutely determined to disturb the peace, ought not to forget that in that event she would have to reckon with Europe. Russia could not look indifferently on at a move on Belgrade which aimed at the humiliation of Serbia. I remarked that I was able to see no humiliation in serious representations by which Serbia was reminded of her international obligations. Mr. Sazonov answered that it would all depend on how the move was carried out; that in no case should there be any talk of an ultimatum. [266]

British officials, too, sensed trouble. Despite Austria's public ambiguity, Bunsen obtained disturbing information about her plans from Heinrich Graf von Lützow, a former Austrian ambassador to Rome. He wired Grey:

I gather that the situation is regarded at the (Austrian) Ministry for Foreign Affairs in a serious light and that a kind of indictment is being prepared against the Serbian

---

[266] G.D. 120, Pourtales to Bethmann-Hollweg, July 21. Sazonov may not have realized that Tisza had initially opposed aggressive measures against Serbia while Berchtold – the "friend of peace" – had favored them. Regarding Forgach, England's ambassador to Russia, George Buchanan, seemingly shared Sazonov's opinion: "Sazonov regards Tisza and Forgach as two very dangerous men and fears that the latter's influence in (Vienna) is all-powerful. I knew Forgach at Sofia and always regarded him with the greatest distrust. He is very intelligent and very ambitious, but utterly unscrupulous." B.D. 164, Buchanan to Nicolson, July 23.

Government for alleged complicity in the conspiracy which led to the murder of the Archduke............My informant (Lutzow) states that the Serbian Government will be required to adopt certain definite measures in restraint of nationalist and anarchist propaganda, and that the Austro-Hungarian Government is in no mood to parley with Serbia, but will insist on immediate unconditional acceptance, failing which force will be used. Germany is said to be in complete agreement with this procedure, and it is thought that the rest of Europe will sympathize with Austria-Hungary in demanding that Serbia shall adopt in the future a more submissive attitude...........

I asked if Russia would be expected to stand by quietly in the event of force being used against Serbia. My informant said that he presumed that Russia would not wish to protect racial assassins, but in any case Austria-Hungary would go ahead regardless of the results. She would lose her position as a Great Power if she stood any further nonsense from Serbia. [267]

Rumbold received similarly foreboding signals from Berlin. Without revealing Austria's specific intentions, Jagow told him: "(I)f a person would or could do nothing to put a stop to a nuisance, the complainant must take remedy into his own hands." [268]

---

[267] B.D. 50, July 16. Bunsen sent a similar note to Nicolson: "(Count Lutzow) put on a serious face and said he wondered if I realized how grave the situation was. (The Austrian) Government was not going to stand Serbian insolence any longer. No Great Power could submit to such audacity as Serbia had displayed, and keep her position in the world.................Austria was determined to have her way this time...............I cannot yet believe Austria will resort to extreme measures, but I think we have an anxious time ahead of us." B.D. 56, July 17.

[268] B.D. 77, Rumbold to Grey, July 22. Rumbold's telegram led Assistant Undersecretary of State for Foreign Affairs Eyre Crowe to comment: "It is difficult to understand the attitude of the German Government. On the face of it, it does not bear the stamp of straightforwardness. If they really are anxious to see Austria kept reasonably in check, they are in the best position to speak at Vienna." Comment of Crowe on ibid. London's doubts about Germany's "straightforwardness" would increase in the coming days.

Grey, to be sure, was less agitated than Sazonov. He retained hope that Vienna would exercise moderation. He explained to Lichnowsky on the 20th: "The more Austria could keep her demand within reasonable limits, and the stronger the justification she could produce for making any demand, the more chance there would be of smoothing things over." [269] Still, he worried that Austria would go further, telling Lichnowsky that he "hated the idea of a war between any of the Great Powers, and that any of them should be dragged into a war by Serbia would be detestable." [270]

And what about Serbia? Initially, Serbian officials were as perplexed as anyone about Vienna's intentions. On the 15th, Serbia's ambassador to Austria, Jovan Jovanovitch, rhetorically asked Pashitch: "What steps will be taken? In what form? What demands will Austria-Hungary make of Serbia?" [271] His puzzlement soon turned to pessimism. He reported to Pashitch on the 20th:

> It is very difficult, indeed almost impossible, to ascertain here (in Vienna) anything positive as to the real intentions of Austria-Hungary. The word has been passed around to maintain absolute secrecy about everything that is being done. Judging by the articles in our newspapers, Belgrade

---

[269] B.D. 68, Grey to Rumbold, July 20.

[270] Ibid. On the 23rd, Lichnowsky informed Berlin of Grey's assumption that Germany would not associate herself with Austrian demands "that are plainly intended to bring on war." G.D. 121, Jagow to Wilhelm. This angered the Kaiser. He blasted Serbia and vented that only Vienna could decide how to deal with her: "The rascals (the Serbs) have added murder to agitation and must be humbled..............I am not called upon to prescribe (to Franz Josef) how to preserve his honor!...................Grey is committing the error of setting Serbia on the same plane with Austria and other Great Powers! That is unheard of! Serbia is nothing but a band of robbers that must be seized for its crimes! I will meddle in nothing of which the (Habsburg) Emperor is alone competent to judge!" Marginal comment of Wilhelm on ibid.

[271] C.D.D., S.B.B., Document No. 25. Serbia's populace was equally mystified. On the 21st, Germany's ambassador to Serbia, Julius von Griesinger, reported to Bethmann-Hollweg: "The excitement among the local population continues, as no one yet knows what steps the Austro-Hungarian Government is going to take against Serbia in the matter of the murder." G.D. 137.

is taking an optimistic view of the questions pending with Austria-Hungary. There is, however, no room for optimism. There is no doubt that Austria-Hungary is making preparations of a serious character. What is chiefly to be feared, and is highly probable, is that Austria is preparing for war against Serbia. The general conviction that prevails here is that it would be nothing short of suicide for Austria-Hungary once more to fail to take advantage of the opportunity to act against Serbia. It is believed that the two opportunities previously missed – the annexation of Bosnia and the Balkans war – have been extremely injurious to Austria-Hungary. [272]

That same day, the Serbian legation in Berlin presented a memorandum to the Germans. It condemned the Archduke's murder, defended Serbia's post-assassination conduct, accused the Austro-Hungarian press of inflaming tensions, and outlined Serbia's efforts to maintain good relations with Austria. [273] The document also asked Germany to mediate between Belgrade and Vienna. [274]

Clearly, Serbia's leadership was getting nervous.

July's first three weeks had been relatively tranquil. Austrian officials quietly obtained Germany's support, determined their course of action, secured Tisza's backing, drafted the ultimatum, and remained publicly vague about their plans. Though dismayed by Austria's slowness, Berlin defended her while revealing few specifics about her intentions. The Central Powers' secrecy seemed to work at first. As the 23rd approached, however, the other Powers suspected that something very bad was coming.

They were right. The period of quiet was about to end.

---

[272] C.D.D., S.B.B., Document No. 31. In a note to Nicolson, Bunsen reported Jovanovitch's (1) frustration that he "can get nothing out of (Vienna) and rather dreads the end of the ominous silence which now prevails there" and (2) view that Serbia "will do anything that can be reasonably asked to put down crime, but that it is useless to ask for the suppression of sentiments felt by every Serbian." B.D. 56, July 17.
[273] G.D. 86, Serbian legation at Berlin to German Foreign Office.
[274] Ibid.

IV

48 HOURS

A. Austria's Brutal Note to Serbia

At 6 p.m. on July 23, Austria presented the following note to Serbia:

On the 31st of March, 1909, the Serbian Minister in Vienna, on the instructions of the Serbian Government, made the following declaration to the Imperial and Royal Government (Austria):

Serbia recognizes that the *fait accompli* regarding Bosnia has not affected her rights and....................in deference to the advice of the Great Powers, Serbia undertakes to renounce from now onwards the attitude of protest and opposition which she has adopted with regard to the annexation since last autumn. She undertakes, moreover, to modify the direction of her policy with regard to Austria-Hungary and to live in the future on good neighborly terms with the latter.

The history of recent years, and in particular the painful events of the 28th of June, have shown the existence of a subversive movement with the object of detaching a part of the territories of Austria-Hungary from the Monarchy. The movement, which had its birth under the eye of the Serbian Government, has gone so far as to make itself manifest on both sides of the Serbian frontier in the shape of acts of terrorism and a series of outrages and murders.

Far from carrying out the formal undertakings contained in the declaration of the 31st of March 1909, the Royal Serbian Government has done nothing to repress these movements. It has permitted the criminal machinations of various societies and associations directed against the Monarchy, and has tolerated unrestrained language on the part of the press, the glorification of the perpetrators of outrages, and the participation of officers and functionaries in subversive agitation. It has permitted an unwholesome propaganda in public instruction; in short, it has permitted all manifestations of a nature to incite the Serbian population to hatred of the Monarchy and contempt of its institutions. This culpable tolerance of the Royal Serbian Government had not ceased at the moment when the events of the 28th of June proved its fatal consequences to the whole world.

It results from the depositions and confessions of the criminal perpetrators of the outrage of the 28th of June that the Sarajevo assassinations were planned in Belgrade; that the arms and explosives with which the murderers were provided had been given to them by Serbian officers and functionaries belonging to the Narodna Odbrana; and finally, that the passage into Bosnia of the criminals and their arms was organized and effected by the chiefs of the Serbian frontier service.

The above-mentioned results of the magisterial investigation do not permit the Austro-Hungarian Government to pursue any longer the attitude of expectant forbearance which they have maintained for years in the face of the machinations hatched in Belgrade, and thence propagated in the territories of the Monarchy. The results, on the contrary, impose on them the duty of putting an end to the intrigues which form a perpetual menace to the tranquility of the Monarchy.

To achieve this end, (Austria) sees (herself) compelled to demand from the Royal Serbian Government a formal assurance that they condemn this dangerous propaganda against the Monarchy; in other words, the whole series of tendencies, the ultimate aim of which is to detach from the Monarchy territories belonging to it, and that they undertake to suppress by every means this criminal and terrorist propaganda.

In order to give a formal character to this undertaking, the Royal Serbian Government shall publish on the front page of their 'Official Journal' of 26 July the following declaration:

'The Royal Government of Serbia condemns the propaganda directed against Austria-Hungary - i.e., the general tendency of which the final aim is to detach from the Austro-Hungarian Monarchy territories belonging to it, and they sincerely deplore the fatal consequences of these criminal proceedings.

The Royal Government regrets that Serbian officers and functionaries participated in the above-mentioned propaganda and thus compromised the good neighborly relations to which the Royal Government was solemnly pledged by its declaration of the 31st of March, 1909.

The Royal Government, which disapproves and repudiates all idea of interfering or attempting to interfere with the destinies of the inhabitants of any part whatsoever of Austria-Hungary, considers it their duty formally to warn officers and functionaries, and the whole population of the (Serbian) Kingdom, that henceforward they will proceed with the utmost rigor against persons who may be guilty of such machinations, which they will use all their efforts to anticipate and suppress.'

This declaration shall simultaneously be communicated to the Royal (Serbian) army as an order by His Majesty the King (of Serbia) and shall be published in the 'Official Bulletin' of the army.

The Royal Serbian Government shall further undertake:
1. To suppress any publication which incites to hatred and contempt of the Austro-Hungarian Monarchy and the general tendency of which is directed against its territorial integrity;
2. To dissolve immediately the society styled 'Narodna Odbrana,' to confiscate all its means of propaganda, and

to proceed in the same manner against other societies and their branches in Serbia which engage in propaganda against the Austro-Hungarian Monarchy. The Royal Government shall take the necessary measures to prevent the societies dissolved from continuing their activity under another name or form;

3. To eliminate without delay from public instruction in Serbia, both as regards the teaching body and also as regards the methods of instruction, everything that serves, or might serve, to foment the propaganda against Austria-Hungary;

4. To remove from the military service, and from the administration in general, all officers and functionaries guilty of propaganda against the Austro-Hungarian Monarchy whose names and deeds the Austro-Hungarian Government reserves to itself the right of communicating to the Royal Government;

5. To accept the collaboration in Serbia of representatives of the Austro-Hungarian Government for the suppression of the subversive movement directed against the territorial integrity of the Monarchy;

6. To take judicial proceedings against accessories to the plot of the 28th of June who are on Serbian territory; delegates of the Austro-Hungarian Government will take part in the investigation relating thereto;

7. To proceed without delay to the arrest of Major Voija Tankositch and of the individual named Milan Ciganovitch, a Serbian State employee, who have been compromised by the results of the magisterial enquiry at Sarajevo;

8. To prevent by effective measures the cooperation of the Serbian authorities in the illicit traffic in arms and explosives across the frontier, and to dismiss and punish severely the officials of the frontier service at Shabatz Loznica guilty of having assisted the perpetrators of the Sarajevo crime by facilitating their passage across the frontier;

9. To furnish (Austria) with explanations regarding the unjustifiable utterances of high Serbian officials, both in Serbia and abroad, who, notwithstanding their official

positions, have not hesitated since the crime of the 28th of June to express themselves in interviews in terms of hostility to the Austro-Hungarian Government; and, finally,

10. To notify the (Austrian) Government without delay of the execution of the measures comprised under the preceding heads.

The (Austrian) Government expects the reply of the Royal Government at the latest by 5 o'clock (later changed to 6 o'clock) on Saturday evening, the 25th of July. [275]

B. Europe's Stunned Reaction to the Ultimatum

If the average European had not heretofore been worried about Sarajevo, he was now. The ultimatum hit the continent like a thunderbolt. [276] There was no longer any question that the situation was deadly serious.

The shock extended to Europe's statesmen. Grey told Mensdorff that the ultimatum was "the most formidable document I had ever seen addressed by one State to another that was independent." [277] He was particularly struck by Demand #5, which appeared to require that Habsburg officials be permitted to enter Serbia to suppress anti-Austrian propaganda. [278] The 48-hour response period also concerned him. Two days was not enough time for the Powers to devise a diplomatic solution. Paul Cambon, France's ambassador to London, felt similarly. He told Grey:

---

[275] Quoted in Horne, *Source Records*, 285-89. See also Geiss, *July 1914*, 160.
[276] In Austria and Germany, though, the ultimatum was a huge hit. Bunsen informed Grey that the note "had given great satisfaction throughout the Dual Monarchy, which felt its very existence was at stake." B.D. 97, July 24. German newspapers, meanwhile, praised Vienna for finally acting against Belgrade. One publication, the *Lokal-Anzeiger*, sneered that Serbia "has now got to pay for past misdeeds," and that she "will fulfill the Austrian demands – or else she will go under." B.D. 159, Rumbold to Grey, July 24.
[277] B.D. 91, Grey to Bunsen, July 24. However, although critical of the ultimatum's tone, Bunsen and France's ambassador to Vienna, Alfred Dumaine, believed that the note contained "many just demands." B.D. 93, Bunsen to Grey, July 24.
[278] B.D. 91.

When two days were over, Austria would march into Serbia, for the Serbians could not possibly accept the Austrian demands. Russia would be compelled by her public opinion to take action as soon as Austria attacked Serbia, and therefore, once the Austrians had attacked Serbia, it would be too late for any mediation. [279]

Grey wanted (1) the 48-hour timeframe extended and (2) "to hear the views of the other Powers," after which negotiations could begin. [280] However, he was less concerned with the Austro-Serbian quarrel *per se* than with its potential expansion into a wider conflict. As he told Rumbold: "I said (to Lichnowsky today) that if the Austrian ultimatum to Serbia did not lead to trouble between Austria and Russia, I had no concern with it." [281] Likewise, he explained to Mensdorff that he saw the crisis "solely from the point of view of the peace of Europe" and that "the merits of the dispute between Austria-Hungary and Serbia............were not (England's) concern." [282]

In France, acting Foreign Minister Jean-Baptiste Bienvenu-Martin also believed that the Habsburg-Serbian dispute concerned Vienna and Belgrade alone. [283] But he otherwise seemed uncertain as to what to do, with Poincare and Prime Minister Rene Viviani out of the country. [284] He soon received instructions from the seaborne Viviani (who learned of the ultimatum via radiogram) to (1) encourage Serbia to accept those demands that were consistent with her honor and sovereignty and (2) convince Vienna to extend the 48-hour period. [285]

---

[279] B.D. 98, Grey to Bertie, July 24. See also B.D. 86, Grey to Bunsen, July 23.

[280] B.D. 91.

[281] B.D. 99, Grey to Rumbold, July 24.

[282] B.D. 91. He even told Mensdorff that if Austria "could make war on Serbia and at the same time satisfy Russia, well and good." B.D. 188, Grey to Bunsen, July 27.

[283] Telegram from Szecsen to Berchtold, July 24, in C.D.D., A.R.B. I, Document No. 13.

[284] Fay, *Origins,* 2:287.

[285] Ibid.

The British-French reaction to the ultimatum, therefore, was one of great surprise and deep concern. Yet neither nation sought to intervene in the Austro-Serbian quarrel.

Russia's reaction, meanwhile, was utterly antagonistic. On the 24th, Sazonov raged at Friedrich Szapary, Vienna's ambassador to Russia:

> I know what it is. You want to go to war with Serbia! I can see what is going on; the German papers are adding fuel to the fire! You are setting fire to Europe! [286]

Regarding Demand #5, he told Szapary: "You will be always wanting to interfere (inside Serbia) and what sort of a life will you make Europe lead!" [287]

Pourtales, too, felt Sazonov's anger. He telegraphed Berlin early on the 25th that Sazonov "was very much excited, and gave vent to boundless reproaches against Austria-Hungary; he stated in the most determined manner that it would be impossible for Russia to admit that the Austro-Serb quarrel could be settled between the parties concerned." [288] Pourtales and Sazonov had another testy discussion later that day:

> (My) (Pourtales's) appeal to the monarchial principle was visibly disconcerting to Mr. Sazonov. He took the stand that in this case the defense of monarchial interests was in no way concerned. Russia, he added angrily, certainly needed to be given no instruction in regard to respect for the sanctity of the monarchical principle............Mr. Sazonov, who, at this stage of the conference, was getting more and more nervous and irritated, sought to avoid this subject, and, by referring to previous assassinations, to

---

[286] Szapary to Berchtold, July 24, quoted in Geiss, *July 1914*, 174. In fact, Sazonov's initial response upon learning of the ultimatum's virulence was, *"C'est la guerre europenne."* ("It's the European war.") Quoted in M.F. Schilling, *How the War Began in 1914, Being the Diary of the Russian Foreign Office* (London: George Allen and Unwin, 1925), 28-29.

[287] Szapary to Berchtold, July 24, quoted in Geiss, *July 1914*, 177.

[288] G.D. 160, Pourtales to German Foreign Office.

take the stand that governments and nations had never yet been held responsible for the acts of individuals............

(He) then gave me to understand that he was not at all convinced by the 'proofs' brought forward by Austria-Hungary; he then broke into the most unmeasured accusations and insinuations against the Austro-Hungarian Government. I could not help expressing to the Minister in response to this most intensely excited outburst my fear that he was wholly under the influence of a blind and implacable hatred of Austria, which unfortunately apparently rendered him insusceptible to all other and reasonable considerations. 'Hatred is no part of my character,' replied the Minister, 'therefore I feel no hatred towards Austria, nothing but contempt'.............

I expressed to the Minister my conviction that even if matters came to extremes, it would only be a matter of a punitive expedition of Austria against Serbia, and that it was far from Austria's intentions to consider making any territorial acquisitions. Mr. Sazonov shook his head incredulously at these arguments, and spoke of far-reaching plans that Austria had in view. First, Serbia was to be eaten up, then it was to be Bulgaria's turn, and then 'we shall have them on the Black Sea.' I remarked to this that such fantastic exaggerations did not appear to me to be in the least worthy of any serious discussion. [289]

Exaggerations though they were, Sazonov did suspect that Vienna was plotting a massive power grab in southeastern Europe. [290] He wrote on the 25th: "The clear aim of (Austria's) procedure – which is apparently supported by Germany – is the total annihilation of Serbia and the disturbance of the political equilibrium in the Balkans." [291]

---

[289] G.D. 204, Pourtales to German Foreign Office, July 25.

[290] Sazonov also suspected that Austria's post-Sarajevo secretiveness about her plans was designed to mislead the Powers. Fay, *Origins*, 2:290-91.

[291] Draft report from Sazonov to Nicholas, quoted in Geiss, *July 1914*, 209.

Sazonov's immediate goal was to gain more time for diplomacy to work. Like Paris and London, he requested that the 48-hour timeframe be extended. A July 25 statement from the Russian government read:

> It is impossible for the Powers in the short time remaining (until the 48-hour period expired) to undertake anything useful towards the settlement of the complications that have arisen. Therefore, in order to avoid the innumerable and universally undesirable consequences to which Austria's course of action could lead, we should think it necessary that she should first of all extend the time limit which she has set Serbia for a reply. Since Austria has declared her readiness to acquaint the Powers with the results of the inquiry on which the accusations are based, the Powers should be given the opportunity to form an opinion on the matter..............The rejection by Austria of our proposal for dealing with the matter would........be openly at variance with international ethics. [292]

So while the Central Powers strived to localize the Austro-Serbian dispute, Sazonov was trying to do the opposite - namely, to *Europeanize* it by getting other countries involved in its resolution. [293] Europeanization would also enable the Powers to take control of the crisis rather than allowing Vienna alone to dictate events.

---

[292] Quoted in Geiss, *July 1914*, 188. See also B.D. 118, Grey to Bunsen, July 25. Despite his anger, Sazonov – like England and France - urged Serbia to accept as many Austrian demands as possible. Geiss, *July 1914*, 166-67.

[293] To Sazonov, the dispute was a European matter because it dealt with whether Serbia had upheld her March 1909 promise to *all* of the Powers – not merely to Austria – that she would get along with Vienna. Fay, *Origins*, 2:297-99. He believed that (1) the Powers should review the evidence against Serbia and (2) it was not for Vienna alone to determine Serbia's level of guilt.

C. Austria Refuses to Yield; Germany Pushes for "Localization" of the Crisis

Yet Austria declined to prolong the timeframe. She believed that granting an extension would make her look weak. Moreover, she utterly distrusted Belgrade. Mensdorff explained to Grey that Vienna had to "stand firm so as to gain for ourselves some sort of guarantees, as hitherto Serbian promises have never been kept." [294] He further said that "there had been so much procrastination on the part of Serbia that a time limit was essential." [295]

Austria also refused to endorse Sazonov's proposed Great Power evidentiary investigation. She felt that this would constitute mediation of the Austro-Serbian dispute. [296] On the 25th, Berchtold arrogantly told Szapary that a memorandum Austria had sent to the Powers explaining her grievances against Serbia "was by no means meant as an invitation to them to inform us of their views on this matter, but simply to convey information as a matter of international courtesy." [297] Austria was essentially telling Europe to butt out of her quarrel with Belgrade.

Still, she tried to mollify the Entente countries (largely to keep them off her back). She stressed that she was acting strictly in self-defense and was not looking to annex Serbian territory; she simply wanted certain guarantees from Belgrade. [298] Berchtold also instructed Mensdorff to indicate to Grey that while Austria would sever diplomatic relations with Serbia should the latter

---

[294] Mensdorff to Berchtold, July 24, in C.D.D., A.R.B. I, Document No. 10.

[295] B.D. 91. See also G.D. 178, Tschirschky to German Foreign Office, July 25.

[296] G.D. 178.

[297] D.D., A.R.B. I, Document No. 21.

[298] Fay, *Origins,* 2:328-29; Berchtold to Szapary, July 24, in C.D.D., A.R.B. I, Document No. 18. Nevertheless, Berchtold directed Szapary to emphasize to Sazonov that it "is a unique event in history that a Great Power should have borne with the seditious intrigues of an adjoining small State for so long a time and with such unparalleled patience as Austria-Hungary has borne with those of Serbia..........(A)ny further toleration of Serbian intrigues would undermine our existence as a State and our position as a Great Power." Berchtold to Szapary, July 25, in C.D.D., A.R.B. I, Document No. 26.

reject the ultimatum, she would not immediately attack her. [299] This undoubtedly relieved Grey because it potentially provided more time for diplomacy.

The Germans, meanwhile, continued to argue that the Austro-Serbian dispute should be left for those two nations to resolve. Austria, they maintained, was in the best position to gauge the threat to her security; Europe had no right to make this determination for her. They also expressed their approval of the ultimatum while insisting that they had no foreknowledge of its terms. [300] Jagow reiterated these things in a July 24 conversation with Jules Cambon, Paris's ambassador to Germany and Paul Cambon's brother:

> I (Cambon) asked (Jagow)..............if it was correct, as announced in the newspapers, that Austria had presented a note to the Powers on her dispute with Serbia, if he had received it, and what view he took of it. Herr von Jagow answered me in the affirmative, adding that the note was forcible, and that he approved it, the Serbian Government having for a long time past wearied the patience of Austria. Moreover, he considers this question to be a domestic one for Austria............
>
> I then said to him that, not having as yet received any instructions, the views which I wished to exchange with him were strictly personal. Thereupon I asked him if the

---

[299] Berchtold to Mensdorff, July 24, in C.D.D., A.R.B. I, Document No. 17. On the 25th, Buchanan informed St. Petersburg that Mensdorff had been authorized "to explain to Sir E. Grey that the step taken at Belgrade was not an 'ultimatum' but a 'demarche' with a time limit." Quoted in Schilling, *How the War Began*, 35-36. The Tsar saw through this amateurish attempt to soften the ultimatum's impact on Grey, writing: "Playing with words." Quoted in ibid., 36.

[300] This was not quite true. Both Jagow and Bethmann-Hollweg saw the ultimatum's text shortly before Serbia received the note. France's acting political director, Philippe Berthelot, questioned Berlin's professed unawareness of Vienna's pre-ultimatum plans: "Was it probable that Germany would have arrayed herself on the side of Austria in such an adventure with her eyes closed?" Note of Berthelot, July 26, quoted in Geiss, *July 1914*, 233.

Berlin Cabinet had really been entirely ignorant of Austria's requirements before they were communicated to Belgrade, and as he told me that that was so, I showed him my surprise at seeing him thus undertake to support claims of whose limit and scope he was ignorant. Herr von Jagow interrupted me, and said, 'It is only because we are having a personal conversation that I allow you to say that to me.'

'Certainly,' I replied, 'but if Peter I (the King of Serbia) humiliates himself, domestic trouble will probably break out in Serbia; that will open the door to fresh possibilities, and do you know where you will be led by Vienna?' I added that the language of the German newspapers was not the language of persons who were indifferent to, and unacquainted with, the question, but betokened an active support. Finally, I remarked that the shortness of the time limit given to Serbia for submission would make an unpleasant impression in Europe. Jagow answered that he quite expected a little excitement on the part of Serbia's friends, but that he was counting on their giving her wise advice.

'I have no doubt,' I then said to him, 'that Russia would endeavor to persuade the Cabinet of Belgrade to make acceptable concessions; but why not ask from one what is being asked from the other, and if reliance is being placed on advice being given at Belgrade, is it not also legitimate to rely on advice being given at Vienna from another quarter?'

(Jagow) went so far as to say that that depended on circumstances, but immediately checked himself; he repeated that the difficulty must be localized. He asked me if I really thought the situation serious. 'Certainly,' I answered, 'because if what is happening is the result of due reflection, I do not understand why all means of retreat have been cut off.' [301]

Notwithstanding the bad impression the ultimatum made on Europe, the Central Powers did not seem especially alarmed by the overall Entente reaction. After all, London and Paris (1) did not publicly blast Austria, (2) essentially recognized her right to some relief, and (3) asked Serbia to be accommodating. And while they requested a time extension, they did not demand one. As for Russia, Sazonov's reaction had been hostile but not entirely unexpected. No wonder Berlin remained unconvinced of Russian intervention. Regarding his above-mentioned July 25 conversation with Sazonov, Pourtales informed Bethmann-Hollweg:

> Mr. Sazonov then explained that in his opinion, Austria was only looking for an excuse to 'devour' Serbia. 'In that event, however,' added the Minister, 'Russia will go to war with Austria.' That was the only time that Mr. Sazonov, who otherwise made use of very little restraint in expressing himself, made any reference to the possibility of an armed intervention on the part of Russia. I should conclude, therefore, despite the great excitement unquestionably predominating in government circles here, that precipitate steps in this direction are not to be looked for at present. [302]

Rumbold, moreover, telegraphed Grey on the 25th:

> (Jagow) said that a reassuring feature of the situation was that Count Berchtold had sent for the Russian representative at Vienna and had told him that Austria-Hungary had no intention of seizing Serbian territory. This

---

[301] Cambon to Bienvenu-Martin, July 25, quoted in Geiss, *July 1914*, 194-95. According to Rumbold, Cambon also told Jagow that if Peter I issued the "army order of the day" per the ultimatum, "the chances were that, in a country like Serbia, he would be assassinated." B.D. 103, Rumbold to Grey, July 24. Rumbold added that Cambon "is inclined to think that the Austro-Hungarian and German Governments are playing a dangerous game of bluff, and that they think they can carry matters through with a high hand." Ibid.
[302] G.D. 204.

step should, in his opinion, exercise a calming influence at St. Petersburg. I asked whether it was not to be feared that, in taking military action against Serbia, Austria would dangerously excite public opinion in Russia. He said he thought not. He remained of the opinion that the crisis could be localized. I said that telegrams from Russia in this morning's papers did not look very reassuring, but he maintained his optimistic view with regard to Russia. [303]

D. Russia Reaches Two Decisions

But there were signs that Pourtales's and Jagow's optimism was misplaced. All of Russia, not merely Sazonov, was outraged over Austria's actions. Oskar von Chelius, Germany's military plenipotentiary at the Russian court in St. Petersburg, informed the Kaiser:

> First, the tone of the (ultimatum). Russia feels herself to be greatly injured by it. Never before, they say, has any nation used such language toward a weaker nation. Russia would have to stand by her racial companion and could not tolerate having Serbia crushed...............'(W)e (Russia) should be breaking our faith with our history if we did nothing but look indifferently on. Austria should have given notice to Russia of such a note; as it is, it constitutes an insult to a Great Power which is friendly to Serbia and which cannot allow the latter to be sacrificed to Austrian high-handedness.' This is the view of the Minister of War.

> Secondly, the refusal to extend the time limit: 'Russia (believes she) showed her good intentions by trying to

---

[303] B.D. 122. Even Zimmerman, who previously deemed the likelihood of a European war to be 90 percent, seemingly grew more optimistic about Russian non-intervention. Schoen had informed Hertling on the 18th that Zimmermann was "counting on the fact that 'bluffing' constitutes one of the most favored requisites of Russian policy, and that while the Russian likes to threaten with the sword, he still does not like so very much to draw it on behalf of others at the critical moment." Quoted in Geiss, *July 1914*, 130.

intervene (diplomatically) even before the termination of the time limit; the refusal is an unbelievable affront on the part of Austria, who treated us (Russia) as if we did not exist. Making full allowance for all the excitement and indignation in Austria at the assassination in Sarajevo, she had no right to act in a manner that is contrary to all diplomatic precedent............' This is the opinion of the entourage of the Tsar..............

Third, the belief that they had known of and approved of the note at Berlin. This has already been denied, but its acceptance has given birth to the impression that after the visit of Poincare, which had brought about a firmer bond between Russia and France, it was intended by the Triple Alliance to deliver a blow in the face of the Russian Monarchy, and that unhappy Serbia had been selected for the purpose, to be trodden under foot while the Entente Powers were being truculently confronted.

These three considerations have fanned excitement (in Russia) to an enormous blaze. [304]

St. Petersburg believed that if it stood aside while Austria smashed Serbia, Russia's pro-Belgrade population would become so infuriated that the Tsar's life might be endangered. [305] It also felt that Vienna could not be permitted to move deeper into southeastern Europe, for this would open the gates for Austro-German expansion through Turkey and the Middle East. The Straits, Russia's dream, could fall into the Central Powers' hands. The Black Sea might become a virtual Germanic lake. Russia's dread of a massive Teutonic advance along her southwestern frontiers was, to be sure, somewhat fanciful. [306] But it was very real - and akin to the Central Powers' fear of a Slavic tsunami.

The Russian government therefore made two important decisions on the 24th and 25th.

---

[304] G.D. 291, July 26.
[305] See G.D. 421, Pourtales to German Foreign Office, July 30.
[306] See G.D. 204.

First, it authorized the mobilization of *some* Russian armies against Austria should circumstances warrant it. [307] "Partial mobilization" - or mobilization of a portion of Russia's forces - was problematic, however. Russia's military leadership had long assumed that war with Austria would mean war with Germany, and vice versa. Hence, there was no plan for Russian mobilization against only one Central Power. [308] The sole blueprint called for mobilization against both countries. Sazonov knew this. Yet he felt that partial mobilization might scare Austria into backing down without requiring Russia to also mobilize against Germany. [309] He did not want to antagonize Berlin. The Tsar accepted Sazonov's logic. Accordingly, General Nicholas Janushkevich, the chief of the general staff, hurriedly prepared a mobilization plan against Austria alone. [310]

The second decision was to immediately initiate the "Period Preparatory to War." This was not actual mobilization. Rather, it involved certain actions *in preparation for* "general mobilization" – or mobilization against both Central Powers. This step was taken because Russia's enormous size and outdated rail system meant that her mobilization would be slower than Germany's or Austria's. St. Petersburg thus wanted to commence its pre-mobilization preparations as early as possible.

Both decisions, of course, were risky. Instead of forcing Austria to ease off, partial mobilization might spur her to mobilize against Russia in response. Furthermore, Berlin would likely learn of Russia's pre-mobilization activities occurring near the German-Russian border and perhaps implement countermeasures. Tensions could escalate dramatically. Regardless, St. Petersburg's decisions indicated that this was not 1909. Russia would not stand aside this time. [311]

---

[307] Geiss, *July 1914*, 190.

[308] Martel, *Origins*, 71.

[309] Fay, *Origins,* 2:307.

[310] Albertini, *Origins,* 2:541.

[311] As England's ambassador to Paris, Francis Bertie, told Grey, Izvolsky believed that allowing Austria "a free hand with Serbia would be as deep a humiliation for Russia as that which he himself (Izvolsky) had had to accept in 1909; he had no choice then, as Russia was not in a position to fight - but things were very different now." B.D. 216, July 28.

That was not all. France, like Russia, was not unwilling to fight. On his own volition, Maurice Paleologue, Paris's ambassador to Russia, promised St. Petersburg on the 24th that France would fulfill her treaty obligations. [312] Making this commitment without approval from Paris was precipitate. Yet Paleologue said nothing that Poincare and Viviani were not already thinking. France was not about to abandon St. Petersburg in this crisis. Paris knew that if it tried to stop Russia from taking steps she deemed vital to her national interests, she might question France's worth as an ally. Indeed, there were certain pro-German officials within Russia's hierarchy. [313] They might use France's non-support as proof of her unreliability and convince the Tsar to instead align with Berlin. [314] A Germany tied to Austria and Russia could – aside from its improved relationship with England - put Paris in largely the same isolated position it was in during Bismarck's days. The French were therefore prepared to stand with Russia should war erupt. England's ambassador to Russia, George Buchanan, perceived this. He wired Grey: "From the French Ambassador's (Paleologue's) language, it almost looked as if France and Russia were determined to make a strong stand." [315]

E. Grey Suggests Mediation

What about the third Entente member?

Paris and St. Petersburg were pressing Britain to proclaim her solidarity with them. They argued that the Austro-German pact would back down if it realized that war with the entire Triple Entente beckoned. Sazonov even intimated to Buchanan that England's failure to support St. Petersburg could damage the Russian-British partnership. [316]

Grey was unmoved. Consistent with Britain's past reluctance to entangle herself in European alliances, he wanted to preserve London's freedom of action. He also believed that the British people would be opposed to getting involved in a Balkan

---

[312] Geiss, *July 1914*, 163; B.D. 101, Buchanan to Grey, July 24.
[313] Martel, *Origins*, 66.
[314] Ibid.
[315] B.D. 101.
[316] Fay, *Origins*, 2:328.

quarrel. They certainly would not fight for Serbia's sake; even after the ultimatum's issuance, British public opinion sympathized with Austria more than with Serbia. Moreover, he feared that siding with France and Russia would make them more willing to go to war – since their chances of victory would be greater - and less interested in a peaceful solution. [317] Buchanan thus told Sazonov on the 24th that England's backing was unlikely:

> I (Buchanan) said (to Sazonov) that I could not speak in the name of His Majesty's (the British) Government..............(but) I could personally hold out no hope that His Majesty's Government would make any declaration of solidarity that would entail an engagement to support France and Russia by force of arms. We had no direct interests in Serbia, and public opinion in England would never sanction a war on her behalf. (Sazonov) replied that the Serbian question was but part of a general European question, and that we could not efface ourselves. [318]

The debate continued the next day:

> (I, Buchanan, said to Sazonov) that England could play the role of mediator at Berlin and Vienna to better purposes as a friend who, if her counsels of moderation were disregarded, might one day be converted into an ally, than if she were to declare herself Russia's ally at once.

> (Sazonov) said that unfortunately Germany was convinced that she could count upon our neutrality............Austria's action was in reality directed against Russia. She aimed at overthrowing the present status quo in the Balkans and establishing her own hegemony there. He did not believe that Germany really wanted war, but her attitude was decided by ours. If we took our stand firmly with France and Russia, there would be no war. If we failed them now,

---

[317] Ibid.
[318] B.D. 101.

rivers of blood would flow, and we would in the end be dragged into war.................

(Sazonov) assured me once more that he did not wish to precipitate a conflict, but that unless Germany can restrain Austria, I can regard the situation as desperate. Russia cannot allow Austria to crush Serbia and become the predominant Power in the Balkans, and, secure of the support of France, she will face all the risks of war. [319]

Disinclined to intercede in the Austro-Serbian dispute, Grey instead focused on preventing a wider war. On the 24th, he proposed that if tensions between Austria and Russia increased, the other Powers would mediate between the two countries. [320]

The Russians were unenthused. They felt that Grey's plan would effectively give Austria a free hand to crush Serbia, for the Powers would only intervene diplomatically between Austria and *Russia*. [321] To St. Petersburg, the Austro-Serbian quarrel was a *European* matter and it was *there* that the Powers should intercede. Nevertheless, surely fearful of alienating England, Russia did not flat-out reject Grey's initiative.

Germany, meanwhile, disliked the idea of any mediation because it might Europeanize the crisis. But Berlin far preferred Austro-Russian mediation to Austro-Serbian mediation. For his part, Lichnowsky urged Jagow not to rebuff Grey:

I deem it my duty to point out to Your Excellency that, according to my conviction, the British Government will strive to maintain toward us a friendly attitude, as unpartisan as possible, just so long as it believes in our honest desire for peace and in our efforts to cooperate with England, hand in hand, to avert the rising European

---

[319] B.D. 125, Buchanan to Grey, July 25. Buchanan also told Sazonov that British support of France and Russia could backfire. Rather than scare Germany into restraining Vienna, it might encourage her to stand up to the Entente. B.D. 170, Buchanan to Grey, July 27.

[320] B.D. 99; G.D. 157, Lichnowsky to German Foreign Office, July 24; Albertini, *Origins,* 2:341.

[321] Paul Cambon also viewed Grey's proposal skeptically. He preferred Austro-Serbian mediation. Fay, *Origins,* 2:370-71, 377.

thunderstorm. To refuse the proposition to mediate between Austria and Russia, however, or a recalcitrant attitude that would justify the supposition that we wished to bring about a war with Russia, would probably have the result of driving England unconditionally over to the side of France and Russia. [322]

Lichnowsky had been cautioning his superiors for some time not to assume England's neutrality in a European war. Yet some in Berlin viewed him as overly alarmist, akin to a frantic old woman. [323] They never took his warnings that seriously. Nor did they completely accept his advice now. On the 25th, Jagow wired Lichnowsky that Germany would help inaugurate Austro-Russian mediation "with the reservation of our known obligations as (Austria's) ally." [324] This caveat indicated that if Austria refused mediation, Berlin would support her decision.

In sum, during the two-day period between the ultimatum's issuance and the late afternoon of the 25th, Britain, France, and Russia each took various diplomatic steps. These included (1) asking that the 48-hour timeframe be extended, (2) encouraging Serbia to accept as many demands as possible, (3) Sazonov's request for an investigation of Austria's evidence against Serbia, and (4) Grey's mediation suggestion. Austria, though, refused to change the timeframe, while Germany insisted that the Austro-Serbian dispute was a local matter.

Just before the deadline for Serbia's reply, things were obviously very serious. But they were not critical. No Power had mobilized for a continental war. There remained time for Austria to pull back or for Germany to compel her to. The Central Powers, however, seemed unwilling to bend. And nothing had yet happened to change Berlin's view that Russia was unlikely to intervene.

---

[322] G.D. 180.

[323] Albertini, *Origins,* 2:432. Furthermore, Bethmann-Hollweg seemingly questioned Lichnowsky's skill in dealing with London, writing: "(Lichnowsky) tells everything to Sir Edward (Grey) in such an awkward fashion." Carnegie Endowment, *German Documents Collected by Karl Kautsky,* 263, footnote 2. See also Appendix C of this book for Jagow's criticisms of Lichnowsky.

[324] G.D. 192.

V

THE REPLY

A. Serbia Responds to Austria's Ultimatum

Needless to say, the ultimatum shocked Belgrade. Germany's ambassador to Serbia, Julius von Griesinger, wired Berlin that Austria's tone and demands "were absolutely unexpected by the Serbian Government." [325] Dayrell Crackanthorpe, England's *charge d'affaires* at Belgrade, reported that Pashitch was "very anxious and dejected." [326] He had reason to be. His country was in real danger. On the 24th, Serbia's Prince Regent begged the Tsar for help:

> We may be attacked at the expiration of the time limit by the Austro-Hungarian army, which is concentrating upon our frontier. We are unable to defend ourselves and we beg Your Majesty to come to our aid as soon as possible. The much appreciated goodwill which Your Majesty has so often shown towards us inspires us with the firm belief

---

[325] G.D. 159, Griesinger to German Foreign Office, July 24. The Kaiser scribbled in response: "Bravo! One would not have believed it of the Viennese!..............How hollow the whole so-called Serbian power is proving itself to be; thus it is seen to be with all the Slavic nations! Just tread hard on the heels of that rabble!" Marginal comment of Wilhelm on ibid.

[326] B.D. 92, Crackanthorpe to Grey, July 24. Crackanthorpe added that Pashitch "begged me earnestly to convey to you (Grey) his hope that (the British) Government will use its good offices in moderating Austria's demands." Ibid.

that once again our appeal to your noble Slav heart will not pass unheeded. [327]

To prepare for the coming storm, the Serbian government ordered mobilization on the afternoon of the 25th. [328] It also began some evacuations of the Belgrade area, which lay across the Danube River from Austria-Hungary. Giesl telegraphed Berchtold that day:

> I hear that the Royal train is being made up; gold belonging to the National Bank and to the railway, as well as the Foreign Office records, are being taken (southward) into the interior of the country..............The garrison has left town (Belgrade) in field order. Ammunition depots in the fortresses were evacuated. Railway station thronged with soldiers. The ambulance trains have left Belgrade, proceeding towards the south. [329]

Nicholas assured the Prince Regent that Russia would "in no case disinterest herself in the fate of Serbia." [330] He added, however, that "so long as the slightest hope exists of avoiding bloodshed, all our efforts must be directed to that end." [331] St. Petersburg thus urged Serbia to be accommodating in her response to Vienna. Belgrade relented. Serbia's violently anti-Austrian population, of course, wanted to refuse every Habsburg demand. But Pashitch knew that this would alienate the Entente nations. It could also undo whatever diplomatic damage Austria inflicted upon herself via the ultimatum's harshness.

Minutes before the 48-hour timeframe expired, Serbia handed her reply to Giesl. It was both conciliatory and slippery. While the document staunchly defended Serbia's behavior since 1909, its tone was pleasant. More importantly, Belgrade appeared

---

[327] C.D.D., R.O.B., Document No. 6.

[328] Albertini, *Origins,* 2:363. Vienna later made the ludicrous argument that because Serbia ordered mobilization before giving her reply, she had "no inclination for a peaceful solution." Berchtold to Mensdorff, July 26, in C.D.D., A.R.B. I, Document No. 29.

[329] C.D.D., A.R.B. I, Document No. 22.

[330] C.D.D., R.O.B., Document No. 40, July 27.

[331] Ibid.

to wholly or substantially agree to Vienna's conditions, save one; Serbia said that accepting Demand #6 would effectively infringe upon her sovereignty:

> The (Serbian) Government considers it its duty as a matter of course to begin an investigation against all those persons who have participated in the outrage of June 28 and who are in its territory. As far as the cooperation in this investigation of specially delegated officials of the (Austrian) Government is concerned, this cannot be accepted, as this is a violation of the constitution and of criminal procedure. [332]

Nonetheless, Serbia offered to have the International Court at The Hague or the Great Powers settle the Austro-Serbian dispute if Vienna was dissatisfied with her reply. [333]

In truth, Belgrade's response – even excluding Demand #6 - was far from a complete acceptance. Many demands had been agreed to with significant, albeit subtle, qualifications. For instance, Serbia agreed to execute Demand #9 (which insisted that Belgrade explain various anti-Austrian statements made by Serbian officials) "(a)s soon as (Vienna) points out in detail where those expressions were made and succeeds in proving that those expressions have actually been made by the functionaries concerned." [334] Vienna was unimpressed, noting:

> The Royal Serbian Government must be aware of the interviews in question. If it demands of the (Austrian) Government that it should furnish all kinds of detail about the said interviews and if it reserves for itself the right of a formal investigation, it shows that it is not its intention seriously to fulfill the demand. [335]

Berchtold had instructed Giesl to deem anything less than an unconditional acceptance of each demand as an unsatisfactory

---

[332] G.W.B., quoted in C.D.D., 421.
[333] Ibid., 423.
[334] Quoted in ibid., 422.
[335] Quoted in ibid.

reply. [336] Serbia's equivocations made Giesl's task much easier. He read Belgrade's response, deemed it insufficient, notified Pashitch of the cessation of Austro-Serbian diplomatic relations, and returned to Austria. [337] Vienna then announced:

> The Royal Serbian Government has refused to accept the demands which we were forced to address to them in order to secure permanently our most vital interests which were menaced by them, and has thereby made it clear that they do not intend to abandon their subversive aims, tending towards continuous disorder in some of our frontier provinces and their final disruption from the Monarchy. Reluctantly, therefore, and very much against our wish, we find ourselves obliged to compel Serbia by the sharpest measures to make a fundamental change in the attitude of enmity she has up to now pursued. [338]

B. London and Paris Grow Frustrated with Austria and Urge Germany to Restrain Her

Yet the *apparent* (rather than the actual) level of Serbia's compliance was what mattered. And Belgrade's slickly-crafted reply greatly impressed Europe. [339] Grey, in particular, was pleased with Serbia's conciliatory attitude – and confounded by Vienna's intransigence. To him, Belgrade had almost completely capitulated. Austria had scored the biggest diplomatic victory in recent memory. What more could she want? What sane country would risk a European war over Demand #6 and a few seemingly minor technicalities? He told Mensdorff that he

> could not understand the construction put by the Austrian Government upon the Serbian reply............(Belgrade's answer) already involved the greatest humiliation to

---

[336] Albertini, *Origins,* 2:373.
[337] Ibid.
[338] Berchtold to Austrian ambassadors at Berlin, Rome, London, Paris, and St. Petersburg, July 26, in C.D.D., A.R.B. I, Document No. 30.
[339] Even Berchtold conceded that Serbia's reply had been masterfully worded. Albertini, *Origins,* 2:460.

Serbia that I (Grey) had ever seen a country undergo, and it was very disappointing to me that the reply was treated by the Austrian Government as if it were as unsatisfactory as a blank negative. [340]

British Prime Minister Herbert Asquith was harsher. He wrote on the 26th:

No one can say what is going to happen in the east of Europe. The news this morning is that Serbia has capitulated on the main point, but it is very doubtful if any reservation will be accepted by Austria, who is resolved upon a complete and final humiliation. The curious thing is that on many, if not most, of the points, Austria has a good and Serbia a very bad case. But the Austrians are quite the stupidest people in Europe. There is a brutality about their mode of procedure which will make most people think that this is a case of a big Power wantonly bullying a little one. [341]

Grey also began to see that the crisis was unresolvable unless the root problem - the Vienna-Belgrade dispute – was addressed. England could not distance herself from it. As Lichnowsky told Berlin:

As long as it remained an Austro-Serbian conflict, he (Grey) held himself in the background. But now he finds himself compelled to take a hand in it, as it threatens to develop into an Austro-Russian and thus into a European conflict. In this way, the Austro-Russian conflict cannot be separated from the Austro-Serbian, as the former is based on the latter, and (Grey) has been talking to me from this point of view. An understanding between Austria and Russia depends on the settlement of the Austro-Serbian quarrel. Without such a settlement, every

---

[340] B.D. 188, Grey to Bunsen, July 27.
[341] Quoted in Herbert Asquith, *Memories and Reflections: 1852-1927*, vol. 2 (Boston: Little, Brown and Company, 1928), 8. Ominously, he added: "(I)t is the most dangerous situation of the last forty years." Quoted in ibid.

attempt at mediation appears entirely hopeless from the English point of view. [342]

With his heightened focus on the Austro-Serbian quarrel, Grey altered his diplomatic strategy. First, he proposed an "ambassadors conference" involving British, French, German, and Italian officials. [343] They would meet to explore ways to resolve the crisis. Russia, Austria, and Serbia, meanwhile, would refrain from military operations pending the conference's results. [344] Second, he started pressing Germany to convince Vienna to accept Serbia's reply or to use it as a basis for negotiations. If Austria would not listen to the Entente countries regarding the need for diplomacy, she would presumably listen to her ally. Lichnowsky wired Berlin on the 27th:

> (Grey stated that) should Austria fail to be satisfied with (Serbia's) reply - in other words, should this reply not be accepted at Vienna as a foundation for peaceful negotiations - or should Austria proceed even to the occupation of Belgrade, which lay quite defenseless before her, it would then be absolutely evident that Austria was only seeking an excuse for crushing Serbia. And thus that Russia and Russian influence in the Balkans were to

---

[342] G.D. 266, Lichnowsky to German Foreign Office, July 27.

[343] Fay, *Origins,* 2:361, 381.

[344] Ibid., 2:380-81. The conference idea apparently originated with Nicolson, who then suggested it to Grey. Ibid., 2:381; B.D. 139, Nicolson to Grey, July 26. Nicolson and William Tyrrell (private secretary to Grey) stressed to Lichnowsky the need for the conference. Lichnowsky telegraphed Berlin: "Both gentlemen (Nicolson and Tyrrell) see in Sir E. Grey's proposal to hold a conference *a' quatre* here, the only possibility of avoiding a general war, and hope that in this way it would be possible to get full satisfaction for Austria, as Serbia would be more apt to give in to the pressure of the Powers and to submit to their united will than to the threats of Austria. But the absolute prerequisite to the bringing about of the conference and the maintenance of peace would be the cessation of all military activities. Once the Serbian border was crossed, everything would be at an end, as no Russian Government would be able to tolerate this, and would be forced to move to the attack on Austria unless she wanted to see her status among the Balkan nations lost forever." G.D. 236, Lichnowsky to German Foreign Office, July 26.

be struck at through Serbia. It was plain that Russia could not regard such action with equanimity, and would have to accept it as a direct challenge. The result would be the most frightful war that Europe had ever seen, and no one could tell to what such a war might lead........

(H)e was turning to us with the request that we should make use of our influence at Vienna either to get them to accept the reply from Belgrade as satisfactory or as the basis for conferences. He was convinced that it lay in our hands to bring the matter to a settlement by means of the proper representations.............

I found (Grey) irritated for the first time. He spoke with great seriousness and seemed absolutely to expect that we should successfully make use of our influence to settle the matter. He is also going to make a statement in the House of Commons today in which he is to express his point of view. In any event, I am convinced that in case it should come to war after all, we should no longer be able to count on British sympathy or British support, as every evidence of ill-will would be seen in Austria's procedure. Also, everybody here is convinced, and I hear it in the mouths of all my colleagues, that the key to the situation is to be found in Berlin, and that if peace is seriously desired there, Austria can be restrained from prosecuting, as Sir E. Grey expresses it, a foolhardy policy. [345]

Lichnowsky himself was irritated. He felt that his superiors' localization strategy was folly. He complained to Berlin:

How can I argue for localization of the conflict when nobody here (in London) has any doubt that by Austria's procedure important Russian interests are in jeopardy, and that Russia will find herself compelled to intervene - even against her own desire - in case no pressure on Vienna is

---

[345] G.D. 258, Lichnowsky to German Foreign Office.

exercised by us? I should be greeted by nothing but a cynical shrug of the shoulders. [346]

London was sufficiently concerned about the situation that on the 26th, the Admiralty ordered the First and Second British Fleets to remain close to home and not to disperse. [347] This hardly meant that England had decided to intervene should a continental war erupt. But it reflected her fear that one might. She thus wanted to prepare her navy for all eventualities.

In Paris, Bienvenu-Martin, too, was exasperated with Vienna's attitude. Yet he was also irritated with Germany. He believed that she was doing virtually nothing to help resolve the crisis. In a July 27 note to Jules Cambon, he even said that if Germany failed to restrain Vienna, she would be responsible for any resultant European war:

> The situation at the moment of writing remains disturbing on account of the incomprehensible refusal of Austria to accept Serbia's submission, of her operations of mobilization (against Serbia), and of her threats to invade Serbia. The attitude taken up from the beginning by the Austrian Government, with German support, her refusal to accept any conversation with the Powers, practically do not allow the latter to intervene effectively with Austria without the mediation of Germany. However, time presses, for if the Austrian army crosses the frontier it will be very difficult to circumscribe the crisis, Russia not appearing to be able to tolerate the occupation of Serbia after the latter has in reality submitted to the Austrian note, giving every satisfaction and guarantee. Germany, from the very fact of the position taken up by her, is qualified to intervene effectively and be listened to at

---

[346] G.D. 266. As early as the 23rd, Lichnowsky warned Jagow that localization was impossible: "(Y)ou will have to admit that such a localization, in the event of a passage of arms with Serbia, belongs in the realm of pious wishes." G.D. 161. See also G.D. 236, in which Lichnowsky warned Berlin against "believing any further in the possibility of localization." Ibid.

[347] Bernadotte Schmitt, *The Coming of the War, 1914*, vol. 2 (New York: Charles Scribner's Sons, 1930), 44.

Vienna. If she does not do this, she justifies all suspicions and assumes responsibility for the war.

The Powers, particularly Russia, France, and England, have by their urgent advice induced Belgrade to yield. They have thus fulfilled their part. Now it is for Germany, who is alone able to gain a rapid hearing at Vienna, to give advice to Austria, who has obtained satisfaction and cannot, for a detail easy to adjust, bring about a general war. [348]

The Franco-British message was clear: the Entente had encouraged Serbia to be accommodating. It was Germany's turn to do likewise with respect to Austria. As Grey told Edward Goschen, Britain's ambassador to Germany: "After the Serbian reply, it is at Vienna that some moderation must be urged." [349]

C. Sazonov Becomes Conciliatory and Requests Direct Austro-Russian Negotiations

Surprisingly, while Grey and Bienvenu-Martin were growing more irked, the person most likely to be angry over Vienna's rebuff of Serbia's reply – Sazonov – had become much calmer! Part of this, perhaps, was simply a reflection of his fickle, up-and-down temperament. [350] Yet he was clearly relieved (1) that Austria did not attack Serbia immediately after breaking relations and (2) by her assurances that she would not annex Serbian territory. He finally seemed to realize that Austria's primary goal was merely to end Belgrade's agitation, not to expand her Balkan influence. Furthermore, he believed that Serbia's reply was nearly

---

[348] Quoted in Geiss, *July 1914*, 246-47.

[349] B.D. 176, July 27. Bunsen, however, seemed to doubt that Austria would pull back: "I believe that Austria-Hungary is fully determined on war with Serbia, that she believes her position as a Great Power is at stake, that her note was drawn up so as to make war inevitable, and that she is unlikely to listen to proposals for mediation until punishment has been inflicted on Serbia." B.D. 175, Bunsen to Grey, July 27.

[350] Fay, *Origins*, 2:282.

a complete acceptance. [351] If he could get Austria to ease up on a few demands, the crisis might be resolved. Pourtales sensed Sazonov's improved mood. He reported to Bethmann-Hollweg on the 27th:

> (A) very striking change has taken place in Mr. Sazonov's attitude, which fact has also been confirmed by my colleagues. The declaration that Austria had no intention of making any territorial acquisitions, and our energetic refutation of the insinuation that we had prodded Austria on with the idea of fomenting a conflict, has plainly had a quieting effect here. They are also breathing easier because of the fact that almost 48 hours have already passed since the unsatisfactory reply from Serbia was received by Austria-Hungary without any news of an Austrian advance into Serbia. They had evidently firmly counted here on the assumption that the refusal of Serbia to accede to the demands of Austria would immediately result in the outbreak of hostilities. Mr. Sazonov.........has even recognized the justice of the Austrian procedure against Serbia in principle, but still continues to feel hopeful that Austria-Hungary might be willing to moderate the form of her demands to a certain extent. [352]

Two demands that Sazonov wanted modified were #4 and #5. [353] He believed that they infringed upon Serbia's sovereignty. He also felt that Belgrade's acceptance of them would so enrage Serbia's populace that the lives of Pashitch and the Serbian royal

---

[351] Chelius informed Berlin of St. Petersburg's satisfaction with Serbia's response: "Prince Troubetzkoi of the entourage of the Tsar expressed himself to me today as follows: 'Now that the Serbian reply has been made public, one is compelled to recognize the satisfactory intention of Serbia to comply wholly and completely with the desires of Austria; otherwise, Serbia would not have replied in so friendly a fashion to Austria's unbelievably sharp note.............Austria would be assuming a heavy responsibility in giving rise to a European conflict by not recognizing Serbia's attitude.'" G.D. 337, Chelius to German Foreign Office, July 28.
[352] G.D. 339. See also G.D. 217, Pourtales to German Foreign Office, July 26.
[353] Sazonov to Schebeko, July 26, in C.D.D., R.O.B., Document No. 25.

family would be endangered. [354] Still, Sazonov was ready to work with Vienna. Pourtales informed Berlin:

> It developed from the discussion (between Sazonov and Szapary) that Sazonov had no objection to a number of the points (in the ultimatum). Concerning some of the other points, (Sazonov) told me, they might be able to come to an agreement as a result of alterations in their form. Perhaps it was only a matter of words. Austria, he said, made some demands which the Serbian Government could not, as a matter of fact, carry out, without altering the Serbian constitution.............But perhaps a method for satisfying Austria might be found without literal compliance with the demands. [355]

To this end, Sazonov asked Vienna to authorize Szapary to negotiate a modification of some of Austria's demands. [356] He also wanted Grey to put his conference proposal on hold. That way, Russian-Austrian talks could proceed unhindered. Grey agreed. He told Goschen that such talks were "the most preferable method of all" for resolving the crisis. [357]

Sazonov now waited for Vienna's response.

D. Germany Remains Confident That the Crisis Can Be Localized

Between the evenings of the 25th and 27th, therefore, the mindsets of certain leading Entente officials shifted. Grey and Bienvenu-Martin became very frustrated with Austria. Sazonov, meanwhile, moved in the opposite direction. In contrast to his earlier anger, he was now quite conciliatory towards Vienna.

But the Central Powers' position did not change during this period. They remained unwilling to yield.

---

[354] Ibid.

[355] G.D. 238, Pourtales to German Foreign Office, July 26. See also Szapary to Berchtold, July 27, in C.D.D., A.R.B. I, Document No. 31.

[356] Sazonov to Schebeko, July 26, in C.D.D., R.O.B., Document No. 25.

[357] B.D. 218, July 28. The prospect of Austro-Russian negotiations led Crowe to comment: "The first ray of hope." Comment of Crowe on B.D. 199, Bunsen to Grey, July 27.

Austria continued to argue that she had to deal firmly with Belgrade, for her existence was at stake. Nikolai Kudaschev, Russia's *charge d'affaires* at Vienna, reported to St. Petersburg on the 26th:

> (Berchtold said that) all (here in Vienna) are firmly convinced..............and in the first place the Emperor himself...............that the purpose of the all-Serbian propaganda is to undermine our (Austria's) house, our dynasty. To endure it any longer would be to confess the downfall of the Monarchy. The destruction of this propaganda, root and branch, is a matter of life or death for Austria-Hungary as a Great Power. We (Austria) must show that we are a Great Power. [358]

Vienna also stressed that Belgrade's reply was much less agreeable than it appeared. As Berchtold said to Mensdorff:

> (T)he offer of Serbia to meet points in our note was only an apparent one, intended to deceive Europe without giving any guarantee for the future. As the Serbian Government knew that only an unconditional acceptance of our demands could satisfy us, the Serbian tactics can easily be seen through: Serbia accepted a number of our demands, with all sorts of reservations, in order to impress public opinion in Europe, trusting that she would not be required to fulfill her promises. [359]

---

[358] Quoted in Schilling, *How the War Began*, 39-40. Kudaschev then added his own thoughts: "It is clearly indispensible to Austria-Hungary to cut through the roots of this ever-growing, threatening danger before it is too late, and to profit by the most favorable opportunity, such as the present is recognized to be, for doing so." Quoted in ibid., 40.

[359] C.D.D., A.R.B. I, Document No. 39, July 28. Vienna similarly told Tschirschky: "(T)he Serbian (reply) is by no manner of means, as Sir Edward Grey seems to think, an assent to all the Austrian demands with but a single exception; on the other hand, reservations are formulated in connection with most of the points, which materially detract from the admissions. Refusal, moreover, concerns just those points that contained some guaranty for the practical attainment of the ends which were their object." G.D. 400, Tschirschky to German Foreign Office, July 29.

In speaking with Grey, Mensdorff said that Serbia had refused "the one thing – the cooperation of Austrian officials and police – which would be a real guarantee" that her agitation would end. [360] He even added that Habsburg action against Serbia would *benefit* Europe by preventing her "from being henceforth an element of general unrest such as she had been for the last ten years." [361]

And Habsburg action was imminent. Late on the 25th, Vienna had ordered mobilization against Serbia. [362] Yet it had not planned to immediately declare war on her. [363] Conrad believed that it would take roughly two weeks to complete Austria's mobilization. Vienna therefore felt that war should be declared around August 12. [364] This alarmed Berlin. Szogyeny wired Berchtold on the 25th:

> I should like to remark that here (in Berlin) the general belief is that if Serbia gives an unsatisfactory answer, our declaration of war and war operations will follow immediately. Here, every delay in the beginning of war operations is regarded as signifying the danger that foreign powers might interfere. We are urgently advised to proceed without delay and to place the world before a *fait accompli*. [365]

Thus, as it had on July 5-6, Berlin urged Austria to act quickly. Otherwise, European diplomatic pressure might force her to accept an unfavorable compromise. Berchtold agreed. He told Conrad that the diplomatic situation would not hold until August 12. [366] Vienna therefore decided to declare war on the 28th or, at the latest, the 29th. [367]

---

[360] B.D. 188, Grey to Bunsen, July 27.
[361] Ibid.
[362] Albertini, *Origins,* 2:386.
[363] Ibid.
[364] Geiss, *July 1914*, 218-19, 227.
[365] Quoted in ibid., 200-01.
[366] Ibid., 227.
[367] Fay, *Origins,* 2:418. Another motivation for accelerating the war declaration could have been the Empire's general mood. Bunsen telegraphed Grey that Austria "has gone wild with joy at the prospect of war" with

While quietly encouraging Vienna to move faster, Berlin publicly continued to insist that the Austro-Serbian quarrel should be localized. Accordingly, Bethmann-Hollweg rebuffed Grey's conference proposal. He wired Lichnowsky on the 27th: "We could not take part in such a conference, as we would not be able to summon Austria before a European court of justice in her case with Serbia." [368] To him, the Powers had no business passing judgment on the Vienna-Belgrade dispute. Also, Austria would have to suspend all military operations during the conference. This would take the initiative from her and give it to the conference participants.

Bethmann-Hollweg knew that Germany's refusal would annoy Grey. To counteract this, Berlin agreed to forward Grey's proposals to Austria for her consideration. Privately, however, Jagow conveyed Berlin's true feelings about them to Vienna. Szogyeny wired Berchtold on the 27th:

> (Jagow) in strictest privacy informed me that very shortly eventual English propositions of mediation would be communicated to Your Excellency through the German Government. The German Government assures in the most decided way that it does not identify itself with these propositions; that on the contrary, it advises to disregard them, but that it must pass them on to satisfy the English Government. [369]

This dismissive, flippant attitude perhaps reflected a belief that England's proposals were meaningless because Russian intervention was unlikely. As late as the 27th, Berlin remained fairly confident that the crisis could be localized. True, the Germans had learned of discreet Russian military preparations. [370] Yet Russia's minister of war, Adjutant-General Vladimir Sukhomlinov, gave the German military *attaché* at St. Petersburg "his word of honor that as yet no mobilization orders of any kind

---

Serbia, and its "postponement or prevention............would undoubtedly be a great disappointment in this country." B.D. 175, July 27.
[368] G.D. 248.
[369] Quoted in Geiss, *July 1914*, 236.
[370] These were ostensibly pursuant to the Period Preparatory to War.

had been issued............nothing but preparatory measures were being undertaken; not a horse was being conscripted, not a reservist called to the colors." [371] Sazonov, moreover, stressed that these measures were purely defensive and that Russia desired a peaceful solution. Indeed, Sazonov seemed as conciliatory as ever. He even said that Serbia deserved "a lesson"! [372] Pourtales telegraphed Berlin on the 27th:

> Your Excellency (Jagow) might remain assured that Russia would not abuse the confidence in her love for peace. (Sazonov) was ready to go to the limt in accommodating Austria, and to exhaust all means to bring the crisis to a peaceful solution. Since Austria had declared her territorial disinterestedness (i.e., no intention to annex Serbian land) and had as yet taken no hostile steps against Serbia, the moment had come, in his opinion, to seek the means by an exchange of views among the Powers 'to build a golden bridge' for Austria. What means should be proposed for the attainment of this end were immaterial to him. The desire to humiliate Austria lay far from his mind. But he urgently requested consideration of the fact that if those Austrian demands which infringed on the rights of Serbian sovereignty should be accepted, there would come into power a revolutionary regime which would be even worse than the present one.
>
> I replied that in any event, Serbia would have to swallow several bitter pills. Austria would probably not let herself be put off with lame excuses; whether some of the points might be formally modified, I was unable to judge. In any case, the Serbian provocations, which had now brought Europe to the verge of war for the third time within five years, must once and for all be put to an end, as present conditions had become simply intolerable for Europe. For

---

[371] G.D. 242, Pourtales to German Foreign Office, July 27.

[372] In fact, Belgrade's troublemaking frequently caused headaches for St. Petersburg. Prince Troubetzkoi (of the Tsar's entourage) told Chelius that while the Russians could not let Austria destroy Serbia, "We do not love the Serbs in the least." G.D. 337.

this reason, Europe ought not to try to stay Austria's arm in her present quarrel with Serbia.

Sazonov did not wish to give up the hope that a moderation of some of the points of the demands put to Serbia might possibly be accomplished. He earnestly requested our cooperation along this line. There must be a way of giving Serbia her deserved lesson while sparing her sovereign rights.

I said in reply that guarantees must also be acquired for the future in order that Serbia should not once again back out of the obligations she had assumed. If Serbia wished to be treated as a member of the European family of nations with equal rights, she would also have to behave herself as a civilized nation. The Minister's objections to this sort of criticism of Serbia were much more feeble than a day or two ago; his speech was just as conciliatory as it was yesterday. [373]

Sazonov's mood reinforced Pourtales's hunch that Russia would not intervene militarily. He told Berlin: "I have the impression that Sazonov............has lost some of his nerve and is now looking for a way out." [374] Tschirschky shared Pourtales's optimism. Bunsen telegraphed Grey on the 26th:

(Tschirschky) has expressed to me his confident belief that Russia, having received assurance that Austria-Hungary will annex no Serbian territory, will keep quiet during the chastisement which Austria-Hungary is determined to inflict on Serbia. I asked if he did not think public opinion might compel the Russian Government to intervene on behalf of a kindred nationality. He said that the days of Pan-Slav agitation in Russia were over. Moscow was perfectly quiet, and everything depended on the personality of the Russian Minister for Foreign Affairs, who could easily resist, if he chose, the pressure of a few

---

[373] G.D. 282, Pourtales to German Foreign Office.
[374] G.D. 238.

newspapers. His Excellency (Tschirschky) did not think that (Sazonov) would be so imprudent as to take a step which would probably bring into the melting-pot many frontier questions in which Russia was interested, such as Swedish, Polish, Ruthene, Romanian, and Persian questions. Nor was France at all in a condition to face war. [375]

German confidence in British neutrality was even higher. The news that England's fleet would remain close to home was, to be sure, disturbing. [376] But this was more than offset by King George's statements to Germany's Prince Henry (George's cousin and the Kaiser's brother). The two met in England. The German naval *attaché* there wired his superiors on the 26th: "King of Great Britain said to Prince Henry that England would maintain neutrality in case war should break out between the Continental Powers." [377] George's words so influenced the Kaiser that he crowed: "I have the word of a king, and that is sufficient for me." [378]

Yet some in London – particularly Nicolson and Assistant Undersecretary of State for Foreign Affairs Eyre Crowe - were getting as irritated with Germany as they were with Vienna. For starters, they found Berlin's view that localization was possible to be foolish and irresponsible. Nicolson wrote on the 27th: "(Tschirschky) is spreading the belief that Russia will keep quiet if

---

[375] B.D. 150.

[376] Albertini, *Origins,* 2:443.

[377] G.D. 207, German naval *attaché* at London to Imperial Naval Office. Henry also wrote to Wilhelm: "(King George)................saw plainly the seriousness of the immediate situation and gave me the assurance that neither he nor his Government would leave anything undone in order to localize the struggle between Austria and Serbia............He said further, to quote his own words, 'We shall try all we can to keep out of this and shall remain neutral.' I am convinced that this statement was made in all seriousness." G.D. 374, July 28. But Henry cautioned that while he himself believed that Britain would be neutral at first, "whether she will be able to keep so permanently, I am not able to judge, but doubt it on account of her relations with France." Ibid.

[378] Quoted in Tirpitz, *My Memoirs,* 361. Wilhelm had read too much into George's words. He perhaps forgot that the monarchy did not control Britain's foreign policy.

no annexations occur! How little can he grasp the real situation." [379] He further commented: "I do not think that Berlin quite understands that Russia cannot and will not stand quietly by while Austria administers a severe chastisement to Serbia." [380] Crowe and Nicolson also felt that Germany was being deceitful. The former wrote:

> So far as we know, the German Government has up to now said not a single word at Vienna in the direction of restraint or moderation. If a word had been said, we may be certain that the German Government would claim credit for having spoken at all. The inference is not reassuring as to Germany's goodwill. At the same time, the rapid succession of fresh proposals and suggestions coming from St. Petersburg made it easier for Germany to find fresh excuses for her inactivity. [381]

Nicolson, meanwhile, told Grey:

> Berlin is playing with us. Jagow did not really adopt your proposal to intervene at Vienna...........but simply 'passed on' your suggestion and told his ambassador to speak about it. This is not what was intended or desired. [382]

He said the same to Buchanan:

> I do not understand after the very satisfactory way in which Serbia has met the Austrian requests how Austria

---

[379] Comment of Nicolson on B.D. 150. He also told Grey: "Prince Henry said that if Russia moved, there would be an internal revolution and the dynasty (would) be upset. This is nonsense.........." B.D. 144, July 26.

[380] Comment of Nicolson on B.D. 264, Goschen to Grey, July 29. Rennell Rodd, London's ambassador to Rome, informed Grey of the opinion of Italy's foreign minister, Marquis Antonio di San Giuliano, that "(t)here seemed to be difficulty in making Germany believe that Russia was in earnest." B.D. 252, July 29. Goschen agreed: "(My) Austrian colleague said to me today that a general war was most unlikely, as Russia neither wanted nor was in a position to make war. I think that opinion is shared by many people here (in Berlin)." B.D. 249, Goschen to Grey, July 28.

[381] Comment of Crowe on B.D. 185, Goschen to Grey, July 27.

[382] B.D. 144, Nicolson to Grey, July 26.

can with any justification proceed to hostile measures against her................(And) Germany has not played a very straight game – at least so far as we are concerned – in all this business. On two occasions, we asked her to use moderating language at Vienna and we promised to support her if she did so. She contented herself with simply passing on our proposal as our proposal, which of course was not what we desired or requested, and again she brushed on one side the idea of a small conference here as being an impractical suggestion. [383]

Yet Berlin remained unworried about England. When Jules Cambon expressed to Jagow his view that the Entente would stand together if war erupted, Jagow responded: "You have your information. We have ours, which is quite to the contrary. We are sure of English neutrality." [384]

As of the early evening of the 27th, Germany's localization strategy remained intact. She still felt that Austria could move against Serbia without triggering a continental war and saw no reason to restrain Vienna. Except for a few glitches – such as Russia's preliminary military measures - things were going largely according to plan.

But this was about to change.

---

[383] B.D. 239, July 28. Responding to a telegram from Goschen to Grey, in which Goschen reported Jagow's insistence that he wanted peace, Nicolson scoffed: "I am a little tired of these protestations and should like to see some practical action." Comment of Nicolson on B.D. 215, July 28. Crowe added: "There is much sound sense in the suggestion that Germany should be asked if, as she says, she is so anxious to work for peace, what *she* proposes the Powers should do." Comment of Crowe on B.D. 215 (emphasis in original).

[384] Quoted in Albertini, *Origins,* 2:429.

VI

ESCALATION

A. The Kaiser Returns to Germany

Wilhelm had been away at sea since early July. This was a godsend for Bethmann-Hollweg. He did not want the unpredictable Kaiser interfering with his and Jagow's management of the crisis. [385] Partly to keep Wilhelm from prematurely returning to Berlin, the chancellor transmitted regular updates to him. They painted the picture that the situation was under control. [386] The Kaiser had other sources of information, however. Some of them indicated that things were more serious than Bethmann-Hollweg believed. [387] Suspicious, the Kaiser departed for Germany, to Bethmann-Hollweg's dismay. Wilhelm's mercurial nature was bad enough. But his sudden return might make Europe think that Berlin was panicking over the crisis. [388]

Wilhelm was back in Germany by the late afternoon of the 27th. [389] By 9 p.m. that evening, several telegrams from Lichnowsky had arrived in Berlin. One was particularly ominous:

---

[385] Albertini, *Origins,* 2:433-34.

[386] Ibid.

[387] Ibid., 2:428, footnote 3.

[388] Ibid., 2:434; Fay, *Origins,* 2:403-04, 406. Tirpitz later wrote that had Wilhelm remained in Germany rather than proceeding with his voyage, he could have exercised more control over the situation and "would probably have found ways and means of evading the danger of war about the middle of the month." Tirpitz, *My Memoirs,* 317.

[389] Albertini, *Origins,* 2:434.

Should we (Germany).............conceive our sympathies for Austria and the exact fulfillment of our alliance obligations to be of so much importance that every other point of view were overshadowed by them, and even the most important item of our foreign policy – our relations with England – subordinated to the special interests of our ally, I believe that it would never again be possible to restore those ties which have of late bound us together.

The impression is constantly gaining force here – and I noticed it plainly at my interview with Sir Edward Grey – that the whole Serbian question has devolved into a test of strength between the Triple Alliance and the Triple Entente. Therefore, should Austria's intention of using the present opportunity to overthrow Serbia..........become more and more apparent, England, I am certain, would place herself unconditionally by the side of France and of Russia in order to show that she is not willing to permit a moral, or perhaps a military, defeat of her group. If it comes to war under these circumstances, we shall have England against us. [390]

At 11:50 p.m., Bethmann-Hollweg wired the following message to Tschirschky:

Since we have already refused one English proposal for a conference, it is impossible for us to waive *a limine* this English suggestion also. By refusing every proposition for mediation, we should be held responsible for the conflagration by the whole world and be set forth as the original instigators of the war. That would also make our position impossible in our own country, where we must appear as having been forced into the war. Our situation is all the more difficult, inasmuch as Serbia has apparently yielded to a very great degree. Therefore, we cannot refuse the mediator's role, and must submit the English proposal to the consideration of the Vienna Cabinet............I request Count Berchtold's opinion on

---

[390] G.D. 265, Lichnowsky to German Foreign Office, July 27.

the English suggestion, as likewise his views on M. Sazonov's desire to negotiate directly with Vienna. [391]

What was this? Here, Bethmann-Hollweg discusses the prospect of a general war. Had he lost confidence that the crisis could be localized? Did he now want to restrain Vienna? The answer to both questions is "no." First off, Bethmann-Hollweg sent his note at Wilhelm's behest, not on his own volition. [392] The Kaiser had sensed England's irritation and wanted to avoid unnecessarily antagonizing her. Bethmann-Hollweg's telegram therefore likely reflected Wilhelm's sentiments more than the chancellor's. Second, while Bethmann-Hollweg speaks of the *possibility* of war, he does not say that Russian intervention was *likely*. Third, he merely asks for Austria's *opinion* on Grey's proposal and Sazonov's request for negotiations. He does not ask or even suggest that she accept them. In fact, his telegram was little different in substance (though more dramatic in tone) from what Jagow told Szogyeny on the 27th – namely, that Berlin would forward Britain's initiatives to Vienna solely to avoid angering London. As seen in this note he sent to Lichnowsky at 2 a.m. on the 28th, Bethmann-Hollweg remained disinclined to curb Austria:

> Sir Edward Grey has expressly and repeatedly stated that the Austro-Serbian conflict did not concern him, but that on the other hand he stood ready to mediate in case of an Austro-Russian conflict, and counted on our assistance in doing so. We had declared ourselves to be in complete agreement with this point of view. Now, Sir Edward has deserted this ground and asks us to mediate to persuade Austria to accept the Serbian reply as satisfactory, or at least to look upon it as a basis for further conferences.
>
> The first petition cannot be acceded to. It is impossible for us to counsel Vienna to give a belated sanction to the Serbian reply, which they had immediately refused as

---

[391] G.D. 277, July 27.
[392] Albertini, *Origins,* 2:444. Early on the 28th, Bethmann-Hollweg notified Wilhelm that he had executed the latter's instruction to submit Grey's proposal to Vienna. G.D. 283, July 27.

unsatisfactory...............We made great concessions to England when we undertook to inaugurate mediation in connection with the second petition...............Austria intends – and it is not only her right but her duty – to secure herself against the continuation of the undermining of her own existence through the Greater Serbia propaganda, which finally resulted in the crime of Sarajevo. That has absolutely nothing at all to do with playing off the Triple Alliance against the Triple Entente.

Deeply as we are engaged in all directions in attempting to maintain the peace of Europe...............we cannot for that reason acknowledge the right of Russia or even of the Triple Entente to take the part of the Serbian intrigues against Austria. [393]

Bethmann-Hollweg's statements regarding Serbia's reply are also revealing. (Incredibly, neither he nor Jagow bothered to ask Vienna for the text of the reply until midday on the 27th!) [394] In his 11:50 p.m. note, he conceded that Serbia had "apparently yielded to a very great degree." [395] Yet his 2 a.m. message showed that he would not push Vienna to accept either the reply or negotiations based thereon.

As dawn arrived on the 28th, therefore, Bethmann-Hollweg's hands-off approach to the Austro-Serbian dispute remained largely intact.

---

[393] G.D. 279. Bethmann-Hollweg's remark about Berlin's "great concessions" in "inaugurating mediation" at Vienna was disingenuous, for he had no intention (at least not yet) of encouraging Austria to accept negotiations. He told Wilhelm: "It will be Austria's business to determine what to do about it (accepting mediation)." G.D. 283.

[394] Albertini, *Origins,* 2:439, 466.

[395] In fact, he felt that it constituted a near acceptance. On the 30th, he rhetorically asked: "What points of the Austrian ultimatum have Serbia refused, anyway? To my knowledge, only the participation of Austrian officials in the judicial proceedings." Marginal comment of Bethmann-Hollweg on G.D. 421, Pourtales to German Foreign Office, July 30. He also told the Prussian Ministry of State: "It must be considered that the Serbian reply had been an actual consent to the Austro-Hungarian demands, except in unimportant points." G.D. 456, Protocol of the Session of the Royal Prussian Ministry of State, July 30.

B. Wilhelm's Pledge Plan

Around mid-morning, the Kaiser reviewed Serbia's reply. He was surprised. It was much more accommodating than he had predicted. He wrote:

> This is more than one could have expected! A great moral victory for Vienna; but with it every reason for war drops away, and Giesl might have remained quietly in Belgrade! On the strength of this, *I* should never have ordered mobilization (against Serbia)! [396]

Wilhelm accordingly dispatched a message to Jagow around 10 a.m. It began:

> After reading over the Serbian reply, which I received this morning, I am convinced that on the whole the wishes of the Danube Monarchy have been acceded to. The few reservations that Serbia makes in regard to individual points could, according to my opinion, be settled by negotiation. But it contains the announcement...........of a capitulation of the most humiliating kind, and as a result, every cause for war falls to the ground.

> Nevertheless, the piece of paper, like its contents, can be considered as of little value so long as it is not translated into deeds. The Serbs are Orientals, and therefore liars, tricksters, and masters of evasion. [397]

This last moronic comment was followed, however, by a wise suggestion:

> In case Your Excellency shares my views, I propose that we say to Austria: Serbia has been forced to retreat in a very humiliating manner, and we offer our congratulations. Naturally, as a result, every cause for war has vanished. But a guaranty that the promises will be carried out is unquestionably necessary. That could be

---

[396] Marginal comment of Wilhelm on G.D. 271 (emphasis in original).
[397] G.D. 293, July 28.

secured by means of the temporary military occupation of a portion of Serbia, similar to the way we kept troops stationed in France in 1871 until the billions (in reparations) were paid. On this basis, I am ready to mediate for peace with Austria. [398]

Wilhelm said many stupid things. But he was no imbecile. He was quite capable of sound, even savvy reasoning. This was such a moment. And despite his never-ending bravado, he had no desire for armed conflict. As Bulow later wrote:

> (Wilhelm) II did not want war. He feared it. His bellicose marginal notes prove nothing. His exaggerations were mainly intended to ring in the ears of Privy Councillors at the Foreign Office, just as his more menacing jingo speeches were intended to give the foreigner the impression that here was another Frederick the Great or Napoleon. [399]

Under Wilhelm's plan, Habsburg forces would temporarily occupy Belgrade (or other areas of Serbia) as a pledge to ensure that the Serbians executed their promises. He felt this would give Austria's army "an ostensible success in the eyes of the world, and to make it possible for it to feel that it had at least stood on foreign soil." [400] It might also mollify Russia because Austria's occupation would be temporary and somewhat limited geographically.

Once a principal supporter of harsh Austrian action, the Kaiser now advocated restraint! Bethmann-Hollweg probably wondered whether Wilhelm's about-face was due to his impulsiveness, a sudden fear of war, or simply a belief that Austria had already won her showdown with Serbia. Regardless, Wilhelm's 10 a.m. message undoubtedly surprised the chancellor. It was one thing for the Kaiser to have Bethmann-Hollweg forward London's proposals to Austria for her mere consideration.

---

[398] Ibid.

[399] Bulow, *Memoirs*, 170.

[400] G.D. 293. Otherwise, Wilhelm feared that "the abandonment of the campaign (against Serbia) might be the cause of a wave of bad feeling (within Austria) against the Monarchy, which would be dangerous in the highest degree." Ibid.

It was quite another for him to essentially say that Austria should not assault Serbia and that negotiations should begin. Per Wilhelm's note, Bethmann-Hollweg now had to actively intervene at Vienna.

C. Bethmann-Hollweg Sends Telegram 174; Berlin's Hopes for Localization Fade

Accordingly, the chancellor sent the following message to Tschirschky at 10:15 p.m. on the 28th; known as "Telegram 174," it began:

> The Austro-Hungarian Government has distinctly informed Russia that it is not considering any territorial acquisitions in Serbia...................(Yet) the reply of the Serbian Government to the Austrian ultimatum, which has now been received, makes it clear that Serbia has agreed to the Austrian demands to so great an extent that, in case of a completely uncompromising attitude on the part of the Austro-Hungarian Government, it will become necessary to reckon upon the gradual defection from its cause of public opinion throughout all Europe.
>
> According to the statements of the Austrian General Staff, an active military movement against Serbia will not be possible before the 12th of August. As a result, the (German) Government is placed in the extraordinarily difficult position of being exposed in the meantime to the mediation and conference proposals of the other Cabinets, and if it continues to maintain its previous aloofness in the face of such proposals, it will incur the odium of having been responsible for a world war, even, finally, among the German people themselves............It is imperative that the responsibility for the eventual extension of the war among those nations not originally immediately concerned should, under all circumstances, fall on Russia. [401]

---

[401] G.D. 323.

Bethmann-Hollweg then suggested that Vienna raise the "pledge plan" with Russia as an equitable solution to the crisis. [402] He added:

> (If St. Petersburg) fail(ed) to recognize the justice of this point of view, it would have against it the public opinion of all Europe, which is now in the process of turning away from Austria. As a further result, the general diplomatic, and probably the military, situation would undergo material alteration in favor of Austria-Hungary and her allies. [403]

He instructed Tschirschky to "discuss the matter along these lines thoroughly and impressively with Count Berchtold, and instigate an appropriate move at St. Petersburg." [404]

Bethmann-Hollweg's telegram to this point is revealing. He appears more uneasy than he did in his 11:50 p.m. note of the 27th. Rather than merely solicit Vienna's *opinion* regarding a negotiated settlement, Tschirschky was to instead "thoroughly and impressively" discuss one with Berchtold. Some of this, again, was Bethmann-Hollweg simply executing Wilhelm's wishes. Yet the chancellor's concerned tone - combined with his statement that Russia must be made responsible for the "eventual extension of the war" – indicates that he now doubted that Austro-Serbian hostilities could be localized. He seems to implicitly acknowledge that Russian intervention was likely. His changed thinking perhaps stemmed from reports on the 28th of increasingly substantial Russian military preparations. Granted, these reports were largely unconfirmed. But the signs that Russia was willing to fight were there.

The chancellor's strategy thus shifted. His prior focus was on localization. [405] Now he wanted Austria to think harder about a

---

[402] Ibid.

[403] Ibid.

[404] Ibid.

[405] Yet Berlin still argued that the Austro-Serbian quarrel was not Russia's business. Sergei Sverbeyev, Russia's ambassador to Berlin, reported to St. Petersburg: "(Jagow said) the Serbian affair in no way concerned Russia and, he, Jagow, could not recognize the role assumed by Russia of official protector of the Balkans. (He said): 'If this were allowed, Germany had an

diplomatic solution so as to (1) avoid war with Russia, (2) convince Europe that the Central Powers wanted peace, and (3) pin the blame on Russia should she decline Wilhelm's proposal. Fair enough. But Bethmann-Hollweg concludes Telegram 174 with the following:

> You will have to avoid very carefully giving rise to the impression that we wish to hold Austria back. The case is solely one of finding a way to realize Austria's desired aim, that of cutting the vital cord of the Greater Serbia propaganda, without at the same time bringing on a world war, and if the latter cannot be avoided in the end, of improving the conditions under which we shall have to wage it, in so far as is possible. [406]

This instruction to "avoid very carefully giving rise to the impression that we wish to hold Austria back" completely undercut Bethmann-Hollweg's earlier directive to discuss Berlin's suggestions with Berchtold "thoroughly and impressively." It showed that while he wanted Austria to *consider* a peaceful solution, he would not strong-arm her into accepting one. [407]

The problem, as we will see, was that unless Berlin really pressured Austria to negotiate, she would remain intransigent.

D. Austria Declares War on Serbia

Such pressure was needed quickly, for Vienna's actions on the 28th led to a serious spike in tensions.

---

equal right with regard to the small Protestant states – for example, Sweden.' It will be understood that I protested energetically against this argument, which was really no argument." Quoted in Schilling, *How the War Began*, 59.

[406] G.D. 323.

[407] This was also evident in an 8:40 p.m. telegram he sent to Lichnowsky that evening: "(Britain) can hardly expect us to go so far in our mediation activities as directly to attempt to compel Austria to give in to Serbia. By doing so, we should contribute to the undermining of the position of Austria-Hungary as one of the Great Powers............We consider the Austro-Serbian procedure as nothing but a means of putting a final end to the Serbian provocations." G.D. 314, July 28.

For starters, Berchtold declined Sazonov's request for Austro-Russian talks (1) on modifying Austria's demands and (2) regarding the text of Serbia's reply. He informed Schebeko: "No one in our country could understand, nor could anyone approve, negotiations with reference to the wording used in the answer which we had designated as unsatisfactory." [408] Bunsen was told the same thing:

> I (Berchtold) thanked the Ambassador (Bunsen) for the communication of Sir E. Grey............(Grey's) point of view was, however, naturally different from mine, as England was not directly interested in the dispute between us and Serbia, and (he) could not be fully informed concerning the serious significance which the questions at issue had for the Monarchy................I had to decline to entertain the idea of a discussion based on the Serbian answer. What we asked for was the integral acceptance of the ultimatum. Serbia had endeavored to get out of her difficulty by subterfuges. We knew these Serbian methods only too well............
>
> In so far as Sir E. Grey desired to be of service to the cause of European peace, he would certainly not find any opposition from us. He must, however, reflect that the peace of Europe would not be saved by Great Powers placing themselves behind Serbia, and directing their efforts to securing that she should escape punishment. For even if we consented to entertain such an attempt at an agreement, Serbia would be all the more encouraged to continue on the path she has formerly followed, and this would, in a very short time, again imperil the cause of peace. [409]

Also, having received reports that Russia might be preparing to mobilize against Austria, Berchtold asked Berlin to

---

[408] Berchtold to Szapary, July 28, in C.D.D., A.R.B. I, Document No. 40.
[409] Berchtold to Mensdorff, July 28, in C.D.D., A.R.B. I, Document No. 41.

reflect whether Russia should, in a friendly manner, be reminded that the mobilization of (Russia's Kiev, Odessa, Moscow and Kazan) districts is equal to threatening Austria-Hungary and would have to be answered by counter-measures of a military character not alone by the (Habsburg) Monarchy, but by the allied German Empire also. [410]

Berchtold essentially wanted the Germans to warn St. Petersburg that they would treat Russian mobilization against Austria as mobilization against Germany as well, thereby compelling both Central Powers to take comparable steps against Russia. Bethmann-Hollweg refused. [411] He felt that such a threat was premature; besides, Jagow had told Jules Cambon on the 27th that Germany would not automatically mobilize if Russia mobilized against Austria. [412] But the fact that Berchtold even made his suggestion – one he hoped would convince Russia not to intervene – indicated that Austria herself had no intention of yielding.

Yet Vienna's most serious action of the 28th was its declaration of war against Serbia. Issued around 11 a.m., the declaration was consistent with what Vienna had decided the day before. [413] It should not have surprised Bethmann-Hollweg, who apparently learned of Austria's decision late on the 27th. [414] Indeed, he neither attempted to block the planned declaration nor warned Wilhelm that it was coming. [415] This suggests that he wanted nothing to interfere with it. [416] Moreover, he did not seem to grasp its significance. He wired Pourtales late on the 28th:

---

[410] Berchtold to Szogyeny, July 28, quoted in Geiss, *July 1914*, 254-55. Russia had not commenced mobilization against Austria at the time Berchtold sent his note.

[411] G.D. 299, Bethmann-Hollweg to Tschirschky, July 28.

[412] Cambon to Bienvenu-Martin, July 27, in C.D.D., F.Y.B., Document No. 67. Jagow warned Cambon, however, that if Russia attacked Austria, "Germany would be obliged to attack at once on her side." Ibid.

[413] Albertini, *Origins,* 2:465.

[414] Ibid., 2:441, 449.

[415] See ibid., 2:470.

[416] See ibid., 2:470-71.

We are constantly striving to persuade Vienna to have a frank discussion with St. Petersburg with the object of making plain to Russia in an unobjectionable and, it is to be hoped, satisfactory, manner, the purpose and extent of the Austrian procedure in Serbia. The declaration of war that has occurred in the meantime need make no difference. [417]

The war declaration may have made no difference to Bethmann-Hollweg. But it would make a huge difference to Sazonov.

E. Russia Decides to Mobilize against Austria

In St. Petersburg, Sazonov had been waiting for Vienna to authorize Szapary to renegotiate Austria's demands. Approximately two days had passed since Sazonov made his request. Although his mood remained conciliatory, Austria's silence disturbed him.

When news of Austria's war declaration against Serbia reached him around 4 p.m. on the 28th, his rage returned. [418] Here he was, trying to accommodate Austria - and then she sneaks behind his back and wrecks his efforts. He promptly discarded the idea of Austro-Russian negotiations. He instead urged London to revive its earlier diplomatic proposals. He hoped that this would forestall Vienna's seemingly imminent invasion of Serbia. (Grey's conference plan, we remember, had called for Austria and Russia to suspend military operations.) Sazonov wired Benckendorff on the 28th:

The Austrian declaration of war clearly puts an end to the idea of direct communications between Austria and Russia. Action by the London Cabinet in order to set on foot mediation with a view to suspension of military operations of Austria against Serbia is now most urgent. Unless military operations are stopped, mediation would

---

[417] G.D. 315.
[418] Albertini, *Origins*, 2:537.

only allow matters to drag on and give Austria time to crush Serbia. [419]

He took a far more important step, however. Consistent with the authorization given to him on the 24th and 25th, he notified Arkadi Bronevski, Russia's *charge d'affaires* at Berlin:

> In consequence of Austria's declaration of war on Serbia, we shall declare mobilization (against Austria) in the military districts of Odessa, Kiev, Moscow and Kazan tomorrow. Kindly bring this to the attention of the German Government and emphasize the absence of any intentions of a Russian attack on Germany. Our Ambassador in Vienna is not being recalled from his post for the time being. [420]

Sazonov's partial mobilization decision was the most dangerous escalation of the crisis to date. Russia was about to become the first Great Power to mobilize against another Power.

And there was more. After Sazonov wired Bronevski, he communicated with Janushkevich. The army chief had not voiced serious opposition on July 24-25 to partial mobilization. [421] Yet he now believed that implementing it on the 29th as planned could prove disastrous. [422] What if, he argued, war with Germany beckoned and Russia needed to mobilize against her? How could partial mobilization be converted midstream into general mobilization without creating a logistical nightmare that would leave Russia's armies completely disorganized and out of position? With war growing more likely anyway, why not proceed directly to general mobilization? Why bother implementing the hastily planned, intermediate step of partial mobilization? We will see whether Sazonov accepted Janushkevich's logic. Clearly, though, the military was starting to assert itself in Russia's decision-making.

---

[419] D.D., B.B.B., Document No. 70(2). Direct Austro-Russian talks, we shall see, were not quite dead. But Sazonov's belief that they were reflected his shock at Austria's war declaration.
[420] Quoted in Geiss, *July 1914*, 262.
[421] Albertini, *Origins*, 2:292-94.
[422] Schmitt, *Coming*, 94-97.

F. The Failure of the "Territorial Disinterestedness" Concept

Sazonov's partial mobilization decision showed the foolishness of Berlin's reliance on "territorial disinterestedness." As we saw, Berlin surmised that Austria's commitment not to annex Serbian soil would satisfy Russia. [423] This had been a cornerstone of German diplomacy since the 26th. Vienna's promise indeed pleased Sazonov. But it alone could not secure Russia's non-intervention. On the 28th, Buchanan asked Sazonov

> whether he would be satisfied with assurances which I (Buchanan) understood the Austrian Ambassador had been instructed to give with regard to Serbia's independence and integrity..............(Sazonov) replied at once that no engagement that Austria might take on these two points would satisfy Russia. [424]

Why was this? For starters, Sazonov perhaps did not believe Austria's assurances. He had, we know, long distrusted her. He may have suspected that she had secret plans to obliterate Serbia. According to Berchtold, Schebeko

> explained (to Berchtold) why our (Austria's) action against Serbia was regarded with such anxiety at St. Petersburg. He said that we were a Great Power which was proceeding against the small Serbian State, and it was not known at St. Petersburg what our intentions in the matter were: whether we desired to encroach on its sovereignty, whether we desired completely to overthrow it, or even to crush it to the ground. Russia could not be indifferent towards the future fate of Serbia, which was linked to Russia by historical and other bonds. [425]

---

[423] G.D. 219.

[424] B.D. 247, Buchanan to Grey, July 28.

[425] Berchtold to Szapary, July 30, in C.D.D., A.R.B. I, Document No. 50. Grey perceived Russia's suspicions of Austria's plans: "The stumbling block hitherto has been Austrian mistrust of Serbian assurances, and Russian mistrust of Austrian intentions with regard to the independence and integrity of Serbia." B.D. 340, Grey to Goschen, July 31. Sverbeyev, moreover, explained to Jagow on the 29th: "With regard to territorial

The main reason for the failure of territorial disinterestedness, however, was that Sazonov felt it was a meaningless assurance unless the ultimatum was modified. [426] Szapary told Berchtold that Sazonov continued

> to hold the opinion that to force on Serbia our conditions would result in Serbia becoming a vassal State. This, however, would upset the equilibrium in the Balkans, and this was how Russian interests became involved. [427]

In other words, Sazonov believed that imposing the whole ultimatum on Serbia would bring her under Vienna's control almost as much as if Habsburg forces permanently occupied part of her territory. Either way, Austria would dominate Serbia.

And this was the central issue for St. Petersburg. Any Austrian move on Serbia – whether via her armies, enforcement of the ultimatum, or both – would damage Russia's position in the Balkans. St. Petersburg believed that this had to be prevented at all costs. Not even France could alter Russia's determination on this point. When Sazonov heard a report that Paris might attempt to restrain Russia, he told Izvolsky: "If it is a question of any (French) pressure for moderation at St. Petersburg, we reject this from the outset, as we have from the beginning adopted an attitude which we cannot modify." [428]

Without question, July 28 was the crisis's worst day thus far. Whereas things on the 27th had been serious but hardly hopeless, tensions increased drastically on the 28th. The catalyst was Vienna's war declaration against Serbia, which triggered Sazonov's partial mobilization decision. With these actions, Austria and Russia moved closer to a collision.

---

annexations............it was possible Austria-Hungary did not desire any at the present moment, but that I knew only too well how wars were waged and how capable they were of bringing about unexpected results." Quoted in Schilling, *How the War Began*, 59.

[426] See G.D. 386, Tschirschky to German Foreign Office, July 29.

[427] C.D.D., A.R.B. I, Document No. 47, July 29.

[428] Quoted in Albertini, *Origins,* 2:401. Sazonov need not have worried. He had Paris's full support.

Whether this would compel Bethmann-Hollweg to restrain Vienna remained to be seen.

VII

MISCALCULATION

A. Wilhelm and Nicholas Communicate

Tsar Nicholas was a peaceful man. He had no wish for armed conflict. Yet after Vienna's war declaration against Serbia, he sensed a European conflagration coming. Around 1 a.m. on the 29th, he urged his cousin, the Kaiser, to halt Austria:

> Am glad you are back (in Germany). In this most serious moment, I appeal to you to help me. An ignoble war has been declared on a weak country. The indignation in Russia, shared fully by me, is enormous. I foresee that very soon I shall be overwhelmed by the pressure brought upon me, and be forced to take extreme measures which will lead to war. To try and avoid such a calamity as a European war, I beg you in the name of our old friendship to do what you can to stop your all(y) from going too far. [429]

The idea of direct correspondence between Nicholas and Wilhelm had also occurred to Bethmann-Hollweg. The chancellor believed that a friendly note to Nicholas could prove beneficial. If Russia intervened after Wilhelm's extension of this olive branch, it would, Bethmann-Hollweg thought, "throw the clearest light on Russia's responsibility" for the war. [430] Wilhelm agreed that he

---

[429] G.D. 332.
[430] G.D. 308, Bethmann-Hollweg to Wilhelm, July 28.

should contact Nicholas. He sent this message to him prior to reading Nicholas's 1 a.m. telegram:

> It is with the gravest concern that I hear of the impression which the action of Austria against Serbia is creating in your country. The unscrupulous agitation that has been going on in Serbia for years has resulted in the outrageous crime to which Archduke Franz Ferdinand fell victim. The spirit that led Serbians to murder their own king and his wife (in 1903) still dominates the country. You will doubtless agree with me that we both, you and me, have a common interest, as well as all Sovereigns, to insist that all the persons morally responsible for the dastardly murder should receive their deserved punishment. In this, politics plays no part.
>
> On the other hand, I fully understand how difficult it is for you and your Government to face the drift of your public opinion. Therefore, with regard to the hearty and tender friendship which binds us both from long ago with firm ties, I am exerting my utmost influence to induce the Austrians to deal straightly to arrive at a satisfactory understanding with you. I confidently hope you will help me in my efforts to smooth over difficulties that may still arise. [431]

Wilhelm's scathing criticism of Serbia surely displeased Nicholas. And his argument that Europe's sovereigns must stand together against regicidal behavior – one that Berlin had been using for several days - had no effect on the Tsar. As for Nicholas's telegram, an irritated Wilhelm wrote: "A confession of his (Nicholas's) own weakness, and an attempt to put the responsibility on my shoulders. The telegram contains a concealed threat and an order-like summons to tie the hands of our ally." [432] Still, the fact that the two emperors were communicating was a positive development.

There would be few others on this day.

---

[431] G.D. 335, July 28.

[432] Marginal comment of Wilhelm on G.D. 332.

B. Germany Warns Russia and France against Further Military Measures

Early on the 29th, Bethmann-Hollweg received a memorandum from Germany's chief of the general staff, General Helmuth von Moltke (whose uncle of the same name conducted Prussia's victorious war against France in 1870-71). Moltke had not contested Bethmann-Hollweg's refusal of Berchtold's July 28 request to warn Russia not to mobilize. [433] However, having received additional reports of Russian and French military preparations, Moltke told Bethmann-Hollweg that Germany could not sit idle indefinitely. [434] He did not yet demand German mobilization. But he indicated that if Russian and French preparations continued, Berlin would have to respond:

> For more than five years, Serbia has been the cause of a European tension which has been pressing with simply intolerable weight on the political and economic existence of nations. With a patience approaching weakness, Austria has up to the present borne the continuous provocations and the political machinations aimed at the disruption of her own national stability by a people which proceeded from regicide at home to the murder of princes in a neighboring land. It was only after the last despicable crime that she took to extreme measures, in order to burn out with a glowing iron a cancer that has constantly

---

[433] Schmitt, *Coming*, 138.

[434] Janushkevich tried to reassure Major Bernhard von Eggeling, Germany's military *attaché* at St. Petersburg, that Russia's military preparations were less significant than they appeared. The *attaché* was not persuaded. Speaking for Eggeling, Pourtales telegraphed Berlin: "We have here (in St. Petersburg) many reports concerning the calling of reservists to the colors that has taken place in various parts of the (Russian) Empire.............(Janushkevich) replied that, on the word of an officer, such reports were mistaken, that it was simply a case of a false alarm here and there. (Janushkevich) admitted movements of troops for the protection of the frontier; those were measures that did not originate with him and were entirely measures of precaution.................In view of the numerous and positive reports about recruitments, I (Eggeling) am forced to consider (Janushkevich's) talk as an attempt to mislead me as to the extent of the measures taken up to the present time." G.D. 370, Pourtales to German Foreign Office, July 29.

threatened to poison the body of Europe. One would think that all of Europe would be grateful to her. All of Europe would have drawn a breath of relief if this mischief-maker could have been properly chastised and peace and order thereby have been restored to the Balkans; but Russia placed herself at the side of this criminal nation.........

(I)t is of the greatest importance to ascertain as soon as possible whether Russia and France intend to let it come to a war with Germany. The further the preparations of our neighbors are carried, the quicker they will be able to complete their mobilization. Thus, the military situation is becoming from day to day more unfavorable for us, and can, if our prospective opponents prepare themselves further, unmolested, lead to fateful consequences for us. [435]

Bethmann-Hollweg agreed. At 12:50 p.m. on the 29th, he sent two telegrams. One went to Germany's ambassador to France, Wilhelm von Schoen:

Reports of French preparations for war are becoming more frequent. Kindly take up the matter with the French Government and call its attention to the fact that such activities would force us to take measures for self-protection. [436]

The other, more foreboding message went to Pourtales:

Kindly call Mr. Sazonov's serious attention to the fact that further continuation of Russian mobilization measures would force us to mobilize, and in that case a European war could scarcely be prevented. [437]

Jagow, we know, had told Jules Cambon that Russian mobilization against Austria would not trigger German

---

[435] G.D. 349, July 29.
[436] G.D. 341.
[437] G.D. 342.

mobilization. [438] Bethmann-Hollweg's note to Pourtales effectively modified this position. Russia was now alerted that mobilization against Austria would eventually compel Germany to mobilize. [439] Berlin's warnings to St. Petersburg and Paris signified that the crisis was expanding geographically. Mobilization activities had thus far been restricted to Austria, Russia, and Serbia. The other Powers had generally confined their actions to the diplomatic sphere. Now two of them - Germany and France - were starting to get sucked into the crisis militarily. The prospect of war was spreading westward across the continent.

C. Russia – Partial or General Mobilization?

We saw earlier how Janushkevich stressed to Sazonov on the 28th the dangers of partial mobilization. The next morning, they secured the Tsar's signature on two *ukases* (orders) - one for partial mobilization, the other for general mobilization. [440] Whichever *ukase* was implemented would depend upon how events unfolded. And the information Sazonov received on the 29th steered him towards general mobilization.

---

[438] Interestingly, Jagow took the news of Russia's partial mobilization far more seriously than his comments to Cambon suggested he would. Sverbeyev, who was with him at the time, informed St. Petersburg: "A paper was brought to Herr von Jagow, which he read with 'horror,' and then handed it to me asking me if the information set forth in it was true. It referred to our mobilization against Austria-Hungary.............(I) emphasized the fact that this was not a hostile measure with respect to Germany.................(Jagow) said that in view of our mobilization against Austria-Hungary, Germany must also mobilize, and that therefore there was nothing more to do but that from now onwards the diplomats must speak through the cannon's mouth. I could not conceal from von Jagow my astonishment at this remark, in that no farther back than on the preceding day he had told Cambon that our mobilization against Austria did not involve mobilization by Germany against us." Quoted in Schilling, *How the War Began*, 61.
[439] Still, Bethmann-Hollweg did not believe that Russian mobilization against Austria required *immediate* German mobilization.
[440] Albertini, *Origins*, 2:544-48.

He learned from Schebeko that Berchtold had declined his request for Austro-Russian negotiations regarding Vienna's demands. [441] This probably did not shock Sazonov in light of Austria's war declaration on Serbia. But the news that Habsburg forces had shelled Belgrade certainly did. Szapary, who was with Sazonov at the time, described the latter's reaction:

> He appeared as if transformed, (and) tried to dish up all his former arguments again in a manner contrary to all logic............'You are only wanting to gain time by negotiations and are meanwhile advancing and bombarding an unprotected city. What else do you want to conquer when you are in possession of the capital?' and other childish utterances to this effect...............'What is the good of our continuing our conversation if you act in this manner?' said he. I left him in a state of great agitation; and also my German colleague, who renewed his call, had – at least for today – to renounce all hope of a calm interview. [442]

Equally disconcerting to Sazonov was Pourtales's delivery of Bethmann-Hollweg's 12:50 p.m. warning sometime between 6 and 7 p.m. [443] A Russian foreign ministry memorandum described the heated exchange that ensued:

> To this communication, Sazonov sharply replied, 'Now I have no further doubts as to the true causes of Austria's intransigence.' Count Pourtales jumped up from his seat, and also sharply exclaimed, 'Minister, I protest with all my might at this insulting assertion.' The Minister drily replied that Germany still had an opportunity for proving

---

[441] See ibid., 2:550. Sazonov apparently construed Schebeko's message to mean that Vienna had refused *all* discussions with St. Petersburg. This, we will see, was a mistaken interpretation.

[442] Szapary to Berchtold, July 29, quoted in Geiss, *July 1914*, 279.

[443] Fay, *Origins,* 2:460-61.

the erroneousness of what he had said. The Minister and the Ambassador parted coolly. [444]

Soon afterwards, Nicholas informed Sazonov of Wilhelm's 1 a.m. telegram, while Sazonov told the Tsar about the German warning. [445] Perplexed, Nicholas telegraphed Wilhelm: "Thanks for your friendly and conciliatory telegram. Whereas official message presented today by your ambassador to my Minister was conveyed in a very different tone. Beg you to explain this divergency............Trust in your wisdom and friendship." [446] Sazonov then met with Janushkevich and Sukhomlinov. He knew that general mobilization would make war very likely. Such an aggressive step could also alienate England. The implications were frightening. But even scarier to him was the prospect of a militarily unprepared Russia. After all that had recently happened - Austria's war declaration, Berchtold's refusal of direct negotiations, the bombardment of Belgrade, and Germany's threat to mobilize – Sazonov doubted that peace could be preserved. Diplomacy had seemingly run its course. The focus, he believed, now had to be on Russia's security. The aforementioned Russian foreign ministry memorandum outlined what he, Janushkevich, and Sukhomlinov decided late on the 29th:

> (A)ll concerned knew how important in respect of our military preparedness even a partial mobilization would be if it were ordered, and still more a general mobilization, as in the first case a partial mobilization would render difficult a general mobilization if such should prove subsequently necessary.

---

[444] Quoted in Geiss, *July 1914*, 297. Pourtales reported the incident to Berlin as follows: "Have just made to Mr. Sazonov the communication as ordered, and stated in doing so that it did not imply a threat, but simply a friendly opinion. (Sazonov), who accepted the communication in a state of great excitement, replied that he would report it to (the Tsar)." G.D. 378, Pourtales to German Foreign Office, July 29.
[445] Geiss, *July 1914*, 297.
[446] G.D. 366, July 29. Nicholas also suggested that the Austro-Serbian dispute be submitted to the Hague Tribunal for arbitration. For ostensibly the same reasons that he eschewed Grey's conference proposal, Bethmann-Hollweg declined Nicholas's recommendation. Fay, *Origins*, 2:427-29.

> After examining the situation from all points, both the Ministers and the Chief of the General Staff decided that in view of the small probability of avoiding war with Germany, it was indispensable to prepare for it in every way in good time, and that therefore the risk could not be accepted of delaying a general mobilization later by effecting a partial mobilization now. The conclusion arrived at..........was at once reported by telephone to the Tsar, who authorized the taking of steps accordingly. [447]

General mobilization it would be. [448] Shortly after approving the trio's decision, however, Nicholas received this message from Wilhelm:

> I received your telegram and share your wish that peace should be maintained. But as I told you in my first telegram, I cannot consider Austria's action against Serbia an 'ignoble' war. Austria knows by experience that Serbian promises on paper are wholly unreliable. I understand its action must be judged as trending to get full guarantee that the Serbian promises shall become real facts. Thus, my reasoning is borne out by the statement of

---

[447] Quoted in Schilling, *How the War Began*, 49-50. As Baron Moritz von Schilling (a top Russian Foreign Ministry official) later explained: "It began.............to be feared in Russia that we might be taken unawares by events and find ourselves face to face with a fully armed opponent before we had rendered our defense secure. It was only gradually that in St. Petersburg the belief developed that Germany could not be relied upon, and that her mediation could not be calculated on for the purpose of settling the Austro-Serbian conflict, which carried with it the danger of a European war...............(T)he loss of all hope of averting war led Russia to mobilize her forces for the purpose of self-defense." Quoted in ibid., 15-17. Indeed, when Pourtales informed St. Petersburg on the 29th that Berlin would try to convince Vienna to make concessions, the Russians questioned "whether Germany really intended to exert serious pressure in Vienna or whether (Pourtales's communication) was only intended to lull us to sleep and so to postpone the Russian mobilization and thus gain time wherein to make corresponding preparations." Quoted in ibid., 47-48.
[448] One argument Sazonov used to persuade Nicholas to approve general mobilization was that it might force the Central Powers to back down, thus avoiding war. Albertini, *Origins*, 2:558.

the Austrian Cabinet that Austria does not want to make any territorial conquests at the expense of Serbia. I therefore suggest that it would be quite possible for Russia to remain a spectator of the Austro-Serbian conflict without involving Europe in the most horrible war she ever witnessed. I think a direct understanding between your Government and Vienna possible and desirable and, as I already telegraphed to you, my Government is continuing its exertions to promote it. Of course, military measures on the part of Russia which would be looked on by Austria as threatening would precipitate a calamity we both wish to avoid and jeopardize my position as mediator, which I readily accepted on your appeal to my friendship and my help. [449]

Desperate to avoid war and encouraged by Wilhelm's assurance that Berlin was continuing to work for an Austro-Russian understanding, Nicholas spoke with Janushkevich and Sukhomlinov. He wanted to revert to partial mobilization. [450] His two subordinates tried to dissuade him. [451] But Nicholas would not budge, telling them: "I will not become responsible for a monstrous slaughter." [452]

Just before midnight, he countermanded the directive for general mobilization and ordered partial mobilization. [453]

D. Austro-Italian Friction; Germany Presses Vienna to Secure Rome's Support

The continued rise in tensions on the 29th likely convinced Bethmann-Hollweg that Russian intervention was not merely probable but almost certain unless Austria showed more conciliation. Yet there was no sign of this. To Bethmann-Hollweg's frustration, Vienna had not responded to his late-night

---

[449] G.D. 359, July 29.
[450] Fay, *Origins,* 2:465.
[451] Ibid.
[452] Quoted in Albertini, *Origins,* 2:558.
[453] Fay, *Origins,* 2:466.

messages of the 27th and 28th. [454] In fact, the 29th passed without a single telegram from Tschirschky regarding Austria's view of the pledge plan. [455] Furthermore, disturbing news from Lichnowsky had arrived:

> The members of the local Austrian Embassy, including Count Mensdorff, have, in their talks with members of this Embassy and with me, never attempted the least concealment of the fact that Austria was solely concerned with the destruction of Serbia, and that the note was intentionally so constructed that it would have to be rejected. When the news that Serbia had submitted was published............these gentlemen were actually stunned. Count Mensdorff told me only yesterday in confidence that in Vienna they were absolutely set on war, as Serbia was to be 'beaten to the earth.' The same gentlemen have also stated that it was the intention to make a present of portions of Serbia to Bulgaria and presumably also to Albania. [456]

This infuriated Bethmann-Hollweg. Mensdorff's statements contradicted Vienna's assurances to Russia of territorial disinterestedness. The chancellor commented: "This duplicity of Austria's is intolerable..............at St. Petersburg, (the Austrians) are lambs with not a wicked thought in their hearts, and in London their Embassy talks of giving away portions of Serbian territory." [457]

Just as irksome to Bethmann-Hollweg was Vienna's attitude towards the third member of the Triple Alliance.

Austro-Italian relations, we know, had been strained for some time. Although the Central Powers did not share the

---

[454] Specifically, his 11:50 p.m. note of the 27th and Telegram 174.

[455] Albertini, *Origins*, 2:525. Agitated over Vienna's silence, the chancellor wired Tschirschky at 10:18 p.m. and 10:30 p.m. on the 29th. His messages, respectively, asked whether Telegram 174 had been received and demanded that Telegram 174's instructions be executed immediately. G.D. 377; Carnegie Endowment, *German Documents Collected by Karl Kautsky*, 332, footnote 3.

[456] G.D. 301, Lichnowsky to German Foreign Office, July 28.

[457] Marginal comment of Bethmann-Hollweg on ibid.

ultimatum's terms with Italy beforehand, the latter suspected that Vienna would demand much of Serbia. The ultimatum's virulence nonetheless shocked Rome. On the 24th, Italy's foreign minister, Marquis Antonio di San Giuliano, and prime minister, Antonio Salandra, met with Hans von Flotow, Germany's ambassador to Rome. As Jagow informed Wilhelm, San Giuliano vented at Flotow in a "more or less excited conference lasting several hours." [458] San Giuliano said that "(t)he substance of the Austrian note was worded so aggressively and so ineptly that the public opinion both of Europe and of Italy would be against Austria" (which spurred Wilhelm to retort, "Rot!"). [459]

More important was what San Giuliano said about Italy's obligations under the Triple Alliance treaty. Article III thereof read:

> If one or two of the high contracting parties should be attacked, without direct provocation on their own part, and should find themselves involved in a war with two or more Great Powers who are not signatories to the present treaty, the *casus foederis* shall be deemed to exist simultaneously for all the high contracting parties. [460]

Article VII stated:

> Austria-Hungary and Italy, having in view only the maintenance, as far as possible, of the territorial *status quo* in the east, bind themselves to use their influence to

---

[458] G.D. 168, Jagow to Wilhelm, July 25. See also G.D. 156, Flotow to German Foreign Office, July 24.

[459] G.D. 168; marginal comment of Wilhelm on ibid. Prior to the 23rd, San Giuliano had urged Vienna to exercise moderation towards Serbia. Naturally, he feared a wider war if Austria used force. But he also questioned whether violence would end Serbia's agitation. Kajetan Merey von Kapos-Mere, Austria's ambassador to Rome, conveyed San Giuliano's position to Berchtold: "In regard to the clearing up of our relations with Serbia, (San Giuliano), as on many previous occasions, explained in detailed arguments that we could remedy them only by adopting a conciliatory attitude (and) not by means of force and the humiliation of a neighboring State." D.D., A.R.B. II, Document No. 3, July 21.

[460] Carnegie Endowment, *German Documents Collected by Karl Kautsky*, 608.

prevent any territorial modification which might be injurious to one or another of the Powers signatory to the present treaty. To this end, they will communicate to each other all information adapted to a mutual enlightenment as to their own intentions as well as to those of other Powers.

In the case, however, that, by reason of the course of events, the maintenance of the *status quo* in the region of the Balkans or on the Ottoman coasts and islands in the Adriatic and in the Aegean Sea should become impossible, and that, whether in consequence of the action of a third Power or otherwise, Austria-Hungary or Italy should find themselves compelled to modify it by a temporary or a permanent occupation on their part, such occupation shall not take place until after a previous agreement between the two Powers; this agreement shall be based on the principle of mutual compensation for every territorial or other advantage which each of the Powers might derive over and above the present *status quo*, and which shall satisfy the interests and the well grounded pretensions of both parties. [461]

San Giuliano made three principal arguments. First, he contended that the Triple Alliance was a defensive pact. It called for mutual support if a member were attacked without provocation. To him, though, Austria was acting *offensively,* not in self-defense; moreover, she was essentially provoking Russia. Thus, Article III did not require Rome to aid Austria if Russia attacked her. Second, Austria's demands on Serbia, if accepted, would tilt the Balkan *status quo* in Vienna's favor. San Giuilano believed that Austria effectively violated Article VII by failing to notify Rome of her intention to alter said *status quo*. Third, under Article VII, Italy was entitled to concessions if Vienna attacked Serbia and occupied part of her territory. In San Giuliano's view, Austria should have agreed - *prior to* the 23rd - to compensate Rome. Accordingly, Flotow informed Berlin:

---

[461] Ibid., 608-09.

(San Giuliano said that) the spirit of the Triple Alliance compact demanded that Austria come to an understanding with her allies before entering upon a move so portentously aggressive. As she had not done so, so far as Italy was concerned, Italy could not consider herself bound in connection with the further consequences of this move. [462]

The Germans did not seem to regret withholding the ultimatum's terms from Italy. Still, they recognized that the Central Powers needed her support in this crisis. [463] Even before the 23rd, they were urging Vienna to obtain it. On the 15th, Jagow told Tschirschky:

Just as Italian public opinion is in general touched with Austrophobia, it has always proved itself up to the present time as Serbophile. So that there is no doubt in my mind that in case of an Austro-Serbian conflict, it would take a pronounced stand by the side of Serbia. Any territorial extension of the Austro-Hungarian Monarchy, even an extension of its influence in the Balkans, would absolutely horrify Italy and would be regarded as damaging to Italy's position there..........

It is of the greatest importance that Vienna should come to some understanding with the Cabinet at Rome.........Italy has, according to her compact with Austria, a right to claim compensation for every change that takes place in the Balkans to the advantage of the Danube Monarchy. [464]

He again told Tschirschky on the 18th: "(A)n early agreement..........between the Cabinets of Vienna and Rome (is)

---

[462] G.D. 156.

[463] Moltke, in particular, wanted Italy's military aid. He believed that her support would (1) compel France to keep troops along the Franco-Italian border, thus diluting the resistance that German armies would face in northern France, and (2) enable Austria to throw her entire strength against Russia and Serbia without having to worry about a surprise Italian attack. See G.D. 662, Moltke to German Foreign Office, August 2.

[464] G.D. 46.

urgently necessary." [465] Similar pleas were conveyed to Vienna over the following days.

But Austria was not listening. The truth was that she (1) had no desire to make concessions to a country she disliked and distrusted, (2) felt that Italy was blackmailing her, (3) feared that giving away territories (e.g., the Trentino) as compensation could set a dangerous precedent, and (4) believed that the Austro-Serbian quarrel was none of Rome's business. Vienna also raised two legal arguments. First, since Austria did not intend to *annex* Serbian territory, a prior agreement with Italy was unnecessary. (This ignored Article VII's verbiage that even a temporary occupation of Balkan territory warranted compensation.) Second, Vienna suggested that Article VII only applied to the occupation of Balkan territory that was under Turkish control when the Article came about. Italy therefore would not deserve compensation if Austria seized areas of Serbia that were not Ottoman-controlled when Article VII became effective. Berchtold outlined Vienna's position regarding Article VII to Kajetan Merey von Kapos-Mere, Austria's ambassador to Rome:

> It would mean a complete misunderstanding of the spirit of the Triple Alliance agreement if Article VII were to be interpreted in such a way as to make a temporary occupation of territory belonging to a neighboring Balkan State at war with Austria-Hungary conditional upon a previous agreement with Italy based on compensations...........
>
> As to the spirit of the treaty..............the Dual Monarchy cannot anticipate an interpretation of the agreement on the part of Italy which would hamper our action against Serbia; especially so, as the object of that action is to obtain guarantees against the continuation of a propaganda which endangers the very existence of the Monarchy. Furthermore, it must not be forgotten that in the spirit of Article VII, the maintenance of the *status quo* existing at that time was said to be desirable in order to prevent any territorial changes which might be of disadvantage to

---

[465] G.D. 68.

either Austria-Hungary or Italy. Since that time, such changes have taken place in a manner decidedly unfavorable to the interests of the Dual Monarchy. Serbia's aggrandizement at the expense of Turkey has accentuated the Great-Serbian utopia to such an extent that the peaceful development of our territories is seriously menaced and Austria-Hungary may be compelled even to resort to force of arms to defend her possessions.

An intervention on the part of the Dual Monarchy for the purpose of changing the *status quo* of the present Turkish possessions or of the territories which at the time of the treaty had been part of the Turkish dominion undoubtedly would necessitate a previous understanding with Italy; on the other hand, it is evident that Austria-Hungary must have a free hand to protect her interests in connection with changes of the *status quo* which have been affected without her intervention. [466]

These arguments failed to impress Italy – or Germany. They instead made Berlin suspect that Vienna had no intention of honestly negotiating with Rome. Bethmann-Hollweg wired Tschirschky on the 26th that Austria *had* to strike a deal with Rome. [467] He added that she "must not evade such an agreement by questionable compact interpretations, but must make up her mind in accordance with the seriousness of the situation." [468] Wilhelm agreed. He deemed it, in Bethmann-Hollweg's words, "absolutely necessary that Austria come to an understanding with Italy on the compensation question in time." [469] Jagow instructed Tschirschky on the 27th to communicate this to Berchtold. [470]

---

[466] D.D., A.R.B. II, Document No. 2, July 20. Berchtold instructed Merey to use these arguments if San Giuliano "endeavored to interpret Article VII of the Triple Alliance Treaty in a way which would conform neither with the sense nor with the wording of it and (tried to) claim compensation." Ibid.
[467] G.D. 202.
[468] Ibid.
[469] Marginal comment of Bethmann-Hollweg on G.D. 244, Flotow to Bethmann-Hollweg, July 25.
[470] G.D. 267.

By the 28th, the pressure from Berlin compelled Berchtold to relent - but only slightly. Summarizing his conversation that day with the Duke of Avarna (Italy's ambassador to Austria), Berchtold told Merey to notify Rome of Vienna's willingness to discuss compensation - on certain conditions:

> The Duke of Avarna called on me today and on behalf of his government made (the following) statement........... 'Should the threatening conflict lead to war and concurrently to an even temporary occupation of Serbian territory, the Italian Government, in accordance with Article VII of the treaty of the Triple Alliance, would reserve its right to claim compensation, with regard to which an agreement should be reached in advance.......'
>
> I replied to the Italian Ambassador that the disagreement with Serbia concerns only ourselves and Serbia; that, besides, we contemplated no territorial conquests, and that an occupation of Serbian territory was therefore not intended. The Duke of Avarna having suggested that it would impress the Powers very favorably if we were to make a formal statement to this effect, I replied that we could not do so, as it was impossible to assume that, in the course of the war, a situation would not arise which would compel us to occupy Serbian territory, even against our will...........
>
> With reference to the claims of compensation based upon Article VII of the Treaty of the Triple Alliance, you (Merey) will make the following declaration (to Rome): 'As already stated to the Italian Ambassador, territorial acquisitions are in no way contemplated by us. Should we, nevertheless, be compelled to decide upon an occupation which could not be considered as merely provisional, we should be prepared to enter upon an exchange of views with Italy concerning an eventual compensation. On the other hand, we fully expect Italy not only not to impede

her ally's action in the pursuance of her aims, but to maintain steadfastly the friendly attitude of an ally.' [471]

Thus, Berchtold would consider compensation if (1) Vienna later decided to permanently occupy Serbian territory and (2) Italy maintained a "friendly attitude" towards Austria during the crisis. He still rebuffed Rome's assertions that a temporary occupation warranted compensation and that an agreement was necessary *now*.

Not surprisingly, Italy declined Berchtold's joke of an offer, later labeling it "vague and unsatisfactory." [472] Rome also said:

> With reference to Count Berchtold's intention to take up the question of compensation when occasion arises, it is clear than an agreement on this point is urgent. As long as an understanding has not been reached, and as long as Austria-Hungary's interpretation of Article VII leaves room for doubt, Italy cannot pursue a policy which would, either now or at a later time, facilitate a temporary or permanent occupation by Austria-Hungary; on the contrary, Italy would have to support every measure calculated to prevent such a possible occupation. [473]

---

[471] D.D., A.R.B. II, Document No. 15, July 28. Berchtold concluded his telegram with this: "For Your Excellency's personal information, I will add that I have determined to make this concession because at the present time great issues are at stake, which in themselves are fraught with great difficulties and which, except for the firm coherence of the Triple Alliance Powers, it would be entirely impossible to accomplish." Ibid. See also G.D. 428, Austro-Hungarian embassy in Berlin to German Foreign Office, July 30. Berchtold's arrogance is amazing. He acted as though he had granted an enormous concession when he should have known it could never satisfy Rome.

[472] Merey to Berchtold, July 31, in D.D., A.R.B. II, Document No. 18.

[473] Merey to Berchtold, July 29, in D.D., A.R.B. II, Document No. 16. Merey vented that Italy "is chiefly concerned (with) the question of compensation…………..and does even shrink from attempts at blackmail." Ibid. He was also irritated at Berchtold. He felt that the latter – under German pressure – had ignored his recommendation to make no concessions to Italy. He sarcastically told Berchtold on the 28th: "As your Ambassador in Rome, I am, at least in rank, the foremost expert in matters concerning Italy…………..I really wonder why we afford ourselves the luxury of an

Appalled by Vienna's obstinance, Bethmann-Hollweg wrote to Jagow on the 29th:

> Is it not necessary to send another telegram to Vienna stating pointedly that we regard the manner in which Vienna is handling the compensation question with Rome as absolutely unsatisfactory and that we rest the responsibility for the attitude that Italy may assume in the event of war directly on Vienna's shoulders? If Vienna threatens in this fashion to blow up the Triple Alliance on the eve of a possible European conflagration, the whole alliance will begin to totter. Vienna's declaration that in case of the permanent occupation of parts of Serbian territory, she will come to an arrangement with Italy is, furthermore, in direct opposition to the assurances of her territorial disinterestedness given at St. Petersburg. The statements made to Rome are certainly known at St. Petersburg. As her ally, we cannot support any double-faced policy.
>
> I consider this to be necessary. Otherwise, we cannot mediate any longer at St. Petersburg and shall find ourselves completely entangled in Vienna's tow-rope. I do not want that, nor do I want to put myself in danger of being accused of double-dealing. [474]

Szogyeny perceived Berlin's grave anxiety about Italy. He telegraphed Berchtold on the 30th:

> If.............the Triple Alliance, so runs the further argument of the German Government, cannot be considered as an integral whole, our chances in the great conflict must be considerably worse. Italy must therefore, absolutely, remain in the Triple Alliance and what is more, as an active factor............This wish of Germany's (to accommodate Italy) is not, according to my

Ambassador at Rome...............and do not rather transfer the representation of our interests in Italy to the German Embassy, which is obviously much more competent." Quoted in Albertini, *Origins,* 3:288-89.
[474] G.D. 340.

opinion, due to a diminution of its fidelity as an ally towards Austria-Hungary, but solely based on the conviction that Austria-Hungary and Germany absolutely need Italy in order to enter the general conflict with safety................I cannot help, in view of the gravity of the situation, absolutely agreeing with the above-reported conviction of the German Government. [475]

We will see in Chapter X whether Berchtold did what was necessary to secure Italy's backing. As for Bethmann-Hollweg, Austria's stubborness with Rome, her rhetoric in London about annihilating Serbia, and her silence regarding the pledge plan led him to wire Tschirschky at 8 p.m. on the 29th:

> I regard the attitude of the Austrian Government and its varying procedure towards the different Governments with increasing astonishment. At St. Petersburg, it announces its territorial disinterestedness; us it leaves entirely at sea regarding its program; Rome is put off with meaningless phrases on the compensation question, and at London Count Mensdorff is giving away portions of Serbia to Bulgaria and Albania and placing himself in direct opposition to Vienna's solemn declarations at St. Petersburg. I must draw from these contradictions the conclusion................that the Government at Vienna is entertaining plans which it finds advisable to keep secret from us in order to assure itself of German support in any event and not to expose itself to a possible refusal of that support by making them public. [476]

Austria was certainly giving Bethmann-Hollweg headaches. Yet the information he received late on the 29th would cause him the most excruciating of pains.

---

[475] Quoted in Geiss, *July 1914*, 302-03.
[476] G.D. 361.

E. Berlin's Confidence in British Neutrality Is Shattered

As of the 27th, Grey had not indicated what Britain would do if war erupted. He still rebuffed Sazonov's pleas for London to stand with the Franco-Russian pact. [477] He insisted on preserving Britain's freedom of action. This likely enhanced Berlin's confidence in English neutrality. Furthermore, since Berlin at that time remained unconvinced that Russia would intervene, it perhaps felt that the question of British intercession could be put aside altogether. Unless Russia went to war, England's intentions were largely moot.

By the 29th, of course, things had changed. Bethmann-Hollweg realized that St. Petersburg would fight, which in turn would likely trigger France's involvement. Britain's potential intervention thus became a bigger issue for Bethmann-Hollweg, particularly considering Grey's frustration with the Central Powers. Lichnowsky, in fact, wired Berlin at 2:08 p.m. on the 29th that Berchtold's refusal to "empower Count Szapary to confer with (Sazonov) about the Austro-Serbian quarrel made a most unpleasant impression" on Grey. [478] In light of the changed situation, Bethmann-Hollweg felt that he had to confirm London's intentions.

But he went about this in a bizarre fashion. On the evening of the 29th, he told Goschen that he understood that England would not accept seeing France fall under German domination. He then proposed the following, as Goschen reported to Grey:

(Bethmann-Hollweg) said he was continuing his efforts to maintain peace, but that in the event of a Russian attack on Austria, Germany's obligation as Austria's ally might, to

---

[477] Grey's position frustrated Izvolsky. The latter believed that war was inevitable because Britain's failure to support Russia and France encouraged Austria's intransigence. B.D. 216, Bertie to Grey, July 28. Asquith, who supported Grey's non-committal stance, wrote in his diary on the 29th: "It is one of the ironies of the case that we, being the only Power who has made so much as a constructive suggestion in the direction of peace, are blamed by both Russia and Germany for causing the outbreak of war." Quoted in Asquith, *Memories,* 9. See also B.D. 320, Bertie to Grey, July 30. Indeed, we will soon examine the Kaiser's crackpot views regarding England's responsibility for the crisis.
[478] G.D. 357, Lichnowsky to German Foreign Office.

his great regret, render a European conflagration inevitable...............The (German) Government was ready to give every assurance to the British Government, provided that Great Britain remained neutral, that in the event of a victorious war, Germany aimed at no territorial acquisitions at the expense of France. In answer to a question from me, His Excellency said that it would not be possible for him to give such an assurance as regards to colonies.

Continuing, His Excellency said he was, further, ready to assure the British Government that Germany would respect the neutrality and integrity of Holland as long as they were respected by Germany's adversaries. As regards Belgium, His Excellency could not tell to what operations Germany might be forced by the action of France, but he could state that, provided that Belgium did not take sides against Germany, her integrity would be respected after the conclusion of the war.

Finally, His Excellency said that he trusted that these assurances might form the basis of a further understanding with England which, as you well know, had been the object of his policy ever since he had been Chancellor. An assurance of British neutrality in a conflict which the present crisis might possibly produce would enable him to look forward to a general neutrality agreement between the two countries, the details of which it would, of course, be premature to discuss at the present moment.

His Excellency asked me how I thought you would view his request. I replied that I thought that you would like to retain full liberty of action, and that personally I did not consider it likely that you would care to bind yourself to any course of action at this stage of events. [479]

---

[479] B.D. 293, July 30. See also G.D. 373, Bethmann-Hollweg to Lichnowsky, July 29.

In fairness, Bethmann-Hollweg was undoubtedly a man under enormous strain. Still, one must wonder whether he had completely lost his mind when he made this idiotic offer. He essentially told Grey: "If war erupts and England remains neutral, we will not annex French or Belgian territory though we might take France's colonies." Whether this reflected blindness, desperation, or both, is debatable. What is certain is that it made a terrible impression on London. It undercut all of Berlin's previous statements about its peaceful intentions. Crowe wrote: "The only comment that need be made on these astounding proposals is that they reflect discredit on the statesman that makes them." [480]

As it turned out, Bethmann-Hollweg need not have made his proposal to get a sense of London's thinking. At 9:12 p.m., the following dispatch from Lichnowsky arrived. Its impact on Berlin was momentous:

> Sir E. Grey just sent for me again. The Minister was entirely calm, but very grave, and received me with the words that the situation was continuing to grow more acute..........
>
> (He) said to me that he had a friendly and private communication to make to me, namely, that he did not want our warm personal relations and the intimacy of our talks on all political matters to lead me astray, and he would like to spare himself later the reproach of bad faith. The British Government desired now as before to cultivate our previous friendship, and it could stand aside as long as the conflict remained confined to Austria and Russia. But if we and France should be involved, then the situation would immediately be altered, and the British Government would, under the circumstances, find itself forced to make up its mind quickly. In that event, it would not be practicable to stand aside and wait for any length of time. 'If war breaks out, it will be the greatest catastrophe that the world has ever seen.' It was far from his desire to express any kind of a threat; he only wanted to protect me from disappointments and himself from the reproach of

---

[480] Comment of Crowe on B.D. 293.

bad faith, and had therefore chosen the form of a private explanation.

> Sir E. Grey added also that the (British) Government of course had to reckon with public opinion. Up to the present, it had in general been in favor of Austria, as the justice of a certain satisfaction due her was recognized; but now it was beginning to turn completely to the other side as a result of Austrian stubbornness. [481]

Now, Grey made no outright threats. He even said that England could stay out of an Austro-Russian war. However, Berlin interpreted his words to mean that if *France* became involved, Britain would probably side with her. Though Lichnowsky had been warning this for some time, his 9:12 p.m. telegram absolutely shocked Berlin. [482] The infuriated Kaiser called Grey "a common cheat." [483] He also accused King George of lying to Prince Henry about English neutrality. [484] His pent-up resentment towards Britain exploded in marginal comments that, even by his standards, were blistering:

> England reveals herself in her true colors at a moment when she thinks that we are caught in the toils and, so to speak, disposed of! That common crew of shopkeepers (one of Wilhelm's choice descriptions of the British people) has tried to trick us with dinners and speeches. The boldest deception, the words of the King to Henry for me: 'We shall remain neutral and try to keep out of this as long as possible.' Grey proves the King a liar, and his words to Lichnowsky are the outcome of an evil conscience because he feels that he has deceived us. At that, it is as a matter of fact a threat combined with a bluff, in order to separate us from Austria and to prevent us from

---

[481] G.D. 368, Lichnowsky to German Foreign Office.

[482] The difference between this telegram and Lichnowsky's past warnings was that he now *quoted* Grey on the intervention issue rather than simply giving his (Lichnowsky's) own opinion. Hearing it from Grey's mouth was what so unnerved Berlin.

[483] Marginal comment of Wilhelm on G.D. 368.

[484] Ibid.

mobilizing, and to shift the responsibility for the war. He knows perfectly well that if he were to say one single, serious, sharp and warning word at Paris and St. Petersburg, and were to warn them to remain neutral, that both would become quiet at once. But he takes care not to speak the word, and threatens us instead!..............England alone bears the responsibility for peace and war, not we any longer! That must also be made clear to the world. [485]

He lashed out again later on the 30th. He elevated George from a "liar" to a "double-tongued liar" and lamented: "God help us in this fight for our existence, brought about by falseness, lies and poisonous envy!" [486]

Bethmann-Hollweg's official reaction to Lichnowsky's telegram was much milder. He wired the ambassador: "Kindly thank Sir E. Grey for his frank explanation and tell him that we are continuing to mediate in Vienna and are urgently advising the acceptance of his proposal." [487] But this outward calmness belied the fact that the 29th had been an extremely bad day for the chancellor. Two of his core assumptions - that Russia would probably not take up arms and, in the unlikely event she and France did, Britain would definitely remain neutral – were exploding in his face. The horrifying prospect of a war against the entire Triple Entente without Italy's support was becoming very real.

Bethmann-Hollweg now had no choice but to pick up the shattered pieces of Berlin's failed diplomacy and attempt to reconstruct something that could avert the potential catastrophe that awaited Germany.

---

[485] Ibid.
[486] G.D. 402, July 30.
[487] G.D. 393, July 30.

VIII

SPARKS

A. The Kaiser's Rage; Bethmann-Hollweg Urges Austria to Accept Negotiations

At 1:45 a.m. on the 30th, this telegram from Nicholas arrived at Wilhelm's palace:

> Thank you heartily for your quick answer...........The military measures which have now come into force were decided five days ago for reasons of defense on account of Austria's preparations. I hope from all my heart that these measures will not in any way interfere with your part as mediator, which I greatly value. We need your strong pressure on Austria to come to an understanding with us. [488]

The message was pleasant enough. But two aspects of it angered Wilhelm. First, it appeared to him that Russia had commenced mobilization five days previously. (This, we know, was not the case.) His second and more valid gripe was Nicholas's claim that Russia's measures were taken in response to Austria's military preparations. Vienna, in fact, had only mobilized against Serbia, not Russia. Wilhelm vented in the telegram's margin:

> No! There is no thought of anything of that sort!!! Austria has only made a partial mobilization against Serbia in the south. On the strength of that, the Tsar – as is openly admitted by him here – instituted military measures which

---

[488] G.D. 390, July 30.

have now come into force against Austria and us and as a matter of fact five days ago. Thus, it is almost a week ahead of us. And these measures are for defense against Austria, which is in no way attacking him!!! I cannot agree to any more mediation, since the Tsar, who requested it, has at the same time secretly mobilized behind my back. It is only a maneuver in order to hold us back and to increase the start they have already got. My work is at an end! [489]

His irritation was evident in his reply to Nicholas:

Best thanks for the telegram. It is quite out of the question that my Ambassador's language could have been in contradiction with the tenor of my telegram. Count Pourtales was instructed to draw the attention of your Government to the danger and grave consequences involved by a mobilization; I said the same in my telegram to you. Austria has only mobilized against *Serbia* and only a *part* of her army. If, as it is now the case, according to the communication by you and your Government, Russia mobilizes against Austria, my role as mediator you kindly

---

[489] Marginal comment of Wilhelm on ibid. He repeated these sentiments after reading a 6 a.m. message from Bethmann-Hollweg stating that Pourtales had confirmed Russia's mobilization against Austria: "According to this, the Tsar has simply been tricking us with his appeal for my assistance, and has deceived us. For one does not ask for help and mediation when one is already mobilizing!..............He (Nicholas) expressly stated in his first telegram that he would presumably be forced to take to measures that would lead to a European war. Thus he takes the responsibility upon himself. Actually, however, the measures were in full swing and he simply lied to me.................I regard my mediation action as brought to an end." Marginal comment of Wilhelm on G.D. 399, Bethmann-Hollweg to Wilhelm, July 30. Later that morning, Bethmann-Hollweg drafted a note for Wilhelm to send to Nicholas. He cautioned Wilhelm: "As this telegram will be a particularly important document historically, I would most humbly advise that Your Majesty do not – as long as Vienna's decision is still outstanding – express in it the fact that Your Majesty's role as mediator is ended." G.D. 408. Clearly, in referring to the document's historical significance, Bethmann-Hollweg wanted to ensure that future generations recognized that Germany was still working for peace.

entrusted me with, and which I accepted at your express prayer, will be endangered if not ruined. The whole weight of the decision lies solely on your shoulders now, who have to bear the responsibility for peace or war. [490]

Yet this was nothing compared to his reaction to the following telegram from Pourtales. The ambassador had spoken with Sazonov shortly after midnight on the 30th:

> (Sazonov tried) to persuade me to advocate participation by my Government in a conference of four, in order to find a way to move Austria by friendly means to drop those demands which infringe on the sovereignty of Serbia. I confined myself to promising to report the conversation, and took the stand that any exchange of opinions appeared to me to be a very difficult if not an impossible matter now that Russia had decided to take the fateful step of mobilization. Russia was demanding of us to do that to Austria which Austria was being reproached for doing to Serbia; to wit, infringing upon her rights of sovereignty. Since Austria had promised to consider Russian interests by her declaration of territorial disinterestedness - which, on the part of a nation at war meant a great deal - the Austro-Hungarian Monarchy ought to be let alone while settling her affairs with Serbia. It would be time enough to return to the question of sparing Serbia's sovereign rights when peace was concluded.

> I added very earnestly that the whole Austro-Serbian matter took a back seat for the moment in the face of the danger of a European conflagration. I took great pains to impress the magnitude of this danger upon the Minister. Sazonov was not to be diverted from the idea that Russia could not leave Serbia in the lurch. No Government could follow such a policy here without seriously endangering the (Russian) Monarchy.

---

[490] G.D. 420, July 30 (emphasis in original).

During the course of the conversation, Sazonov wanted to argue the inconsistency between the telegram of (Wilhelm) to the Tsar and (Berlin's July 29 threat to mobilize). I decidedly denied any, and pointed out that even if we had already mobilized, an appeal by (Wilhelm) to the common interests of monarchs would not be inconsistent with such a measure. I said that the communication I had made to him..............had been no threat, but a friendly warning in the shape of a reference to the automatic effect that the mobilization here (in St. Petersburg) would have to have on us in consequence of the German-Austrian alliance. Sazonov stated that the order for mobilization (against Austria) could no longer possibly be retracted, and that the Austrian mobilization was to blame for it.

From Sazonov's statements, I received the impression that (Wilhelm's) telegram did not fail of an effect on the Tsar, but that (Sazonov) is busily striving to make sure that the Tsar stands firm. [491]

Wilhelm testily rebuffed Sazonov's claim that Russia's mobilization could not be retracted. [492] He then tore into his favorite target: England. In a ludicrous, near-paranoiac tirade, he essentially accused London of masterminding a gigantic plot to isolate and annihilate Germany:

I have no doubt left about it: England, Russia and France have agreed among themselves – after laying the foundation of the *casus foederis* for us through Austria – to take the Austro-Serbian conflict for an excuse for waging a war of extermination against us. Hence, Grey's cynical observation to Lichnowsky 'as long as the war is confined to Russia and Austria, England would sit quiet, only when we and France mixed into it would he be compelled to make an active move against us;' i.e., either we are shamefully to betray our allies, sacrifice them to

---

[491] G.D. 401, Pourtales to German Foreign Office, July 30.
[492] Marginal comment of Wilhelm on ibid.

Russia – thereby breaking up the Triple Alliance, or we are to be attacked in common by the Triple Entente for our fidelity to our allies and punished, whereby they will satisfy their jealousy by joining in totally ruining us. That is the real naked situation *in nuce*, which, slowly and cleverly set going, certainly by Edward VII, has been carried on, and systematically built up by disowned conferences between England and Paris and St. Petersburg; finally brought to a conclusion by George V and set to work. And thereby the stupidity and ineptitude of our ally is turned into a snare for us.

So the famous 'circumscription' of Germany has finally become a complete fact, despite every effort of our politicians and diplomats to prevent it. The net has been suddenly thrown over our head, and England sneeringly reaps the most brilliant success of her persistently prosecuted purely anti-German world policy, against which we have proved ourselves helpless, while she twists the noose of our political and economic destruction out of our fidelity to Austria, as we squirm isolated in the net. A great achievement, which arouses the admiration even of him who is to be destroyed as its result! Edward VII is stronger after his death than am I who am still alive!

And there have been people who believed that England could be won over or pacified by this or that puny measure!!! Unremittingly, relentlessly, she has pursued her object with notes, holiday proposals, scares, Haldane, etc., until this point was reached. And we walked into the net and even went into the one-ship-program in construction with the ardent hope of thus pacifying England!!! All my warnings, all my pleas were voiced for nothing. Now comes England's so-called gratitude for it!

From the dilemma raised by our fidelity to the venerable old Emperor of Austria, we are brought into a situation which offers England the desired pretext for annihilating us under the hypocritical cloak of justice, namely, of helping France on account of the reputed 'balance of power' in Europe, i.e., playing the card of all the European nations in England's favor against us! This whole business must now be ruthlessly uncovered and the mask of Christian peaceableness publicly and brusquely torn from its face in public, and the pharisaical hypocrisy exposed on the pillory!! And our consuls in Turkey and India, agents, etc., must fire the whole Mohammedan world to fierce rebellion against this hated, lying, conscienceless nation of shopkeepers; for if we are to be bled to death, England shall at least lose India. [493]

Meanwhile, Bethmann-Hollweg, though not as animated as Wilhelm, was nonetheless beginning to panic. He knew that the crisis was getting totally out of control. He wired Pourtales: "Russian mobilization on the Austrian border will, I presume, be followed by corresponding Austrian measures. To what extent the rolling stone can then be checked, it is hard to say, and I fear that Mr. Sazonov's peaceful intentions can never be realized." [494] It should have been obvious to him early on the 30th that with Russia refusing to fold, the only way to avoid a holocaust was to restrain Vienna.

But Austria did not seem particularly interested in a negotiated solution. This was evident in a message from Tschirschky that arrived in Berlin at 1:30 a.m. – over 27 hours after Bethmann-Hollweg sent Telegram 174. It was the first indication from Tschirschky of Vienna's reaction to the pledge plan. [495] It was not encouraging. Tschirschky reported that

---

[493] Marginal comment of Wilhelm on ibid.

[494] G.D. 380, July 29. To make sure that Sazonov recognized Berlin's mediation efforts, Bethmann-Hollweg added: "In order still to avoid if possible the threatening catastrophe, we are working in Vienna to get the Austro-Hungarian Government to once more declare formally to Russia, in confirmation of its earlier assurance, that it has no idea of territorial acquisitions in Serbia, and that its military measures contemplate solely a temporary occupation in order to force from Serbia a guaranty of future good behavior. If Austria-Hungary should make such a declaration, Russia will have obtained all she desires. That Serbia must receive 'the deserved lesson,' Mr. Sazonov himself has admitted to Your Excellency." Ibid.

[495] Albertini, *Origins,* 2:525.

Berchtold intended to reemphasize to Russia the Habsburg realm's territorial disinterestedness. [496] However,

> so far as the further declaration with reference to military measures (i.e., limiting Austria's occupation of Serbian territory via the pledge plan) is concerned, Count Berchtold says that he is not in a position to give me a reply at once. In spite of my representations as to the urgency of the matter, I have up to this evening received no further communication. [497]

It is unclear whether Bethmann-Hollweg saw this telegram before sending the following note to Tschirschky at 2:55 a.m. [498] But his message would have been the same regardless: Austria *had* to consider a diplomatic settlement. To ensure that Vienna got the point, the chancellor – worried that Italy and Romania would not back the Central Powers - painted a scary picture in which Rome ultimately aligned with the Entente:

> We stand, in case Austria refuses all mediation, before a conflagration in which England will be against us; Italy and Romania to all appearances will not go with us, *and we two shall be opposed to four Great Powers.* On Germany, thanks to England's opposition, the principal burden of the fight would fall. Austria's political prestige, the honor of her arms, as well as her just claims against Serbia, could all be amply satisfied by the occupation of Belgrade or of other places. She would be strengthening her status in the Balkans as well as in relation to Russia by the humiliation of Serbia. Under these circumstances, we must urgently and impressively suggest to the consideration of the Vienna Cabinet the acceptance of mediation on the above-mentioned honorable conditions.

---

[496] G.D. 388, Tschirschky to German Foreign Office, July 29.
[497] Ibid.
[498] Albertini, *Origins,* 2:525-26, footnote 6. At 12:30 a.m. on the 30th, Bethmann-Hollweg forwarded Lichnowsky's 2:08 p.m. telegram of the 29th to Tschirschky. He instructed the latter to notify Berchtold of it "at once." G.D. 384, July 29. He added that mediation could ensue "if founded on an occupation of a portion of Serbian territory as a hostage." Ibid.

The responsibility for the consequences that would otherwise follow would be an uncommonly heavy one both for Austria and for us. [499]

Minutes later, at 3 a.m., he sent another note to Tschirschky. It concluded:

We cannot expect Austria to deal with Serbia, with whom she is at war. The refusal to hold any exchange of opinions with St. Petersburg, however, would be a serious error, as it would be a direct provocation of Russia's armed interference, which Austria-Hungary is beyond all else interested to prevent.

We are, of course, ready to fulfill the obligations of our alliance, but must decline to be drawn wantonly into a world conflagration by Vienna without having any regard paid to our counsel. Also, Vienna appears to disregard our advice in regard to the Italian question. Please talk to Count Berchtold at once with all impressiveness and great seriousness. [500]

And at 4:10 a.m., he again wired Tschirschky:

Russia complains that neither through Mr. Schebeko nor Count Szapary have the (Austro-Russian) conferences made any headway. Hence, we must urgently request, in order to prevent a general catastrophe, or at least to put Russia in the wrong, that Vienna inaugurate and continue with the conferences according to Telegram 174. [501]

These messages to Vienna were certainly stronger than his ones of the 27th and 28th.
But were they strong enough?

---

[499] G.D. 395 (emphasis added).
[500] G.D. 396.
[501] G.D. 385.

B. *The Attitude of France*

Paris had thus far been very supportive of Russia. Paleologue, we know, had promised St. Petersburg his country's virtually unqualified backing. France also undertook certain pre-mobilization military measures in case hostilities erupted. [502] None of this meant, however, that Paris was encouraging Russia to go to war or to eschew peace proposals. Indeed, the still-seaborne Viviani had instructed Paleologue on the 27th:

> Please say to M. Sazonov that France, appreciating as fully as Russia how highly important it is for the two countries to affirm their complete agreement with regard to the other Powers and to neglect no effort to bring about a solution of the conflict, is ready to give full support to the action of the (Russian) Government for the purpose of maintaining the general peace. [503]

Viviani's stance remained intact when he and Poincare returned to Paris on the 29th. That afternoon, the two discussed the crisis with Cabinet officials. [504] While Viviani reassured Izvolsky that evening that France would fulfill her alliance obligations, he – like the Cabinet – wanted to continue all efforts to avert war. He therefore could not have been pleased when, early on the 30th, Izvolsky conveyed to him a message from Sazonov. [505] After mentioning Berlin's July 29 warning to St. Petersburg, Sazonov's note said:

> As we cannot comply with the wishes of Germany, we have no alternative but to hasten our own military preparations and to assume that war is probably inevitable. Please inform the French Government of this, and add that we are sincerely grateful to them for the declaration which

---

[502] Fay, *Origins*, 2:482-83. One measure involved positioning French troops near the German border. Schmitt, *Coming*, 234-35. These forces, however, were to remain about 10 kilometers back from the frontier so as to (1) avoid border clashes and (2) convince London of France's peaceful intentions. Ibid.
[503] Quoted in Schmitt, *Coming*, 89.
[504] Ibid., 227; Fay, *Origins*, 2:483.
[505] Fay, *Origins*, 2:483.

the French Ambassador made to me on their behalf to the effect that we could count fully upon the assistance of our ally, France. In the existing circumstances, that declaration is especially valuable to us. [506]

Viviani perhaps wondered whether Paleologue's enthusiastic promise of support had given the Russians the impression that France wanted them to take aggressive measures. [507] To make certain that St. Petersburg understood Paris's position, he wired Paleologue on the 30th:

> As I have stated in my telegram of 27 July, the Government of (France) is determined to neglect no effort towards a solution of the conflict and to support the action of the (Russian) Government in the interest of general peace. On the other hand, France is resolved to fulfill all the obligations of the alliance. But, in the same interest of general peace and in view of the fact that conversations have begun between the Powers not directly interested, I think it would be well that in taking any precautionary measures of defense to which she thinks she must proceed, Russia should not immediately take any step which may offer Germany a pretext for a total or partial mobilization of her forces. [508]

Yet Viviani's note in no way demanded that Russia not mobilize. Nor did it hint that she risked losing Paris's support if she did. In fact, two other top French officials merely recommended to Russia that if she accelerated her military preparations, she should do so quietly. Izvolsky telegraphed Sazonov on the 30th:

> (Bruno Jacquin de) Margerie (in the French Foreign Ministry)............told me that the French Government, without wishing to interfere in our military preparations, would consider it extremely desirable, in view of the

---

[506] Sazonov to Izvolsky, July 29, in C.D.D., R.O.B., Document No. 58.
[507] Schmitt, *Coming,* 231.
[508] Quoted in ibid., 231-32.

negotiations still pending for the preservation of peace, that these preparations should be carried on in the least open and least provocative manner. The Minister of War (Adolphe Messimy), on his part, expressing the same idea, told Count (Alexei) Ignatiev (Russia's military *attaché* in Paris) that we could declare that, in the higher interests of peace, we were willing to slow down temporarily our mobilization measures, which would not hinder us from continuing and even strengthening our military preparations, while refraining, as much as possible, from the transportation of masses of troops. [509]

In sum, France's position in the week following the ultimatum was that while she wanted to avoid war and preferred that Russia not take openly provocative measures, she refused to prevent St. Petersburg from doing what it deemed necessary to protect its vital interests. [510] Paris hoped for peace and supported the various diplomatic proposals that arose but was prepared to stand with Russia should war erupt. [511]

---

[509] Quoted in Fay, *Origins,* 2:484-85.

[510] Nicolson perceived this back on the 25th, writing: "The moment has passed when it might have been possible to enlist French support in an effort to hold back Russia. It is clear that France and Russia have decided to accept the challenge thrown out to them. Whatever we may think of the merits of the Austrian charges against Serbia, France and Russia consider that these are the pretexts, and that the bigger cause of the Triple Alliance versus the Triple Entente is definitely engaged." Comment of Nicolson on B.D. 101.

[511] Notwithstanding Paris's peace hopes, Schoen detected a haughty attitude in the French press. He wired Berlin on the 30th: "The tone of the local press today is arrogant, as the result of the conviction that in the case of war English assistance can certainly be counted on. Delcasse is said to have stated that the English fleet could starve Germany out. A large portion of the press seems to think that the chances for peace lie materially in the fact that war would be too dangerous a game for Germany in view of the firm coherence of the Triple Entente." G.D. 430, Schoen to German Foreign Office.

C. Grey Declines to Side with Paris and Continues His Peace Efforts

Not surprisingly, Grey had zero interest in Bethmann-Hollweg's harebrained neutrality offer of the 29th. Grey instructed Goschen on the 30th:

> You must inform the German Chancellor that his proposal that we should bind ourselves to neutrality on such terms cannot for a moment be entertained. He asks us in effect to engage to stand by while French colonies are taken and France is beaten so long as Germany does not take French territory as distinct from the colonies. From the material point of view, such a proposal is unacceptable, for France could be so crushed as to lose her position as a Great Power, and become subordinate to German policy without further territory in Europe being taken from her. But apart from that, for us to make this bargain with Germany at the expense of France would be a disgrace from which the good name of this country would never recover. [512]

Angry, even insulted though Grey sounded, his position regarding British intervention did not change. Indeed, in his July 29 conversation with Lichnowsky that so unnerved Berlin, he had merely indicated that French involvement in the war might trigger British intercession. He did not say that Britain *would definitely* intervene. As he explained to Paul Cambon: "If Germany became involved and France became involved, we had not made up our minds what we should do; it was a case that we should have to consider.........We were free from engagements, and we should have to decide what British interests required us to do." [513]

Grey's stance irked Paris. Francis Bertie, England's ambassador to France, reported to London:

> (Poincare) is convinced that the preservation of peace between the Powers is in the hands of England, for if (the

---

[512] B.D. 303. Jagow later told Goschen that Bethmann-Hollweg would never have made his offer had Lichnowsky's 9:15 p.m. telegram of the 29th arrived earlier. B.D. 305, Goschen to Grey, July 30.
[513] B.D. 283, Grey to Bertie, July 29.

British) Government announces that, in the event of a conflict between Germany and France resulting from present differences between Austria and Serbia, England would come to the aid of France, there would be no war, for Germany would at once modify her attitude.

I explained to him how difficult it would be for (Britain) to make such an announcement. He, however, said that he must maintain that it would be in the interests of peace.............(and) that if there were a general war on the continent England would inevitably be involved in the course of it for the protection of her vital interests, and a declaration by her now of her intention to support France, who desires to remain at peace, would almost certainly prevent Germany from embarking on a war. [514]

But Grey would not budge. As we saw, there were several reasons for his non-committal position. First, he wanted to keep England's options open. Second, he feared that a pronouncement of British support would encourage Franco-Russian belligerence. As Crowe wrote: "What must weigh with (the British) Government is the consideration that (it) should not by a declaration of unconditional solidarity with France and Russia induce and determine these two Powers to choose the path of war." [515] Bertie agreed: "If we gave an assurance of armed assistance to France and Russia now, Russia would become more exacting and France would follow in her wake." [516] Third, the British people, including many Cabinet members, had no interest in fighting a war on the European mainland - especially over a Balkan dispute. [517] Grey told Paul Cambon:

(P)ublic opinion here (in England) approached the present difficulty from a quite different point of view from that taken during the difficulty as to Morocco a few years ago. In the case of Morocco, the dispute was one in which

---

[514] B.D. 318, Bertie to Grey, July 30.
[515] Comment of Crowe on ibid.
[516] B.D. 320, Bertie to Grey, July 30.
[517] Schmitt, *Coming,* 280-88.

France was primarily interested and in which it appeared that Germany, in an attempt to crush France, was fastening a quarrel on France on a question that was the subject of a special agreement between France and us. In the present case, the dispute between Austria and Serbia was not one in which we felt called to take a hand. Even if the question became one between Austria and Russia, we should not feel called upon to take a hand in it. It would then be a question of the supremacy of Teuton or Slav – a struggle for supremacy in the Balkans, and our idea had always been to avoid being drawn into a war over a Balkan question. [518]

Bertie seemed aggravated that Paris did not understand this. He wrote Grey: "The feeling here (in Paris) is that peace between the Powers depends on England...........(But) people do not realize or do not take into account the difficulty for the British Government to declare England's *solidaire* with Russia and France in a question such as the Austro-Serbian quarrel." [519] He even told Grey that Paris should try to restrain Russia instead of pestering England: "(France) should be encouraged to put pressure on the Russian Government not to assume the absurd and obsolete attitude of Russia being the protectress of all Slav States whatever their conduct, for this will lead to war." [520]

Naturally, Grey did not want Britain to *have* to make a decision on intervention. He therefore continued pushing for a diplomatic settlement. The lack of progress frustrated him, however. He lamented to Mensdorff: "The Powers were not allowed to help in getting satisfaction for Austria, which they might get if they were given an opportunity." [521] Similarly, he told Lichnowsky:

(Berlin) seemed to think that the particular method of conference, consultation, or discussion, or even conversations *a quatre* in London, too formal a method. I

---

[518] B.D. 283.
[519] B.D. 320.
[520] B.D. 192, July 27.
[521] B.D. 282, Grey to Bunsen, July 29.

urged (to Lichnowsky) that the German Government should suggest any method by which the influence of the four Powers could be used together to prevent war between Austria and Russia. France agreed. Italy agreed. The whole idea of mediation or mediating influence was ready to be put into operation by any method that Germany could suggest if mine was not acceptable. In fact, mediation was ready to come into operation by any method that Germany thought possible if only Germany would 'press the button' in the interests of peace. [522]

Mensdorff reported Grey's rising apprehension to Berchtold on the 29th:

I have just spoken to Sir Edward Grey, who declared that the situation had grown far more serious and that he was very anxious..............The danger of a great European complication is hourly increasing. He repeatedly said that we (Austria) should probably have the support and the sympathy of all the Powers if we were satisfied by Serbia's acceptance of all our demands and that, moreover, all the Powers would guarantee to us the keeping of these promises. I pointed out that after the (Austrian) declaration of war and the beginning of hostilities, this might be too late. 'Then it is perhaps also too late for the prevention of the general war,' he exclaimed.

I insisted that it was necessary to separate the Austro-Hungarian-Serbian conflict from the question of a European war and that Russia needed to be influenced not to provoke it by its intervention. Hereupon Grey

---

[522] B.D. 263, Grey to Goschen, July 29. Nicolson, however, did not think the Central Powers would accept mediation: "I ask myself what is the use of exchanging views at this juncture. To my mind, the only possible way of avoiding a conflict is to ask Austria to take no military action pending conversations; it is quite clear that such a request would be peremptorily rejected and would not be supported by Germany. I am of the opinion that the resources of diplomacy are, for the present, exhausted." Comment of Nicolson on B.D. 252, Rodd to Grey, July 29.

remarked: 'If the Powers are only to intervene in Russia in order that it remains passive, this would be equal to giving you a free hand, a thing that Russia will not accept. You must give us something, however small, that we could make use of in St. Petersburg.' [523]

Grey clearly had doubts that peace could be preserved. Nevertheless, he forged ahead. He suggested to Lichnowsky on the 30th that "it would seem............to be a suitable basis for mediation if Austria, after occupying Belgrade, for example, or other places, should announce her conditions." [524] He further explained his initiative - which had similarities to Wilhelm's pledge plan - to Buchanan:

> If Austria, having occupied Belgrade and neighboring Serbian territory, declares herself ready, in the interest of European peace, to cease her advance and to discuss how a complete settlement can be arrived at, I hope that Russia would also consent to discussion and suspension of further military preparations, provided that other Powers did the same. It is a slender chance of preserving peace, but the only one I can suggest if the Russian Minister for Foreign Affairs can come to no agreement at Berlin. [525]

Wilhelm's proposal, we recall, envisioned the temporary holding of Serbian territory as a hostage to force Serbia to fulfill her guarantees. While it did not require Serbia to accept the entire ultimatum (the few reservations Belgrade had would be negotiated), it did not call for the ultimatum to be substantially modified, either. Grey's plan, too, allowed Austria to occupy parts of Serbia temporarily. [526] The key difference was that Grey

---

[523] Quoted in Geiss, *July 1914*, 276.

[524] G.D. 368.

[525] B.D. 309, July 30. See also B.D. 285, Grey to Goschen, July 29.

[526] Indeed, despite his irritation with Austria, Grey still believed that she deserved redress. Lichnowsky telegraphed Berlin on the 29th: "To my Italian colleague, who has just left me, Sir E. Grey said that he believed if mediation were accepted, that he would be able to secure for Austria every possible satisfaction; there was no longer any question of a humiliating retreat for Austria, as the Serbs would in any case be punished and compelled, with the

seemed more focused than Wilhelm on preserving Serbia's sovereignty and integrity. This would require Austria to water down the ultimatum. The Kaiser's plan, therefore, was primarily an enforcement mechanism; only minor points would be negotiated. Grey, however, appeared to envision much broader mediation. Notwithstanding this distinction, though, having Germany and England on board with some variation of a "Halt in Belgrade" formula was a positive sign.

D. Russia Opts for General Mobilization

There were other glimmers of hope on the 30th.

As we know, Sazonov had learned of Berchtold's refusal of direct Austro-Russian negotiations. But Sazonov had misunderstood Vienna's position. He thought that Berchtold had declined *all* talks with Russia. In actuality, he had only refused to discuss altering the ultimatum or accepting Serbia's reply. [527] Berchtold instructed Szapary to inform Sazonov that Austria was very willing to (1) *explain* the ultimatum's text to him and (2) converse with St. Petersburg on "questions directly concerning our relations with Russia............which might clear up many matters which, I regret to say, are not quite clear and which might assure the so much desired peaceful development of neighborly relations." [528] It appeared that the two sides would be talking in depth again.

---

consent of Russia, to subordinate themselves to Austria's wishes. Thus Austria could obtain guarantees for the future without a war that would jeopardize the peace of Europe." G.D. 368. But Grey cautioned Lichnowsky that while Austria should not be humiliated, the question was "how far Austria meant to push the humiliation of others. There must, of course, be some humiliation of Serbia, but Austria might press things so far as to involve the humiliation of Russia." B.D. 284, Grey to Goschen, July 29.

[527] Fay, *Origins,* 2:434. See also Berchtold to Szapary, July 30, in C.D.D., A.R.B. I, Document No. 50.

[528] Quoted in Geiss, *July 1914,* 302. See also C.D.D., A.R.B. I, Document No. 50. Schebeko, in fact, informed Sazonov of his "impression that Austria really desires to come to an understanding with us." Schebeko to Sazonov, July 30, quoted in Schmitt, *Coming,* 179. She indeed did – though Schebeko failed to see that Austria only wanted an agreement on *her* terms.

Also, Sazonov's discussions with Pourtales seemed more constructive than they had been on the 29th. When they spoke on the 30th, Sazonov reiterated that Austria's territorial disinterestedness alone would not placate Russia. [529] Pourtales asked Sazonov what he sought, stressing that for there "to be the least prospect of a peaceful solution, (Russia) would absolutely have to agree to some sort of compromise." [530] Sazonov responded:

> If Austria declares that in recognition of the fact that its conflict with Serbia has assumed the character of a question of European interest (and) it declares itself ready to eliminate from its ultimatum those points which infringe on Serbia's sovereign rights, then Russia agrees to suspend all military preparations. [531]

This was, to be sure, almost as much of a threat as a proposal. Sazonov essentially said that unless Austria modified her demands, Russia would fight. Moreover, he did not say that Russia would *revoke* her military preparations. (He previously told Pourtales that mobilization could not be retracted.) [532] Nonetheless, his initiative showed that even after recommending general mobilization the previous evening, he still desired a negotiated solution.

Yet despite these marginally favorable developments, the overriding problem remained. *Specifically, the diplomatic*

---

[529] G.D. 421, Pourtales to German Foreign Office, July 30. Yet Berlin *still* pushed the territorial disinterestedness concept. On the 30th, Jagow told several German embassies abroad: "(If Russia intervenes), she would be adopting as her own the Serbian efforts to undermine the existence of the Austro-Hungarian Monarchy, and she alone will be responsible if a European war results............This Russian responsibility is as clear as day, and weighs all the more heavily since Count Berchtold has officially announced to Russia that (Austria) desires neither to acquire any Serbian territory nor to encroach upon the Kingdom of Serbia, but is merely anxious to put an end to the Serbian intrigues which are endangering its existence." G.D. 423.
[530] G.D. 421.
[531] Ibid. Interestingly, Sazonov's initiative did not call for Austria to suspend her military operations against Serbia. See ibid. This was likely a mere oversight on his part.
[532] G.D. 401.

stalemate was unresolvable unless St. Petersburg or Vienna retreated from its respective position. Either Russia would have to accept the ultimatum's demands or Austria would have to modify them. And neither country was willing to bend. Sazonov believed that as long as Austria remained unyielding, Russia had to continue her armed preparations. But he and the generals worried that Nicholas's reversal of general mobilization would hamper these preparations and endanger Russia. They felt that Russia should commence general mobilization *now*. Otherwise, Germany and Austria, with their faster mobilizations, might launch a rapid, devastating blow against Russia's disorganized forces. Around midday on the 30th, Nicholas's subordinates set out to change his mind. As outlined in a Russian foreign ministry memorandum:

> Between 9 and 10 a.m., the Minister for Foreign Affairs spoke to the Minister for Agriculture (Alexander Krivoshein) by telephone. Both of them were greatly disturbed at the stoppage of the general mobilization, as they fully realized that this threatened to place Russia in an extremely difficult position in the event of relations with Germany becoming acute. Sazonov advised Krivoshein to beg an audience with the Tsar in order to represent to His Majesty the dangers called forth by the change.

> At 11 a.m., the Minister for Foreign Affairs again met the Minister for War and the Chief of the General Staff. Information received during the night still further strengthened the opinion which they all held that it was imperative to prepare for a serious war without loss of time. Accordingly, the Ministers and the Chief of Staff adhered to the view, which they had expressed yesterday, to the effect that it was indispensible to proceed to a general mobilization. Adjutant-General Sukhomlinov and General Janushkevich again endeavored by telephone to persuade the Tsar to revert to his decision of yesterday to permit a general mobilization. His Majesty decidedly

refused to do so, and finally shortly declared that the conversation was at an end. [533]

At Sazonov's request, however, Nicholas agreed to see him that afternoon. [534] After the Tsar hung up, Janushkevich asked Sazonov to let him know if Nicholas later decided to reinvoke general mobilization. [535] Janushkevich then said: "After that, I shall go away, smash my telephone and generally adopt measures which will prevent anyone from finding me for the purpose of giving contrary orders which would again stop our general mobilization." [536]

At Nicholas's afternoon meeting with Sazonov (which Major-General Ilja Tatistchev also attended), the following discussion ensued:

> During the course of nearly an hour, the Minister proceeded to show that war was becoming inevitable, as it was clear to everybody that Germany had decided to bring about a collision, as otherwise she would not have rejected all the pacificatory proposals that had been made and could easily have brought her ally to reason. Under these circumstances, it only remained to do everything that was necessary to meet war fully armed and under the most favorable conditions for ourselves. Therefore, it was better to put away any fears that our warlike preparations would bring about a war, and to continue these preparations carefully rather than by reason of such fears to be taken unawares by war.

> The firm desire of the Tsar to avoid war at all costs, the horrors of which filled him with repulsion, led His Majesty in his full realization of the heavy responsibility which he took upon himself in this fateful hour to explore every possible means for averting the approaching danger. Consequently, he refused during a long time to agree to

---

[533] Quoted in Schilling, *How the War Began*, 62-63.

[534] Ibid., 63.

[535] Ibid., 63-64.

[536] Quoted in ibid., 64.

the adoption of measures which, however indispensible from a military point of view, were calculated, as he clearly saw, to hasten a decision in an undesirable sense.

The tenseness of feeling experienced by the Tsar at this time found expression, amongst other signs, in the irritability most unusual with him, with which His Majesty interrupted General Tatistchev. The latter, who throughout had taken no part in the conversation, said in a moment of silence: 'Yes, it is hard to decide.' His Majesty replied in a rough and displeased tone: 'I will decide' – in order by this means to prevent the General from intervening any further in the conversation.

Finally, the Tsar agreed that under the existing circumstances it would be very dangerous not to make timely preparations for what was apparently an inevitable war, and therefore gave his decision in favor of an immediate general mobilization. Sazonov requested the Imperial permission to inform the Chief of the General Staff of this immediately by telephone, and this being granted, he hastened to the telephone on the ground floor of the palace. Having transmitted the Imperial order to General Janushkevich, who was waiting impatiently for it, the Minister, with reference to their conversation that morning, added: 'Now you can smash your telephone.' [537]

Nicholas did not lose all hope of a peaceful outcome. But with Russia's general mobilization bound to trigger similar measures by both Central Powers, a European conflagration seemed probable.

E. Germany's Generals Press Bethmann-Hollweg for Preliminary Military Steps

Berlin was unaware of the debate in St. Petersburg over partial versus general mobilization. It only knew that partial

---

[537] Quoted in ibid., 64-66.

Russian mobilization had been announced. Pourtales stressed to Sazonov the dangers of mobilization:

> (Sazonov) sought to convince me (Pourtales) that in Russia, mobilization was far from meaning war, as it did among the western European nations; that the Russian army would doubtless be able to remain under arms for weeks to come without crossing the frontier. Russia wanted to avoid war, if it were in any way possible. I replied that these statements were not sufficient to satisfy me. The danger of every preparatory military measure lays in the counter-measures of the other side. It was obvious that the general staffs of the possible opponents of Russia would not be willing to sacrifice the advantage of getting a start over Russia in the matter of mobilization and would press for counter-measures. I earnestly begged him to consider this peril. Mr. Sazonov assured me most solemnly once again that not the least thing was to happen to us. [538]

Notwithstanding his July 29 warning to St. Petersburg, Bethmann-Hollweg did not believe that Russian mobilization against Austria warranted *immediate* German mobilization. Initially, Moltke did not seriously challenge this view. [539] In fact, he told Captain Fleischmann of the Austro-Hungarian General Staff that (1) Russia's partial mobilization did not yet require Germany to mobilize and (2) Austria should not declare war on Russia but should instead let the Russians attack first. [540]

By 1 p.m. on the 30th, Moltke's stance had changed. [541] The threat to Austria now greatly alarmed him. He believed that Germany would soon have to come to her defense. [542] He also worried about Russia's head start over the Central Powers in the mobilization race. For these reasons, he felt that a "state of

---

[538] G.D. 343, Pourtales to German Foreign Office, July 29.

[539] According to Falkenhayn, Moltke on the 29th had rendered only very slight opposition to Bethmann-Hollweg's stance. Albertini, *Origins,* 3:7.

[540] Fay, *Origins,* 2:506-07; Schmitt, *Coming,* 182.

[541] Albertini, *Origins,* 3:7. Moltke's changed position surprised Falkenhayn. Ibid.

[542] Fay, *Origins,* 2:507.

threatening danger of war" should be declared in Germany. [543] At a meeting with Bethmann-Hollweg that afternoon, he undoubtedly told the chancellor this. [544]

The problem was that a state of threatening danger of war was the stage of military preparations immediately preceding mobilization. And for Germany, mobilization meant war. [545] This was due to her strategy for fighting the Franco-Russian pact – the famed Schlieffen Plan. [546]

The German high command believed that Germany – even with Austria fighting alongside her - lacked the manpower to win a long, attritional war against Russia and France. (Russia's population alone was about two-and-a-half times that of Germany's.) It also believed that this inferiority in troop numbers would be coupled with a disparity in resources. Heavily dependent on imports for food and raw materials, Germany would be cut off from Russian grain and, if Britain intervened, blockaded from the oceans. [547] The only realistic way, it was thought, for Germany to defeat the Paris-St. Petersburg alliance was to hurl most of her forces against one foe in hopes of a quick victory while temporarily fighting on the defensive against the other. The goal was to rapidly knock out one opponent so that Germany's entire strength could be concentrated against her remaining adversary.

The high command deduced that Russia's mobilization would be slow. Furthermore, her armies (once deployed) could withdraw eastward into the vast Russian interior to avoid battle. [548] A quick triumph over Russia was deemed doubtful. The Germans therefore wanted to use the war's opening weeks - when Russia would still be mobilizing - to crush France.

The Schlieffen Plan envisioned a massive attack on France with the overwhelming preponderance of Germany's total troop strength. (The very small remainder of Germany's forces would

---

[543] Albertini, *Origins,* 3:7-8.

[544] Ibid.

[545] See G.D. 456.

[546] The plan's namesake was General Alfred von Schlieffen. He was chief of Germany's general staff from 1891 through 1905. He died in 1913.

[547] Jack Snyder, *The Ideology of the Offensive: Military Decision Making and the Disasters of 1914* (Ithaca, NY: Cornell University Press, 1984), 108.

[548] Ibid., 141.

defend northeastern Germany against whatever armies Russia could mobilize early on.) The high command felt that invading France across the Franco-German border could be difficult and time-consuming in light of the strong French fortifications in eastern France. The attack's main thrust would therefore come via central Belgium. These forces would advance through Belgium into northern France. The right (northwestern-most) part of the invasion force would march to the *west* of Paris, thus enveloping the city and most of France's armies, which were expected to be well east of Paris. This gigantic flanking movement reflected the Germans' hope that a single campaign could finish France off; Germany's victorious forces could then move east to battle Russia.

The plan was based on two main assumptions. First, it would take Russia about six weeks to complete her mobilization. Second, France could be beaten within that same period. If she were not defeated before Russia fully mobilized, Germany would likely have to prematurely transfer forces eastward to meet the Russian threat. With her armies in France thus weakened, she would conceivably (1) lack the manpower to win in the West and (2) be condemned to the drawn-out, two-front war that the Schlieffen blueprint was designed to avoid.

Obviously, to rest the Schlieffen Plan's fate – and perhaps the fate of Germany herself - on the notion that France's armies could be encircled and destroyed in only six weeks was very risky. The Schlieffen Plan was a huge gamble. [549] Germany's generals knew it. But France or Russia had to be quickly eliminated. And neither Schlieffen nor his successor, Moltke, saw a better alternative than a mammoth flanking offensive against the French.

With the need to promptly defeat France, speed and precision in Germany's mobilization were critical. Everything from troop movements to transport schedules had been planned in great detail so that the offensive began smoothly. Any significant delay in these timetables could disrupt everything. For this reason, once German mobilization began, it could not be stopped.

---

[549] It is important to note that the Schlieffen Plan was, generally speaking, merely a broad strategic blueprint for war against France and Russia. It did not, for instance, prescribe the movements of units within various army corps. In fact, several historians have questioned the degree to which the plan was even committed to paper.

Moreover, there was no concrete plan that enabled Germany to mobilize yet keep her forces within her borders indefinitely. Nor was there a firm strategy in 1914 for war against Russia alone; Berlin assumed that hostilities with one Franco-Russian pact member would bring in the other. [550] Thus, the moment the button was pressed and Germany's mobilization commenced was effectively the moment that war with France and Russia began. [551]

Despite Moltke's pressure, Bethmann-Hollweg on the 30th declined to proclaim a state of threatening danger of war. He knew that such a declaration would lead to mobilization and war. [552] He was not yet prepared to take such a draconian step. However, he promised Moltke that the German government would make a final decision by 12 noon on the 31st. [553] This essentially meant that if no diplomatic breakthrough occurred by then, Germany would get ready for war.

Moltke was not satisfied. He felt it was pointless and dangerous to delay preparing for a conflict that, to him, seemed inevitable. Agitated, he sent for Austria's military *attaché* at Berlin, Lieutenant-Colonel Baron von Bienerth. [554] Telegraphing Conrad at 5:30 p.m., Bienerth conveyed Moltke's advice:

> (Moltke) considers the situation critical unless the Austro-Hungarian Monarchy mobilizes at once against Russia. The declaration made by Russia concerning her mobilization makes countermeasures necessary on the part of Austria-Hungary…….………Every hour of delay makes

---

[550] Germany previously had a mobilization plan that deployed most of her forces in the East against Russia. But Moltke scrapped it in 1913. This left only the western-focused mobilization plan. Gerhard Ritter, *The Sword and the Scepter: The Problem of Militarism in Germany*, vol. 2 (1965; reprint, Coral Gables, FL: University of Miami Press, 1970), 202; Konrad Jarausch, *The Enigmatic Chancellor: Bethmann-Hollweg and the Hubris of Imperial Germany* (New Haven, CT: Yale University Press, 1973), 174. See also Albertini, *Origins*, 3:241.

[551] See G.D. 456.

[552] As he told the Prussian Ministers of State on the 30th: "Declaration of a 'state of threatening danger of war' meant mobilization, and that, under present conditions – mobilization on both sides – meant war." G.D. 456.

[553] Fay, *Origins*, 2:513.

[554] Schmitt, *Coming*, 196-97.

the situation worse, for Russia gains a start.........Decline the renewed advances of Great Britain for the maintenance of peace. A European war offers the last chance of preserving Austria-Hungary. Unconditional support of Germany. [555]

Shortly thereafter, Moltke wired Conrad directly. He stated in part: "Stand fast against Russian mobilization. Austria-Hungary must remain preserved; mobilize at once against Russia. Germany will mobilize." [556]

This was a gross interference in matters that, strictly speaking, were none of Moltke's business. The circumstances under which Germany would support Austria were for the government, not Moltke, to decide. He had no right to go behind Bethmann-Hollweg's back and give Austria diplomatic advice. Telling Vienna to rebuff England's proposals was particularly egregious considering that Bethmann-Hollweg was still pursuing a negotiated settlement. At a Prussian Ministry of State meeting around 5 p.m. on the 30th, the chancellor said:

> His Majesty (Wilhelm) had consented that, before any further decisions were arrived at, the (diplomatic) move at Vienna..........should be brought to a conclusion...........Presumably, the Vienna decision concerning the English and the German proposals would be given today.

> So far as the attitude of other nations was concerned, any hope based upon England was nil. England would probably take sides with (Russia and France). Italy's attitude was not quite clear. The Austro-Serbian conflict was unpopular in Italy, as they saw in it the danger to Italian interests in the Balkans.............He had tried to use his influence with Austria to persuade her to come to an understanding with Italy, but so far this had not been brought to pass, as, in fact, Austria was very uncompromising in the prosecution of her policies..........

---

[555] Quoted in ibid.
[556] Quoted in ibid., 197.

All the Governments, including that of Russia, and the great majority of the nations were peaceable themselves, but control had been lost, and the stone had started rolling. As a politician, he would not yet give up his hope nor his efforts to maintain peace, as long as his *demarche* at Vienna had not been repelled. The decision might come in a very short time, then another marching route would be chosen. [557]

Though conceding that the crisis had spiraled out of control, Bethmann-Hollweg's main message was that he was unwilling to take up arms before Vienna's final answer was received. [558]

F. Why Austria Remained Intransigent and Why Germany Refused to Abandon Her

Just before 5:30 p.m. on the 30th, two telegrams from Tschirschky arrived in Berlin. Neither contained Austria's decision. But they shed light on her general thinking.

One note reported that "instructions (from Berchtold) have gone to Count Szapary for him to begin conversations with Mr. Sazonov." [559] More importantly, Berchtold planned to tell Schebeko:

The Monarchy has no idea of making any territorial acquisitions in Serbia, and that, after the conclusion of peace, it intends to occupy Serbian territory purely

---

[557] G.D. 456; Albertini, *Origins*, 3:14.

[558] German officials attempted to get Vienna's answer. Wilhelm von Stumm of the foreign ministry telephoned the German embassy in Vienna throughout the 30th for information. See Albertini, *Origins*, 3:29. The Kaiser himself telegraphed Franz Josef at 7:15 that evening: "I should be honestly obliged to you if you would favor me with your decision as soon as possible." G.D. 437.

[559] G.D. 433, Tschirschky to German Foreign Office, July 30. This spurred Wilhelm to comment: "In view of the colossal war preparations of Russia now discovered, this is all too late, I fear. Begin! Now!" Marginal comment of Wilhelm on ibid. Again, though, Berchtold only permitted Szapary to *explain* the ultimatum's terms to (Sazonov). *Modifying* the ultimatum was out of the question.

temporarily, in order to compel the Serbian Government to the complete fulfillment of its demands and for the creation of guarantees for future good behavior. Just to the extent that Serbia fulfills the conditions of peace, the evacuation of Serbian territory by the Monarchy will follow. [560]

This *sounded* very encouraging. Austria had seemingly agreed to hold Serbian territory only provisionally. Once her conditions were met, her forces would leave. The Kaiser believed that Vienna had consented to his pledge plan. He wrote: "Thus, practically my proposition accepted and handled as I telegraphed it to the Tsar as my view. Good!" [561]

But the truth was quite different. First off, Austria insisted on "the complete fulfillment of (her) demands." This indicated that she still meant to impose the whole ultimatum on Serbia. Neither Wilhelm nor Grey had contemplated this. (The Kaiser, we recall, believed that Serbia's reservations could be negotiated.) Second, the term "conclusion of peace" implied that Vienna intended to continue its war against Serbia until she folded completely. This was inconsistent with the "Halt in Belgrade" concept, which was largely intended to limit Austria's offensive action so Russia would not intervene. [562] Wilhelm had obviously misread Tschirschky's note.

The other telegram discussed Vienna's reaction to San Giuliano's statement that - according to Serbia's *charge d'affaires* at Rome - Belgrade might accept Demands 5 and 6 of the ultimatum. [563] This, in the *charge d'affaires*'s eyes, would constitute Serbia's "integral acceptance" of the entire ultimatum. [564] Berchtold disagreed:

(Berchtold) said that to claim that with the acceptance of Articles 5 and 6 of the Austrian note, the note would be

---

[560] G.D. 433.
[561] Marginal comment of Wilhelm on ibid.
[562] Indeed, nothing in Tschirschky's telegram indicated that Austria would restrict her occupation of Serbian territory to Belgrade or other small pockets.
[563] G.D. 432, Tschirschky to German Foreign Office, July 30.
[564] Ibid.

accepted in its entirety, was an error, as Serbia had made reservations with regard to various other points. The integral acceptance of the demands of the note would have sufficed here as long as a peaceful termination of the conflict between Serbia and the Monarchy was still possible. Now, since a state of war had supervened, Austria's conditions would naturally be different. [565]

So even if Serbia now accepted the ultimatum without reservations, it might be too late. This was a very serious development. Since the 23rd, the central problem, we know, had been the ultimatum's wording. It now appeared that resolving this issue would still not end the crisis because Austria planned to impose new, tougher demands on Serbia.

Bethmann-Hollweg must have been as confounded as the rest of Europe by Vienna's obstinance. Did Austria, he undoubtedly wondered, not realize how dangerous the situation was? Did she not understand that war with Russia, France, *and* Britain loomed? And that she should take steps to diffuse the crisis? She had already humiliated Serbia and bombarded her capital. Was it worth a world war for Vienna to be able to rub Serbia's nose in it some more? [566]

We revisit the reasons for Austria's attitude. First, she believed that only harsh measures would end Serbia's agitation. Second, she feared that mediation would lead to an undesirable compromise for her. Third, the Austro-Hungarian populace would

---

[565] Ibid. Lichnowsky, too, informed Berlin that Serbia might agree to Demands 5 and 6 if "certain interpretations as to the mode of participation of Austrian agents" were given. G.D. 357, Lichnowsky to German Foreign Office, July 29. Serbia would then accept these demands on the Great Powers' "advice." Ibid. This would presumably make them more amenable to her because she would be yielding to *Europe*, not Austria. See B.D. 202, Rodd to Grey, July 27. But nothing came of this. As Berchtold informed Tschirschky, acceptance of Demands 5 and 6 was not enough.

[566] Princess Daisy of Pless told Wilhelm as much: "Belgrade has fallen. Serbia is punished. Let Austria return now so that the peace of Europe is assured. Only Your Majesty can influence this and hold Russia back, otherwise under such conditions I fear for Germany. God be with Your Majesty now and always." G.D. 470, July 31.

not tolerate a weak response to the assassination. Fourth, Austria felt that she had to show strength in order to preserve her Great Power status, if not her actual existence. If she backed down even an inch, she believed, her enemies would be emboldened, her prestige would be shattered, and the Empire would crumble all the same.

Yet there was another, more basic reason. Austria was remaining intransigent because – well, because she could. She had received a promise of German support on July 5-6. With this, she felt free to take the hardest possible line against Serbia. Bethmann-Hollweg did try to restrain her. He used polite suggestions, strong recommendations, and even urgent pleas. But he failed to utter the words that would have stopped Vienna: "Either you accept the 'Halt in Belgrade' formula or you will lose Germany's backing. You will be on your own against Russia." [567] Austria would never have committed certain suicide by taking on Russia without Germany's military support. She absolutely would have agreed to negotiations. Absent such a threat of abandonment, however, Vienna saw no need to bend. And Bethmann-Hollweg refused to make the threat.

Why? The reason was Berlin's fear of alienating Austria and wrecking their alliance. Bethmann-Hollweg alluded to this after the war:

> (The Archduke's) murder was the bloody signal that Greater Serbia believed its hour (had) come. But the fatal hour of the Danube Monarchy had also struck. For if it passively suffered this attempt to overthrow it from its status, then its final dissolution could not be long delayed............Had we any option as to whether we should leave Austria to its fate in so vital a question as this?................(Germany) saw its one reliable ally doomed to early destruction if denied the power of damaging the mines that had been driven under the foundations of its house. If this ally collapsed or deserted to the enemy's camp from the failure of its friends to

---

[567] His 3 a.m. telegram of the 30th was the closest he came to saying this. Yet it was far from an unequivocal threat to desert Austria. He merely insisted that Vienna *pay regard to* Germany's advice. G.D. 396.

protect its vital interests, then Germany would (have been) completely isolated. [568]

He was indeed worried that Austria would desert "to the enemy's camp." He told the previously referenced post-war commission: "Turning aside from Austria would have brought us no new friends................Austria, however, would have been in the position to choose new friends." [569]

But was he overly worried? To be sure, Austria would have been furious had Berlin forced mediation on her after promising its support. It would have appeared that Vienna had humiliatingly caved in to Russia. The Austro-German alliance would have become very strained. Yet it would not have collapsed. It was virtually inconceivable that Austria, in her anger, would have left Germany after 35 years and allied herself with Russia, France, or Britain. Russia was a virtual enemy. And the notion of Austria's sizeable German population one day fighting alongside Franco-British forces against Germany seemed ludicrous. More importantly, neither France nor England would have gone to war to protect Austria from her Slavic enemies.

Germany, on the other hand, was the lone European country to view her security as contingent upon Austria's. Even had Berlin made Vienna accept negotiations, Austria knew that Germany in most circumstances would take up arms for her. The Entente nations would not. It is therefore difficult to fathom Austria, recognizing her military and economic reliance on Germany, trading the security that Germany provided for the questionable friendship of London and Paris.

But Bethmann-Hollweg could not see this. Incredibly, he seemed to believe that alienating Vienna would prove more damaging to Germany than fighting a war against the entire Triple

---

[568] Bethmann-Hollweg, *Reflections*, 104, 112-113. See also G.D. 412, Pourtales to German Foreign Office, July 30, in which Pourtales explained that he told Sazonov: "(I)t was a very ticklish thing (for Germany) to try to stay the hand of a Great Power (Austria) that had decided to take to arms for a just cause. We should, by doing so, run the risk of seriously disturbing our relations with our neighbor and of undermining her status as a Great Power, which was of the utmost importance to ourselves." Ibid.
[569] Carnegie Endowment, *Official German Documents,* 13.

Entente - one that she and Austria, on paper at least, would probably lose. [570] Tirpitz later wrote:

> Bethmann-Hollweg showed himself oversensitive for the dignity of the Austro-Hungarian State, which was not identical with the German Empire, but which the policy of the Chancellor at that time had bound to us for life or death...............He failed to realize how unenviable his position and how enormous his responsibility before history would be if he appeared as the man who had left Germany's future in the hands of the Vienna Government without any further control. [571]

In failing to make the threat that would stop Austria, Bethmann-Hollweg was effectively allowing Vienna – rather than Berlin – to decide whether Germany went to war. His paranoia over preserving the alliance with Austria no matter the consequences was - to use words he had expressed to Jagow - completely entangling Germany "in Vienna's tow-rope." [572]

G. Bethmann-Hollweg's Final Plea to Vienna

At 9 p.m. on the 30th, Bethmann-Hollweg dispatched what turned out to be his last request for Vienna to accept negotiations. In a note (known as "Instruction 200") to Tschirschky, he said:

> If Vienna declines to give in in any direction, especially along the lines of the last Grey proposal...............it will hardly be possible any longer to place the guilt of the outbreak of a European conflagration on Russia's shoulders. His Majesty undertook intervention at Vienna

---

[570] Lichnowsky, in fact, expressed to Berlin "his humble wish that our policy be guided solely and alone by the need of sparing the German nation a struggle in which it has nothing to gain and everything to lose." G.D. 236. He also informed Berlin of Tyrrell's opinion that Germany and Austria "would not stand the test of a world war." G.D. 355, Lichnowsky to German Foreign Office, July 29.
[571] Tirpitz, *My Memoirs,* 328, 341-42.
[572] G.D. 340.

at the request of the Tsar, since he could not refuse to do so without creating the incontrovertible suspicion that we wanted war. The success of this intervention is, of course, rendered difficult, inasmuch as Russia has mobilized against Austria. This we have announced to England today, adding that we had already suggested in a friendly tone, both at Paris and St. Petersburg, the cessation of French and Russian war preparations, so that we could take a new step in this direction only through an ultimatum, which would mean war.

We suggested to Sir Edward Grey, nevertheless, that he work energetically along this line at Paris and St. Petersburg, and have just received through Lichnowsky his assurance to that effect. If England's efforts succeed, while Vienna declines everything, Vienna will be giving documentary evidence that it absolutely wants a war, into which we shall be drawn, while Russia remains free of responsibility. That would place us, in the eyes of our own people, in an untenable situation. Thus we can only urgently advise that Austria accept the Grey proposal, which preserves her status for her in every way.

Your Excellency will at once express yourself most emphatically on this matter to Count Berchtold, perhaps also to Count Tisza. [573]

Moltke learned of Bethmann-Hollweg's telegram. [574] He was aghast. He did not want Austria to waste time contemplating negotiations when Russia was mobilizing against her; Vienna instead needed to prepare for war. [575] The matter was raised with

---

[573] G.D. 441. Bethmann-Hollweg believed that the German people would be more supportive of the war if Germany appeared as the victim; hence his statement regarding the German government's "untenable position" if Russia were not made responsible for the war.

[574] Albertini, *Origins*, 3:23.

[575] Ibid. Moltke also felt that negotiations would be dangerous for Germany for two reasons. First, it would give the appearance that St. Petersburg had forced Berlin to cave in. Second, Russia and France might secretly complete their mobilizations during the talks. If war ultimately erupted, Germany

Bethmann-Hollweg. At 11:20 p.m., the chancellor wired Tschirschky:

> Please do not carry out Instruction No. 200 for the present. [576]

Zimmermann crafted a follow-up note for Bethmann-Hollweg to send to Tschirschky:

> I cancelled the order of instructions in No. 200, as the General Staff just informs me that the military preparations of our neighbors, especially in the east, will force us to a speedy decision if we do not wish to expose ourselves to the danger of surprise. The General Staff earnestly desires to be informed definitely and immediately as to Vienna's decisions, particularly those of a military nature. Please use your utmost endeavor to get us a reply tomorrow (July 31). [577]

This draft indicates that Berlin wanted Austria's decision immediately. Tschirschky was to cease his efforts to persuade Vienna to accept mediation. The message was ready to be sent when Bethmann-Hollweg learned of this telegram from King George to Prince Henry:

> So pleased to hear of (Wilhelm's) efforts to concert with Nicky (the Tsar) to maintain peace. Indeed, I am earnestly desirous that such an irreparable disaster as a European war should be averted. My Government is doing its utmost suggesting to Russia and France to suspend further military preparations if Austria will consent to be satisfied with the occupation of Belgrade and neighboring Serbian territory as a hostage for the satisfactory settlement of her demands, other countries meanwhile suspending their war preparations. Trust (Wilhelm) will use his great influence

---

would be so far behind in her military preparations that the Schlieffen Plan – with its emphasis on crushing France before Russia fully mobilized – would fail. Schmitt, *Coming*, 212.

[576] G.D. 450.

[577] G.D. 451, July 30.

to induce Austria to accept this proposal, thus proving that Germany and England are working together to prevent what would be an international catastrophe. Pray assure (Wilhelm) that I am doing and shall continue to do all that lies in my power to preserve the peace of Europe. [578]

The chancellor put aside Zimmermann's draft. He instead wired Tschirschky at 2:45 a.m. on the 31st:

I cancelled the order of instructions in No. 200 in consideration of the following telegram from the King of England to Prince Henry. (Telegram quoted.) Your Excellency will communicate the telegram to Count Berchtold without delay...............A definite decision in Vienna during the course of today (the 31st) is urgently desired. [579]

As in Zimmermann's version, Bethmann-Hollweg cancels Instruction 200. Yet he now instructs Tschirschky to communicate George's telegram to Berchtold. Did he want Tschirschky to continue trying to get Vienna to bend? Probably not; it appears that he merely wanted Tschirschky to use George's note to remind Vienna of Berlin's preference for negotiations. Tschirschky's foremost priority, however, was to get Vienna's decision - whatever it was - quickly.

Thus ended Bethmann-Hollweg's efforts to pull Austria back.

While the 28th and 29th saw tensions escalate dramatically, no further significant increase in friction occurred during the first two-thirds of the 30th. Things generally remained as they were when the 29th ended. There were even a few rays of hope. First, London accepted the "Halt in Belgrade" formula. Second, Berchtold was ready to converse with St. Petersburg (at least with respect to general Austro-Russian relations). Third, Sazonov proposed to suspend Russia's military preparations if Austria met certain conditions. Nevertheless, the diplomatic deadlock

---

[578] G.D. 452, July 30.
[579] G.D. 464.

continued because neither Russia nor Austria would back down. The former wanted Vienna to modify its demands on Serbia. Austria refused; in fact, she planned to make tougher demands.

This stalemate would soon fade into the background, however. Russia's general mobilization and Berlin's revocation of Instruction 200 late on the 30th signified that the Russian and German militaries were seizing control of events from the civilians.

IX

DETONATION

A. Grey Maintains His Non-Committal Stance

We have witnessed Grey's ongoing refusal to align England with France and Russia. On the 31st, he had the following discussion with Paul Cambon:

> M. Cambon referred today to a telegram that had been shown to Sir Arthur Nicolson this morning from the French Ambassador in Berlin, saying that it was the uncertainty with regard to whether we would intervene which was the encouraging element in Berlin, and that if we would only declare definitely on the side of Russia and France, it would decide the German attitude in favor of peace.
>
> I (Grey) said that it was quite wrong to suppose that we had left Germany under the impression that we would not intervene. I had refused overtures to promise that we should remain neutral. I had not only definitely declined to say that we would remain neutral; I had even gone so far this morning as to say to the German Ambassador that if France and Germany became involved in war, we should be drawn into it. That, of course, was not the same thing as taking an engagement to France, and I told M. Cambon of it only to show that we had not left Germany under the impression that we would stand aside.

M. Cambon then asked me for my reply to what he had said yesterday (about English intervention on France's side). I said that we had come to the conclusion in the Cabinet today that we could not give any pledge at the present time............Though we should have to put our policy before Parliament, we could not pledge Parliament in advance. Up to the present moment, we did not feel, and public opinion did not feel, that any treaties or obligations of this country were involved. Further developments might alter this situation and cause the Government and Parliament to take the view that intervention was justified............

M. Cambon............repeated his question of whether we would help France if Germany made an attack on her. I said that I could only adhere to the answer that, as far as things had gone at present, we could not take any engagement............M. Cambon urged that Germany had from the beginning rejected proposals that might have made for peace. It could not be to England's interest that France should be crushed by Germany. We should then be in a very diminished position with regard to Germany. In 1870, we had made a great mistake in allowing an enormous increase of German strength, and we should now be repeating the mistake. He asked me again whether I could not submit his question to the Cabinet again.

I said that the Cabinet would certainly be summoned as soon as there was some new development, but at the present moment the only answer I could give was that we could not undertake any definite engagement. [580]

Cambon must have been totally confused after this conversation. On the one hand, Grey goes beyond his July 29 warning to Lichnowsky that Britain could well intervene in a Franco-German conflict. He now tells Cambon that Britain *would* be "drawn into" such a war; though unsaid, England's intercession would obviously be on Paris's side. And yet Grey still would not

---

[580] B.D. 367, Grey to Bertie, July 31.

promise to support France! Grey's slipperiness and mixed signals were no doubt causing frustration and worry in Paris.

But strangely enough, they were having the opposite effect on – of all people – Lichnowsky. At 9:30 a.m. on the 31st, he sent the following note to Berlin:

> I have today for the first time the impression that the improved relations with Germany of late years and perhaps also some friendly feeling for Germany in the Cabinet makes it appear possible that, in case of war, England will probably adopt an attitude of watchful waiting. [581]

Coming from someone who had been so doubtful of British neutrality, this statement was striking! Why the change? One factor could have been his conversation with Grey early on the 31st. Grey later related to Goschen:

> I (Grey) said to the German Ambassador this morning that if Germany could get any reasonable proposal put forward which made it clear that Germany and Austria were striving to preserve European peace, and that Russia and France would be unreasonable if they rejected it, I would support it at St. Petersburg and Paris and go to the length of saying that if Russia and France would not accept it, *His Majesty's Government would have nothing more to do with the consequences.* [582]

Remarkably, Grey appears to tell Berlin that if it made a decent diplomatic proposal that Russia and France unreasonably declined, Britain would remain neutral! It indeed seemed that despite his statement to Cambon that England would be drawn into a Franco-German war, Grey had not ruled out non-intervention.

He also made another proposal on the 31st. He asked Goschen to discuss the following with Jagow:

---

[581] G.D. 484, Lichnowsky to German Foreign Office. He urged Berlin, however, to continue mediating at Vienna so as to "kill the suspicion, still in evidence here (London), that we have unconditionally supported the Austrian point of view." Ibid.

[582] B.D. 340, July 31 (emphasis added).

The stumbling-block (to a diplomatic resolution) hitherto has been Austrian mistrust of Serbian assurances, and Russian mistrust of Austrian intentions with regard to the independence and integrity of Serbia. It has occurred to me that in the event of this mistrust preventing a solution being found by Vienna and St. Petersburg, Germany might sound Vienna, and I would undertake to sound St. Petersburg, whether it would be possible for the four disinterested Powers to offer to Austria that they would undertake to see that she obtained full satisfaction of her demands on Serbia, provided that they did not impair Serbian sovereignty and the integrity of Serbian territory...............Russia might be informed by the four Powers that they would undertake to prevent Austrian demands going the length of impairing Serbian sovereignty and integrity. All Powers would, of course, suspend further military operations or preparations. [583]

Grey thus sought to bridge the Austro-Russian diplomatic gap by essentially having the other four Powers guarantee that both countries' concerns were addressed. The problem, as always, was that Austria would be required to modify her demands. And this was not going to happen. Though well-meaning, Grey's proposal went nowhere.

Despite Grey's ongoing desire for a negotiated compromise, there was one thing on which he would not compromise: Belgium. In 1839, Britain signed a treaty with other European countries (including Prussia) that guaranteed Belgium's independence and neutrality. [584] London took this obligation seriously. This was not merely out of sentiment for Belgium. There were also strategic considerations. If a Power hostile to England (e.g., Germany) occupied Belgium, it would acquire naval bases relatively close to British shores. Grey explained to Paul Cambon on the 31st: "The preservation of the neutrality of Belgium might be, I would not say a decisive, but an important factor in determining our attitude. Whether we proposed to Parliament to intervene or not to

---

[583] B.D. 340.
[584] Tuchman, *Guns*, 18.

intervene in a war, Parliament would wish to know how we stood with regard to the neutrality of Belgium." [585]

Accordingly, Grey asked Paris and Berlin whether they would respect Belgium's neutrality if war erupted. [586] France said that she would, provided no other Power violated Belgian neutrality. [587] But Germany was evasive. Belgium, we know, had an important role in the Schlieffen Plan. Goschen informed Grey:

> (Jagow) said that he could not possibly give me an answer before consulting the Emperor and the Chancellor. I said that I hoped that the answer would not be too long delayed. He then gave me to understand that he rather doubted whether they could answer at all, as any reply they might give could not fail, in the event of war, to have the undesirable effect of disclosing to a certain extent part of their plan of campaign. [588]

Jagow's failure to straightforwardly answer Grey's simple question effectively revealed Berlin's intentions. [589]

To summarize, Grey still refused to formally promise France that England would support her. Even Lichnowsky became slightly optimistic that London would remain neutral.

The Belgian question, however, loomed ominously on the horizon.

---

[585] B.D. 367.

[586] See B.D. 348, Grey to Bertie, July 31.

[587] Viviani to French ambassadors at London and Berlin and to French minister at Brussels, August 1, in C.D.D., F.Y.B., Document No. 122.

[588] B.D. 383, July 31.

[589] Of course, Bethmann-Hollweg effectively divulged Germany's plans for Belgium in his July 29 neutrality offer. Crowe noted at the time: "Germany practically admits the intention to violate Belgian neutrality." Comment of Crowe on B.D. 293, July 30.

B. Austria Finally Responds to Bethmann-Hollweg's Peace Recommendations

At 1:35 a.m. on the 31st, Tschirschky dispatched a telegram to Berlin. It described his efforts to persuade Berchtold to consider the recommendations in Bethmann-Hollweg's 2:55 a.m. note of the 30th:

> (The 2:55 a.m. telegram), which arrived at noon (on the 30th), was brought to me immediately after being decoded at the Ministry of Foreign Affairs, while I was breakfasting with Count Berchtold. Immediately after getting up from the table, I carried out the instructions contained in it relative to Count Berchtold, in the presence of Count Forgach. The Minister (Berchtold), who listened, pale and silent, while it was read twice – Count Forgach taking notes – said at the conclusion that he would make a report to his Emperor at once about it.
>
> I called the attention of the Minister particularly to the fact that the justifiable claims of Austria would seem to be fully protected by a castigation of Serbia together with the acquisition of guarantees for the latter's future good behavior by the acceptance of the mediation proposal, and that the object declared from the beginning by the Monarchy to be that of the action against Serbia would thus be attained without unchaining a world war. Under these circumstances, it seemed to me that a complete refusal of the mediation was out of the question. The honor of the Austrian arms would be satisfied by the occupation of Serbian territory by Austro-Hungarian troops. That this military occupation was to take place with the express consent of Russia unquestionably meant an important strengthening of Austrian influence with regard to Russia and in the Balkans. I begged both gentlemen to keep in mind the incalculable consequences of a refusal of the mediation.
>
> When Count Berchtold left the room to change his dress for his audience with the Emperor, I appealed very

seriously to Count Forgach's conscience; he, too, expressed it as his opinion that agreement to the mediation was requisite. Just the same, the restriction of the military operations now in progress appeared to him to be scarcely possible.

This afternoon, both before and after the telephone conversation with Mr. von Stumm, I again took occasion to speak very seriously, from our point of view, with Count Forgach and Count Hoyos. Both of them assured me that restriction of the military operations was, in their opinion, out of the question, in view of the feeling in the Army and among the people. Count Tisza will appear in Vienna early tomorrow. His opinion must be obtained on this far-reaching decision. [590]

This interim but, as usual, discouraging response from Austria said this: we *might consider* mediation, but our war against Serbia *must* go on. Nothing indicated an intention to draw back.

Berchtold's meeting with Franz Josef later on the 30th (which Conrad and Krobatin also attended) largely confirmed this. [591] They agreed that (1) Austria's demands were non-negotiable and (2) military operations against Serbia would continue. [592] Franz Josef also agreed with Berchtold's suggestion to "carefully avoid accepting the English offer on its merits" but to give the appearance that Austria "desired to meet England's wishes and thus also meet the wishes of the German State Chancellor by not offending the Government." [593]

The question of whether to mobilize against Russia was harder to resolve. Conrad argued that Russia's mobilization compelled Austria to do likewise. Berchtold had reservations:

Berchtold:	That (mobilization against Russia) will cost millions.
Conrad:	The Monarchy is at stake.

---

[590] G.D. 465, Tschirschky to German Foreign Office, July 30.
[591] Schmitt, *Coming,* 183.
[592] Ibid., 183, 213.
[593] Quoted in Geiss, *July 1914,* 320.

Berchtold:	If the army is stationed in Galicia (a province in northeastern Austria-Hungary bordering Russia), it will mean war with Russia. [594]

How could Berchtold not have realized well before the 30th that defensive measures against Russia would eventually be necessary - especially considering his July 7 acknowledgment that Russian intervention was likely? And that it was his refusal to temper Austria's demands, rather than stationing forces in Galicia, that would cause war with Russia? His comments to Conrad reflected either (1) sheer blindness as to the real reasons for Russia's willingness to fight or (2) growing nervousness now that a European conflagration stared him in the face.

Conrad assured Berchtold that mobilization against Russia did not necessarily mean war with her. He said: "If the Russians do nothing against us, we need do nothing against them." [595] This must have worked, for Berchtold agreed that the threat from Russia required Austrian general mobilization. [596]

Berchtold also felt reassured of Germany's support. Bethmann-Hollweg's recent telegrams had made him suspect that Berlin wanted to end the crisis. Around 8:30 a.m. on the 31st, however, he learned of Bienerth's and Moltke's messages to Conrad urging Austrian mobilization and promising Germany's support. [597] As these messages seemed inconsistent with Bethmann-Hollweg's desire for negotiations, Berchtold exclaimed, "How odd! Who runs the government: Moltke or Bethmann?" [598] He then told Tisza and Sturgkh, who were with him: "I have asked you to come here because I had the impression that Germany was weakening. But now I have received the most reassuring declaration from the most competent authority." [599] Berchtold's determination of who ran Germany was apparently based on whose advice he liked better. And Moltke's bold,

---

[594] Quoted in Albertini, *Origins,* 2:670.
[595] Quoted in Schmitt, *Coming,* 183.
[596] Ibid., 184.
[597] Ibid., 213.
[598] Quoted in Albertini, *Origins,* 2:674.
[599] Quoted in Schmitt, *Coming,* 213, 219.

supportive language was far more appealing than Bethmann-Hollweg's wavering.

The Habsburg Cabinet Council for Common Affairs met later that morning. Berchtold began by discussing the overall situation and his conference with Franz Josef the previous day. [600] He noted that the Emperor "had instantly declared that the cessation of hostilities against Serbia was impossible." [601] According to the Council minutes, Berchtold then outlined the tenets of Vienna's planned response to Berlin's peace recommendations:

> The reply to the German Government had not yet been elaborated, but he (Berchtold) could already say now that three fundamental principles had been observed in its wording:
>
> 1. The warlike operations against Serbia must continue.
> 2. We cannot negotiate concerning the English offer as long as the Russian mobilization has not been stopped.
> 3. Our demands must be accepted integrally and we cannot negotiate about them in any way. [602]

Continuing, Berchtold expressed skepticism about Grey's proposal:

> If this whole action ended in nothing else than a gain of prestige, it would...............have been undertaken altogether in vain. A mere occupation of Belgrade would be of no good to us, even if Russia would allow it. All this was moonshine. Russia would pose as the savior of Serbia and especially of the Serbian army; the latter would remain intact and in two or three years we could expect a renewed attack of Serbia under far more unfavorable conditions. He (Berchtold) therefore had the intention of replying most courteously to the English offer, making at

---

[600] Geiss, *July 1914*, 319-20.
[601] Quoted in ibid., 320.
[602] Quoted in ibid.

the same time the aforementioned conditions and avoiding the discussion of facts. [603]

The other attendees generally agreed with this. However, Leon von Bilinski, the Habsburg finance minister, said that Austria's mobilization had created "a completely new situation." [604] He explained that "proposals which might have been acceptable at an earlier date are no longer acceptable now." [605] Tisza then asked whether they should "inform the Powers of our new demands on Serbia." [606] The thinking seemed to be that if Berchtold's third principle (regarding Austria's conditions) were included in Vienna's response, it could give the false impression that acceptance of the ultimatum would satisfy Austria. [607] The Council therefore decided against discussing Vienna's demands in its answer.

Around midday, Franz Josef signed the order for general mobilization. [608] At 3:45 a.m. on August 1, Berchtold instructed Szogyeny to inform Berlin of the following:

> (W)e fully appreciate England's endeavors for the preservation of world peace and would be quite willing to enter more closely into Sir E. Grey's proposal to mediate between Serbia and ourselves. The prerequisites for our acceptance would, however, naturally be that our military action against (Serbia) should, for the time being, take its course, and that the British Cabinet should prevail upon the Russian Government to bring to a standstill the mobilization of its troops against us, in which event we would naturally also put an immediate end to the

---

[603] Quoted in ibid., 321. Vienna also opposed the pledge concept for military reasons. If Habsburg forces stopped in Belgrade, the Serbs would gain time to bolster their defenses. If negotiations failed and Austria had to assault Serbia after all, she would have a tougher go of it. Schmitt, *Coming,* 181.

[604] Quoted in Geiss, *July 1914,* 321.

[605] Quoted in ibid.

[606] Quoted in ibid.

[607] Schmitt, *Coming,* 218.

[608] Fay, *Origins,* 2:518.

defensive military countermeasures in Galicia to which we have been compelled by Russian mobilization. [609]

Austria's acceptance of mediation was thus contingent upon (1) being permitted to continue her war on Serbia and (2) Russia suspending her mobilization against Austria. Vienna had to know that Russia would not accept these conditions. Consequently, Austria's response amounted to a refusal of the "Halt in Belgrade" concept. Her apparent readiness to "enter more closely into (Grey's) proposal" was likely mere window-dressing designed to get Berlin off her case.

After three days of waiting, Bethmann-Hollweg was about to get Vienna's final answer.

But it no longer mattered.

C. Germany Proclaims a "State of Threatening Danger of War" and Sends an Ultimatum to Russia

By dawn on the 31st, Moltke had received indications that Russia had commenced general mobilization. [610] He further learned around 7 a.m. that (1) red placards announcing general mobilization had been posted in Russia and (2) Russian forces had closed the border with Germany. [611] Still, no confirmation from Pourtales of Russian general mobilization had arrived. Until it did or until he obtained additional evidence of Russian mobilization, Moltke was reluctant to advise Wilhelm to order German mobilization. [612]

As for Bethmann-Hollweg, the lack of favorable news from Vienna was disheartening. But he probably doubted that war could be avoided anyway due to the situation in the East. Just before 10 a.m., Goschen gave him London's answer to his July 29 neutrality proposal. [613] Their conversation went elsewhere, however. Goschen reported to Grey in two separate notes:

---

[609] Quoted in Geiss, *July 1914*, 323.

[610] See Fay, *Origins*, 2:513.

[611] Ibid.

[612] Ibid.

[613] Albertini, *Origins*, 3:32.

(Bethmann-Hollweg) informs me that he has just received news to the effect that Russia has burnt her cordon of houses along the German frontier, sealed her public offices in the neighborhood of the frontier, and carried off her money chests into the interior. He has been unable to get absolute confirmation of this intelligence, as the Russo-German frontier was now entirely closed, but if, as he thinks, it is true, it can only mean that Russia looks upon war as certain, and that she is now taking military measures on the German frontier............

The Chancellor added that he himself had done everything possible, and even more perhaps than the Austro-Hungarian Government liked, at Vienna to preach moderation and peace, but his efforts had been seriously handicapped by the mobilization of Russia against Austria. If now the news he had received proved true and military measures were also being taken against Germany, he could not remain quiet, as he could not leave his country defenseless while other Powers were gaining time. [614]

I read (to Bethmann-Hollweg) a paraphrase containing the exact words of your answer to his appeal for British neutrality in the event of war. (He) was so taken up with the news (of Russia's military activities) that he made no remarks whatever upon your communication. He asked me whether I would let him have the paraphrase I just read to him as an *aide-memoire*, as his mind was so full of

---

[614] B.D. 337, July 31. Bethmann-Hollweg's statement that he had done "everything possible" to "preach moderation" at Vienna was disingenuous. First off, the preaching only began late on the 28th; before then, Berlin had recommended aggressive Austrian measures. Second, as we have seen, he failed to take the step that would have diffused the crisis: threatening Austria with abandonment. In addition, his remark that Russia's partial mobilization had hampered his peacemaking efforts – besides being untrue – was, as Crowe commented, "an endeavor to throw the blame for military preparations on Russia." Comment of Crowe on ibid.

grave matters that he could not be certain of remembering all I had said. [615]

Ominously, Bethmann-Hollweg added that because of Russia's actions:

> It was quite possible that in a very short time, perhaps even today, (Germany) would take some very serious step. [616]

Yet Wilhelm, who was in Potsdam (roughly 20 miles from Berlin), was confident that peace would be preserved! [617] As we saw, he believed that Berchtold had largely accepted his pledge plan. He also thought that Bethmann-Hollweg was still working with Vienna to finalize a settlement. The fact that (1) Austria had *not* agreed to his proposal and (2) Bethmann-Hollweg had ended his peace efforts and was bracing for war, indicates that Wilhelm was overly optimistic and not attuned to what his subordinates were doing. [618]

Reality was about to hit him. Just before the noon deadline for the German government's final decision - and with no news from Vienna regarding a peace deal - Bethmann-Hollweg conferred with Moltke and Falkenhayn. [619] During the meeting, this telegram from Pourtales arrived:

> General mobilization of (Russia's) army and fleet ordered. First day of mobilization, July 31. [620]

---

[615] B.D. 336, July 31.

[616] B.D. 337.

[617] Albertini, *Origins,* 3:36.

[618] Ibid., 3:35-37.

[619] Ibid., 3:33-34.

[620] G.D. 473, Pourtales to German Foreign Office, July 31. Sverbeyev informed St. Petersburg of Jagow's reaction to Russia's general mobilization: "At 2 p.m. (on the 31st), Herr von Jagow requested me to come to him, and on the basis of a telegram received from Count Pourtales, informed me of our general mobilization, adding that after this there was nothing more to be done, that the (German) Government was under the necessity of proclaiming at once that the fatherland was in danger and of issuing orders for general mobilization in Germany. I expressed some doubt as to the authenticity of

Bethmann-Hollweg immediately telephoned Wilhelm, who left for Berlin. [621] Before departing, he sent a message to King George that conveyed his shock and disappointment:

> Your proposals coincide with my ideas and with the statements I got this night from Vienna, which I have had forwarded to London. I just received news from the chancellor that official notification has reached him that...............Nicky has ordered the mobilization of his whole army and fleet. He has not even awaited the results of the mediation I am working at and left me without any news. I am off to Berlin to take measures for ensuring the safety of my eastern frontier, where strong Russian troops are already posted. [622]

About an hour later, he wired Nicholas:

> On your appeal to my friendship and your call for assistance, I began to mediate between yours and the Austro-Hungarian Government. While this action was proceeding, your troops were mobilized against Austria-Hungary, my ally. Thereby, as I have already pointed out to you, my mediation has been made almost illusory.

> I have nevertheless continued my action. I now receive authentic news of serious preparations for war on my eastern frontier. Responsibility for the safety of my empire forces preventive measures of defense upon me. In my

---

this information..............as I had received no direct announcement of any kind concerning it. Jagow again began to refer to the exchange of telegrams between our Sovereigns, and said that Emperor Wilhelm, apparently at the request of my august monarch, had accepted the role of mediator and had even telegraphed to the Emperor Franz Josef, and then 'at this very moment you mobilize your whole army,' he added.............When we parted, Herr von Jagow repeated that in consequence of our mobilization, the situation was hopeless, to which I replied that as an optimist by nature I never employ the word 'finished' until the end has really come, but that, speaking unreservedly, I could not see what more could be done to obviate war." Quoted in Schilling, *How the War Began*, 74-76.
[621] Fay, *Origins,* 2:523.
[622] G.D. 477.

endeavors to maintain the peace of the world, I have gone to the utmost limit possible. The responsibility for the disaster which is now threatening the whole civilized world will not be laid at my door. In this moment, it still lies in your power to avert it. Nobody is threatening the honor or power of Russia, who can well afford to await the result of my mediation. My friendship for you and your empire, transmitted to me by my grandfather on his deathbed, has always been sacred to me and I have honestly often backed up Russia when she was in serious trouble..........

The peace of Europe may still be maintained by you if Russia will agree to stop the military measures which must threaten Germany and Austria-Hungary. [623]

With Pourtales's confirmation of Russian mobilization against Germany, the outcome of Bethmann-Hollweg's meeting with the generals was certain. In Germany's eyes, all outstanding peace proposals were now moot. The longer Germany waited to implement the Schlieffen Plan, the less time she would have to defeat France before Russia's threat to her eastern frontiers became acute. As Bethmann-Hollweg later told Lichnowsky:

It will have to be the duty of Your Excellency to awaken British comprehension to the fact that our geographical and military position did not permit us to do otherwise than to reply immediately to the Russian mobilization...............We could not sit back quietly and wait to see whether a more common sense view would gain the upper hand at St. Petersburg, while at the same time the Russian mobilization was proceeding at such speed that, if the worst came, we should be left completely outstripped in a military sense. Should Russia complete her mobilization without ourselves mobilizing, (eastern Germany) would be left helpless at the mercy of the Russians.................A mobilized Russian army on our borders when we ourselves have not mobilized is a deadly

---

[623] G.D. 480.

menace to us even without any 'provocative action' (by Russia). The provocation of which Russia is guilty towards us in having mobilized against us when we were mediating in Vienna at her request is in itself so strong that no German would understand it if we failed to reply to it with strong measures. [624]

Consequently, on the afternoon of the 31st, Germany declared a state of threatening danger of war. [625] At 3:30 p.m., Bethmann-Hollweg telegraphed Pourtales:

> In spite of the still pending negotiations for mediation and although we ourselves have up to the present hour taken no mobilization measures of any kind, Russia has mobilized her entire army and navy, thus against us also. For the security of the (German) Empire, we have been compelled by these Russian measures to declare a state of threatening danger of war, which does not yet mean mobilization. Mobilization must follow, however, in case Russia does not suspend every war measure against Austria-Hungary and ourselves within 12 hours and make to us a distinct declaration to that effect. Please inform Mr.

---

[624] G.D. 529, August 1.

[625] Lieutenant-Colonel Alick Russell, Britain's military *attaché* at Berlin, reported the German declaration to Goschen, who forwarded the message to Grey: "A state of imminent national danger............has been proclaimed by the Emperor this afternoon throughout the Empire, except Bavaria, where, however, a similar ordinance has also been issued. It appears from the official pronouncement...............that the military measures to be taken consequent upon this proclamation are the following: (1) all the necessary steps on the frontier and for the protection of the railways; (2) limitation of postal, telegraph and railway traffic to meet military requirements................(3) proclamation of a state of war throughout the Empire; (4) prohibition of publications regarding movements of troops and measures of defense............Certain further ordinances have been issued regarding the prohibition of the export of foodstuffs and certain articles and materials, prohibition regarding publication of news of military interest, etc." B.D. 509, August 1.

Sazonov of this at once, and wire the hour of your communication. [626]

At the same time, the chancellor wired Schoen in Paris. After reporting Russia's general mobilization, he said:

> (W)e have declared a state of threatening danger of war, which must be followed by mobilization in case Russia does not suspend every war measure against Austria and ourselves within 12 hours. Mobilization will inevitably mean war. Please ask the French Government if it intends to remain neutral in a Russo-German war. Answer must be given within 18 hours. Telegraph immediately the hour at which the inquiry is made. Utmost haste necessary. [627]

A secret caveat to this note read:

> If, as is not to be presumed, the French Government declares its intention to remain neutral, Your Excellency will inform the French Government that we shall have to demand the turning over of the fortresses of Toul and Verdun as a pledge of neutrality; these we would occupy and return after the completion of the war with Russia. Reply to the last proposition must be here by four o'clock tomorrow afternoon. [628]

The countdown to war had begun.

D. Moltke and Conrad Prepare

Moltke spent much of the 31st getting ready for war. This included communicating with Conrad to coordinate the Central Powers' military efforts.

---

[626] G.D. 490.

[627] G.D. 491.

[628] Ibid. The high command believed that the Toul-Verdun pledges were militarily necessary. Berlin wanted assurances that if German armies were deep inside Russia, France would not use the occasion to attack Germany. Bethmann-Hollweg, *Reflections*, 146.

But such coordination was proving problematic.

Austria had two blueprints for war with Serbia and Russia. "Plan B" involved stationing three armies in Galicia in a defensive deployment while three other armies assaulted Serbia. [629] Under "Plan R," four armies would face Russia and two would handle Serbia. [630] As of midday on the 31st, Conrad did not believe that Austro-Russian hostilities were imminent. [631] The two countries were merely mobilizing against each other. [632] And Russia's mobilization would presumably be slow. Conrad thought that he would have time to crush Serbia before Russia posed a real danger; he therefore chose Plan B. [633] Austria would stay on the defensive in Galicia; the attack on Serbia would continue.

This stunned Moltke. He felt it was imperative to keep Russia off-balance in the war's opening weeks. She could not be permitted to attack Germany *en masse* while most of Germany's forces were in France. Moltke wanted Vienna to not only focus on Russia (rather than Serbia) but also to go on the offensive against her. He had the following message telephoned to Conrad late on the 31st:

> The Chief of the General Staff (Moltke) has received a telephone communication from His Excellency Conrad that Austria does not intend to wage war against Russia. Germany will proclaim mobilization of her entire military forces probably on 2 August and open hostilities against Russia and France. Will Austria leave her in the lurch? [634]

The Kaiser, too, stressed to Franz Josef the Galician Front's significance:

> It is of the utmost importance in this grave struggle that Austria oppose her principal forces to Russia, and not

---

[629] Alan Clark, *The Eastern Front, 1914-1918: Suicide of the Empires* (1971; reprint, Gloucestershire: The Windrush Press, 1999), 44-46.

[630] Ibid.

[631] Fay, *Origins*, 2:518.

[632] And as we saw, he told Berchtold on the 30th: "If the Russians do nothing against us, we need do nothing against them."

[633] Schmitt, *Coming*, 185.

[634] Quoted in Albertini, *Origins*, 3:47.

fritter away her strength by a simultaneous offensive against Serbia. This is of all the more importance as a great part of my army will be employed against France. Serbia plays, in this gigantic fight upon which we are entering shoulder to shoulder, a very subordinate role, which requires of us only the defensive measures absolutely necessary. Success in the war, and with it the continued existence of our monarchies, can only be hoped for if we both oppose our new and powerful opponent with all our forces. [635]

Now *Conrad* was stunned. Contrary to his assumption that a continental war was not imminent, he learned that Germany (1) was about to take on Russia and France and (2) expected Austria to strike Russia. With little choice and consistent with Berlin's wishes, he agreed to focus Austria's main effort on Russia. [636] Yet the forced change of plans irritated him. His long-dreamt-of, all-out assault on the hated Serbs had suddenly become a war against Russia in which Austria, not Germany, would bear the brunt of the initial fighting.

But Conrad had only himself to blame. For starters, his view that he could defeat Serbia before the Galician Front became critical was somewhat reckless. Though comparatively small, Serbia's battle-hardened army was no pushover. Moreover, Moltke had warned Conrad for several years that Austria's fate in a European war would depend upon Germany's success in the West. With Russia's mobilization and her obvious willingness to fight, Conrad should have recognized that (1) war with her was near and (2) Berlin would request that his forces concentrate on Russia.

E. Eleventh-Hour Peace Initiatives from St. Petersburg

Notwithstanding Russia's general mobilization, Sazonov and Nicholas still sought to avoid war. On the 30th, Buchanan had

---

[635] G.D. 503, July 31. For his part, Bethmann-Hollweg wired Tschirschky on the 31st: "We expect from Austria immediate active participation in the war against Russia." G.D. 479.
[636] Fay, *Origins,* 2:519.

notified Sazonov of Grey's "Halt in Belgrade" suggestion, while Sazonov had informed Buchanan of his own offer to suspend Russia's military preparations. At Grey's request, Sazonov revised his proposal to more resemble Grey's. On the 31st, Sazonov wired several of his ambassadors:

> The British Ambassador, on the instructions of his Government, has informed me of the wish of the London Cabinet to make certain modifications in the formula which I suggested yesterday to the German Ambassador. I replied that I accepted the British suggestion. I accordingly send you the text of the modified formula, which is as follows:
>
> 'If Austria consents to stay the march of her troops on Serbian territory, and if, recognizing that the Austro-Serbian conflict has assumed the character of a question of European interest, she admits that the Great Powers may examine the satisfaction which Serbia can accord to the Austro-Hungarian Government without injury to her rights as a sovereign State or her independence, Russia undertakes to maintain her waiting attitude.' [637]

Sazonov was therefore willing to let Habsburg forces temporarily occupy parts of Serbia if Austria agreed that this was a European crisis requiring the Powers' diplomatic intervention. [638] This was a painful concession for him. He later wrote:

---

[637] C.D.D., R.O.B., Document No. 67. In sending to Buchanan his request that Sazonov alter his July 30 proposal (see B.D. 309), Grey did not mention the Austrian ultimatum. Lichnowsky had told him that the statement in Sazonov's proposal regarding the modification of Vienna's demands was unacceptable. G.D. 439, Lichnowsky to German Foreign Office, July 30. Sazonov's revised offer was therefore silent about Austria's demands.

[638] Meanwhile, the shelling of Belgrade continued. Crackanthorpe wired Grey on August 1: "British Vice-Consul telephones that the situation is becoming critical in Belgrade. There is a general panic, and the inhabitants are hiding in cellars during intermittent bombardment." B.D. 435. Crowe commented: "The bombardment of Belgrade does seem an unnecessary piece of vandalism, and gives the impression that the object is the destruction of the Serbian capital as a form of punishment. This is unfortunately quite in

> Sir Edward Grey's version went considerably beyond my statement (to Pourtales), for he agreed to Austria temporarily occupying certain parts of Serbian territory and thus came near Kaiser Wilhelm's idea about 'Austrian hostages' in Serbia. Grey merely demanded that Austria should refrain from sending her troops any further; he trusted that the Powers would be able to satisfy the Austrian demands without infringing upon the sovereign rights of Serbia and the integrity of her territory.
>
> Much as I disliked this new formula, I asked the Tsar's permission to accept it in the interests of the European peace, although I fully realized that being essentially unjust it could not lead to a proper solution of the Austro-Serbian conflict or establish stable and satisfactory relations between the parties in dispute. In spite of his profound love of peace, the Tsar was unpleasantly surprised by Sir Edward Grey's new offer, and it was as difficult for me to persuade him to agree to it as it had been for me to decide to ask his consent. [639]

Nonetheless, every Power but one had now agreed to the overall "Halt in Belgrade" concept.

And Sazonov thought that the lone holdout - Austria - might be ready to fold. His cautious optimism stemmed from (1) his talks with Szapary and (2) Schebeko's telegrams from Vienna; Schebeko, for instance, conveyed to Sazonov his belief that Austria "really desires to come to an understanding with us." [640] However, neither Schebeko nor Szapary seemed to make clear to Sazonov that Austria would never modify her demands. Consider Szapary's account of his talk with Sazonov on the 31st:

---

accordance with Austrian methods." Comment of Crowe on B.D. 332, Crackanthorpe to Grey, July 30.
[639] Sergei Sazonov, *Fateful Years, 1909-1916: The Reminiscences of Serge Sazonov* (1928; reprint, New York: Ishi Press International, 2008), 209. His desire not to alienate Britain undoubtedly encouraged him to accept Grey's formula.
[640] Quoted in Schmitt, *Coming*, 179.

I (said to Sazonov) that Your Excellency's (Berchtold's) two instructions started from the misunderstanding that we had declined further negotiations with Russia. This was, as I had already informed him without instructions, a mistake. Your Excellency was not only ready to negotiate with Russia on a broad basis, but especially inclined to discuss the text of our note as far as its interpretation was concerned.

I knew, of course, that the Russian point of view was that the form of the note should be modified, whilst Your Excellency was of the opinion that its meaning could be explained. This resulted in a discrepancy, which could not be overlooked, though on the whole it seemed to me that it came to the same thing.

Mr. Sazonov said that this was good news, for he still hoped in this way that the matter might be directed into that channel which he had from the first imagined the best. I insisted on the fact that Your Excellency's instructions to me were a proof of good will............Mr. Sazonov replied that he took note with satisfaction of this proof of good will. Also, he would like to draw my attention to the fact that negotiations in St. Petersburg would seem, for reasons easily understood, to promise less hope of success than those on the neutral ground of London. I answered that Your Excellency, as I had already explained, started from the point of view of direct contact with St. Petersburg, so that I was not in a position to give any opinion concerning his suggestion about London, but that I would report to Your Excellency on the subject.

Mr. Sazonov seemed greatly relieved by my information and to consider it of exaggerated importance, so that I always had to point out again the modified situation, the discrepancy of our initial views, and so forth. Moreover, during the conversation, two principal points were completely avoided: on my part, the purely retrospective and theoretical character of a conversation about the text of the note as I gathered it from Your Excellency's telegram;

on his part, the question of what should become of the military operations during the eventual negotiations. [641]

Szapary, it appears, never unequivocally says to Sazonov that the ultimatum would not be modified. And unless Sazonov was point-blank told this, he would seize any diplomatic opening he could. Indeed, his meeting with Szapary spurred him to send the following proposal to his Great Power ambassadors on the 31st:

> The Austrian Ambassador called on me and conveyed to me the consent of his Government to enter into a discussion on the content of the ultimatum presented to Serbia. I expressed my satisfaction over this and indicated to the Ambassador that it would be preferable that the negotiations should be carried on in London with the participation of the Great Powers. We hope that the English Government will undertake to preside over these discussions, whereby it would earn the gratitude of all Europe.
>
> For a successful prosecution of such negotiations, it would be very important that Austria should suspend her military operations on Serbian territory. [642]

Sazonov's first sentence was technically correct. Vienna *was* prepared to discuss and explain the ultimatum's contents. But his implication was that Austria had agreed to revise her demands. [643]

---

[641] Szapary to Berchtold, August 1, quoted in Geiss, *July 1914*, 340-42.

[642] Quoted in Albertini, *Origins,* 2:683.

[643] Schebeko and Bunsen thought that Vienna had caved in. Bunsen later wrote: "As between (Russia and Austria), an arrangement seemed almost in sight, and on August 1, I was informed by M. Schebeko that Count Szapary had at last conceded the main point at issue by announcing to M. Sazonov that Austria would consent to submit to mediation on the points in the note to Serbia which seemed incompatible with the maintenance of Serbian independence................Austria, in fact, had finally yielded, and that she herself had at this point good hopes of a peaceful issue is shown by the communication made to you on the 1st August by Count Mensdorff, to the effect that Austria had neither 'banged the door' on compromise nor cut off the conversations. M. Schebeko to the end was working hard for peace. He was holding the most conciliatory language with Count

This was nonsense. Furthermore, his suggestion that the talks be held in London "with the participation of the Great Powers" was pure fantasy; it differed little from the other conference proposals that Austria had previously declined.

St. Petersburg made yet another proposal on the 31st. Though Nicholas's ongoing correspondence with Wilhelm was growing futile, the Tsar wired his cousin at 2:55 p.m.:

> I thank you heartily for your mediation, which begins to give one hope that all may yet end peacefully. It is technically impossible to stop our military preparations, which were obligatory owing to Austria's mobilization. We are far from wishing war. So long as the negotiations with Austria on Serbia's account are taking place, my troops shall not take any provocative action. I give you my solemn word for this. I put all my trust in God's mercy and hope in your successful mediation in Vienna for the welfare of our countries and for the peace of Europe. [644]

Thus, so long as Austro-Russian talks continued, St. Petersburg would undertake no aggressive action beyond mobilization. And Sazonov again stressed to the Central Powers that Russia's mobilization was strictly defensive. He told Szapary:

> The (Russian) mobilization had no significance, and Emperor Nicholas had pledged his word to Kaiser Wilhelm that the army would not budge so long as a conversation tending towards an agreement was still going on with Vienna............As concerned the Russian army, it was so well-disciplined that the Emperor with one word could make it retire from the frontier. [645]

Berchtold.................and M. Schebeko repeatedly told me he was prepared to accept any reasonable compromise." B.D. 676, Bunsen to Grey, September 1. Obviously, he and Schebeko were wrong in believing that Vienna had "yielded" or that an Austro-Russian deal was near.

[644] G.D. 487. Nicholas's implication that Austria's general mobilization had preceded Russia's was incorrect. As we saw, Russian general mobilization was ordered on the 30th, a day before Austrian general mobilization.

[645] Szapary to Berchtold, August 1, quoted in Geiss, *July 1914*, 341.

Naturally, Austria recognized Russia's mobilization as a serious step. But she did not consider it a fatal one. Berchtold informed his ambassadors on the 31st:

> As mobilization has been ordered by the Russian Government on our frontier, we find ourselves obliged to take military measures in Galicia. These measures are purely of a defensive character and arise exclusively under the pressure of the Russian measures, which we regret exceedingly, as we ourselves have no aggressive intentions of any kind against Russia, and desire the continuation of the former neighborly relations.
>
> *Pourparlers* between the Cabinets at Vienna and St. Petersburg appropriate to the situation are meanwhile being continued, and from these we hope that things will quiet down all around. [646]

In fact, Austro-Russian tensions – the heart of the crisis for the past week – were easing. German-Russian tensions, however, were suddenly soaring, for Berlin viewed Russia's general mobilization as a war-triggering act. [647] As Bunsen later wrote: "(On and after July 31), the tension between Russia and Germany was much greater than between Russia and Austria............(T)he conversations (between) St. Petersburg and Vienna were cut short by the transfer of the dispute to the more dangerous ground of a direct conflict between Germany and Russia." [648] Russia's peace initiatives of the 31st were all for naught. [649]

---

[646] C.D.D., A.R.B. I, Document No. 53. Such *pourparlers* suited Berchtold perfectly. By dragging out talks with St. Petersburg, Austria would gain more time to smash Serbia.

[647] The Tsar may not have understood this. He told Pourtales on the 31st that peace remained entirely possible if Germany would restrain Austria. G.D. 535, Pourtales to German Foreign Office, July 31. Knowing the impact that Russia's general mobilization would – and did - have on Berlin, Pourtales concluded that Nicholas was "not yet conscious of the gravity of the situation." Ibid.

[648] B.D. 676.

[649] As indicated earlier, Germany essentially refused to entertain any new or existing diplomatic proposals once Russia's general mobilization had been confirmed. Goschen reported to Nicolson on the 1st: "I did my very best and

F. Germany Declares War on Russia

Pourtales delivered the German ultimatum to Sazonov around midnight on the 31st. [650] Sazonov's reaction was surprisingly tame. While noting the technical impossibility of suspending Russia's mobilization, he emphasized that negotiations could continue. [651] He also asked whether German mobilization meant war. [652] Pourtales "replied in the negative, but added that we were very near it." [653] The ambassador summarized their conversation in a 1 a.m. telegram to Berlin. It closed with this:

> I put to the Minister (Sazonov) the direct question: could he give me a guarantee that Russia intended to keep the peace, even in the event that an agreement with Austria was not reached? The Minister was unable to give me an affirmative answer to this question. In that case, then, I replied, nobody can blame us for our unwillingness to allow Russia a longer start in mobilization. [654]

Later that morning, Pourtales sent an emotional, last-minute plea to Count Fredericks, the Russian minister of the household:

> The mobilization of the entire Russian army has made the most unfortunate impression in Berlin. They cannot understand how this order could have been given while the mediation of my Sovereign was in progress and had not yet met with failure. Do not forget that it is only a few days since we were informed in a formal manner that mobilization would be put through only on the Austrian

---

hardest last night to persuade Jagow, notwithstanding all mobilizations and ultimatums, not to relax his efforts to prevent one of the biggest catastrophes - in fact the biggest - of modern times and to work in the direction indicated by (England). He was sympathetic but apparently absolutely determined that nothing more could be done until Russia said she would demobilize." B.D. 510.

[650] G.D. 536, Pourtales to German Foreign Office, August 1.
[651] Ibid.
[652] Sazonov to Russian representatives abroad, August 1, in C.D.D., R.O.B., Document No. 70.
[653] Ibid.
[654] G.D. 536.

frontier and not on that of Germany. Consequently, the situation has become extremely serious, and I am seeking everywhere the means to avert a catastrophe, for a war would be an enormous danger to all monarchies.........We cannot conceal from ourselves that in such an event we are but a finger's breadth from war – a war that neither you nor we desire. I know how difficult it is to stop a machine set in motion. But the Emperor of Russia can do everything in this connection. I entreat you - do what you can to prevent a catastrophe. [655]

In Berlin, the hours passed. No further news from Pourtales arrived. Around 1 p.m., Jagow instructed Pourtales to deliver the following message to Sazonov; it stated in part:

Russia, without awaiting the result (of the Kaiser's mediation), proceeded to the mobilization of her entire land and sea forces. As a consequence of this threatening measure, occasioned by no military preparation on the part of Germany, the German Empire found itself face to face with a grave and imminent danger. Had the (German) Government failed to prepare itself to meet this peril, it would have endangered the security and the very existence of Germany. The (German) Government, therefore, felt itself compelled to address the Government of (Russia), insisting upon the suspension of the said military activities. Russia having (failed to do so)...........I have the honor, on behalf of my Government, to inform Your Excellency as follows:

His Majesty, the Emperor, my august Sovereign, accepts the challenge in the name of the (German) Empire, and considers himself as being in a state of war with Russia. [656]

At 5 p.m., Wilhelm signed the order for mobilization. [657] Pourtales, meanwhile, again saw Sazonov. In his memoirs, Sazonov described what happened:

---

[655] G.D. 539.
[656] G.D. 542.

Count Pourtales came to see me at seven o'clock in the evening, and after the very first words asked me whether the Russian Government was ready to give a favorable answer to the ultimatum presented the day before. I answered in the negative, observing that although general mobilization could not be cancelled, Russia was nevertheless disposed, as before, to continue negotiations with a view to a peaceful settlement.

Count Pourtales was much agitated. He repeated his question, dwelling upon the serious consequences which our refusal to comply with the German request would involve. I gave the same answer. Pulling out of his pocket a folded sheet of paper, the Ambassador repeated his question for the third time in a voice that trembled. I said that I could give no other answer. Deeply moved, the Ambassador said to me, speaking with difficulty:

'In that case, my Government charges me to give you the following note.' And with a shaking hand, Pourtales handed me the Declaration of War..........

After handing the note to me, the Ambassador, who had evidently found it a great strain to carry out his orders, lost all self-control and leaning against the window burst into tears. With a gesture of despair, he repeated: 'Who could have thought that I should be leaving St. Petersburg under such circumstances!' In spite of my own emotion, which I managed to overcome, I felt sincerely sorry for him. We embraced each other and with tottering steps he walked out of the room.

Count Pourtales had not always been successful as an intermediary between the German and the Russian Governments.............I nevertheless believe that he was sincerely anxious to avoid a breach between his own country and Russia, not only from a natural love of peace but also because he realized what the consequences of

---

[657] Schmitt, *Coming,* 323.

such a breach were likely to be. When he had to take part in the drama, the picture of these consequences probably rose before his imagination so vividly that he was overwhelmed with despair at the thought that something irrevocable and too awful to conceive had been done. [658]

Not the first Great Power to mobilize in this crisis, Germany *was* the first to declare war on another Power. Yet not everyone in Berlin supported the declaration. Tirpitz was particularly dismayed. Berlin had seemingly scored a diplomatic victory when Russia mobilized first and, to some degree, made herself appear as the aggressor. [659] This might influence Italy's, Romania's, and even England's attitude. Tirpitz believed that Bethmann-Hollweg had thrown this advantage away. He later explained:

> On August 1, I learned...............that we had sent a declaration of war against Russia after the ultimatum. I considered that very unfavorable for Germany. In my opinion, we ought to have turned to account diplomatically the advantage that we were militarily on the defensive with regard to Russia by leaving the declaration of war to the Russians. We ought not to have inspired the *moujik* with a conviction that the (Kaiser) intended to attack the White Tsar. The depreciation of our alliance treaty with Romania was also of importance. This treaty, just like that with Italy, had been made by Prince Bismarck for defense; both States were only pledged to help us if Russia or France attacked us. By our declaration

---

[658] Sazonov, *Fateful Years*, 212-13. Though sympathetic towards Pourtales, Sazonov was furious at Berlin. Wiring London and Paris on August 1 about Nicholas's July 31 promise to Wilhelm, he fumed that "in the face of such a guarantee, Germany had no right to doubt that we would accept any peaceful way out compatible with the dignity and independence of Serbia." Quoted in Schilling, *How the War Began*, 81. Predictably, Russia and Germany blamed each other for initiating hostilities. Russia argued that Berlin grossly overreacted to her general mobilization. Germany claimed that St. Petersburg's provocative actions forced Berlin to end its peacemaking efforts and to go to war.

[659] Bethmann-Hollweg also used Russia's mobilization to convince the German people that the war had been forced on Germany. Jarausch, *Enigmatic Chancellor*, 177.

of war on Russia, we formally gave the Romanians the right to leave us alone in the war............Did not Bethmann-Hollweg really consider the enormous disadvantages which were created for us by our not leaving the act of a declaration of war to the enemy?

I had the impression that our action.........was completely unconsidered.........and my feelings revolted at our having to assume the odium of the attacking party in the face of the world...........although we could not at all intend to march into Russia, and although we were in reality the attacked party. I therefore asked the Chancellor.........why the declaration of war had to coincide with our mobilization? [660]

Bethmann-Hollweg responded that the declaration was needed because Germany "would immediately send troops over the frontier." [661] Tirpitz assumed that this meant the Russian frontier. He recalled:

(The chancellor's) reply astonished me, because at the most it could only be a question of patrols (going over the Russian border)..............When I asked Moltke afterwards about the actual relation between the crossing of the frontier and our declaration of war, he denied any intention of sending troops over the frontier forthwith. He also told me that he attached no value to the declaration of war from his own point of view. Thus the riddle - why we declared war first - remains unsolved for me. [662]

---

[660] Tirpitz, *My Memoirs*, 363-64. Tirpitz's fears were realized. Lichnowsky informed Berlin that Germany's declaration of war on Russia "has created an unfavorable impression here (in London), since they think that the Tsar was still striving to mediate further, and had given his word that no soldier should pass the frontier so long as there was hope of a peaceful solution." G.D. 676, Lichnowsky to German Foreign Office, August 2.

[661] Tirpitz, *My Memoirs*, 364.

[662] Ibid., 364-65. Tirpitz also described Bethmann-Hollweg's temperament around this time: "Through all these days, Bethmann was so agitated and overstrained that it was impossible to speak with him. I can still hear him as he repeatedly stressed the absolute necessity of the declaration of war, with

The war declaration likely had much to do with France. Bethmann-Hollweg apparently reasoned that an attack on France could be justified under international law only if Germany was already at war with France's ally, Russia. [663] He implied in his memoirs that the offensive in the West could not begin until a formal German-Russian state of war existed:

> Falkenhayn thought it was a mistake to declare war on Russia, not because he considered that war could be avoided after Russia had mobilized, but because he feared that the political effect would be prejudicial to us............(Moltke) was, on the other hand, in favor of declaring war because our plan of mobilization, providing for a war on two fronts, required that military actions be immediately taken, and because our hope of success against an enormous superiority in numbers was dependent on the extreme rapidity of our movements. I myself agreed with the view of General von Moltke. I was, of course, under no illusion as to the effect on the question of responsibility for the war that our declaration of war would have and actually did have. But it was impossible at a moment when the existence of the country was entirely dependent on military action to oppose the military arguments, quite reasonable in themselves, of that general who was responsible for military operations. [664]

---

his arms uplifted, and consequently cut short all further discussion." Ibid., 364. The sentiment in the German Foreign Office, meanwhile, was - according to Goschen - one of "considerable depression." B.D. 510. Goschen told Nicolson: "Zimmermann said to Cambon yesterday, 'This is the most tragic day for 40 years and it happens just as we were settling down to what we thought were improved relations all around'............He (Zimmermann) was very angry and excited about the whole thing, (and) expressed regret that Germany, France 'and perhaps England' had been drawn in, none of whom wanted war in the least and said that it came from 'this d-----d system of alliances, which were the curse of modern times.'" Ibid.

[663] Albertini, *Origins,* 3:186.

[664] Bethmann-Hollweg, *Reflections,* 137-38. Note Bethmann-Hollweg's and Tirpitz's differing accounts of Moltke's view regarding the need to declare war.

With Germany now at war with Russia, Bethmann-Hollweg awaited France's response to Berlin's July 31 note to her. He fully expected an unfavorable answer. [665]

G. *Elation (and a Huge Misunderstanding) in Berlin*

Before discussing the various emotions in Berlin late on August 1, let us examine events in France.

By the 31st, Paris recognized that war was very likely. It thus focused on two issues: (1) military preparations and (2) obtaining England's support.

The first was resolved fairly quickly. Paleologue's confirmation of Russian general mobilization did not arrive in Paris until 8:30 p.m. on the 31st, though French officials got wind of Russia's action through Schoen, Jules Cambon, and other sources. [666] The news did not change Paris's determination to stand alongside Russia. In fact, France's chief of the general staff, General Joseph Joffre, alarmed by reports (albeit exaggerated ones) of German military preparations, urged the government on the 31st to order mobilization. In a 3:30 p.m. message to Messimy, he warned that if France's leadership failed to act, he would not be responsible for the consequences:

> (I)f the Germans, under the cover of diplomatic conversations, continue to take the various steps comprised in their plan for mobilization – though without pronouncing that word – it is absolutely necessary for the (French) Government to understand that, starting with this evening, any delay of 24 hours in calling up our reservists and issuing orders prescribing covering operations, will have as a result the withdrawal of our concentration points by from 10 to 12 miles for each day of delay; in other words, the initial abandonment of just that much of our

---

[665] G.D. 492, Bethmann-Hollweg to Flotow, July 31.

[666] Albertini, *Origins,* 3:89; Fay, *Origins,* 2:531.

territory. The Commander-in-Chief must decline to accept this responsibility. [667]

The next morning, Joffre reemphasized the need for mobilization. [668] He later recalled: "I felt it was necessary to point this out to the Government and to indicate the responsibility which it would incur if there was any delay in taking this step." [669] The government agreed. The mobilization order was signed that afternoon. [670]

The issue of British support, however, remained troublesome for Paris. Grey still would not shift from his non-committal position. He spoke with Paul Cambon on the 1st:

> After the Cabinet (meeting) today, I (Grey) told M. Cambon that the present position differed entirely from that created by the Morocco incidents. In the latter, Germany made upon France demands that France could not grant, and in connection with which we had undertaken special obligations towards France. In these, public opinion would have justified the British Government in supporting France to the utmost of their ability. Now..........(France) was bound by an alliance to which we were not parties, and of which we did not know the terms. This did not mean that under no circumstances would we assist France, but it did mean that France must take her own decision at this moment without reckoning on an assistance that we were not now in a position to promise.
>
> M. Cambon said that he could not transmit this reply to his Government, and he asked me to authorize him to say that the British Cabinet had not yet taken any decision. I said that we had come to a decision: that we could not propose to Parliament at this moment to send an expeditionary military force to the continent. Such a step had always

---

[667] Quoted in Joseph Joffre, *The Memoirs of Marshal Joffre*, vol. 1 (London: Geoffrey Bles, 1932), 125.

[668] Ibid., 127.

[669] Ibid.

[670] Ibid., 128.

been regarded here as very dangerous and doubtful. It was one that we could not propose and Parliament would not authorize unless our interests and obligations were deeply and desperately involved.

M. Cambon said that the French coasts were undefended. The German fleet might come through the Straits any day and attack them. [671]

Poincare was so concerned about England's stance that he appealed directly to King George:

It is, I believe, on the language and attitude of the English Government that the last possibilities of a peaceful solution now depend. We, ourselves, from the beginning of the crisis have recommended to our ally a moderation from which they have not departed. In accord with the English Government and conformably to Sir Edward Grey's suggestions, we shall continue to act in the same sense. But if all efforts for conciliation are applied on the same side, and if Germany and Austria can calculate on English abstention, the Austrian demands will remain inflexible, and an accord between her and Russia will become impossible. I am deeply convinced that the more England, France and Russia at the present moment give a strong impression of unity in their diplomatic action, the more it will still be legitimate to count on peace being preserved. [672]

Poincare was obviously trying to convince George that Paris had done everything possible to avoid war. Yet he blatantly exaggerated – if not outright lied about - France's efforts to restrain Russia, which we know were very limited. [673] Such, perhaps, was his desperation to secure England's backing. [674]

---

[671] B.D. 426, Grey to Bertie, August 1.
[672] Quoted in Albertini, *Origins,* 3:68.
[673] See ibid.
[674] See ibid., 3:69.

Hence was the situation in Paris when, at 4:23 p.m. on the 1st, an incredible telegram from Lichnowsky arrived in Berlin. At that moment, Germany's leadership had many worries – an imminent war with France, the prospect of British intervention, and Italy's and Romania's likely neutrality. Lichnowsky's message erased most of them:

> Sir E. Grey has just had me informed through Sir W. Tyrrell that he hopes, as the result of a Ministerial Council now in session, to be able to give me this afternoon some facts which may prove useful for the avoidance of the great catastrophe. Judging from Sir William's hints, this would appear to mean that in case we did not attack France, England would remain neutral and would guarantee France's neutrality. I shall learn more this afternoon.
>
> Sir E. Grey has just called me on the telephone and asked me if I thought I could assure him that in case France should remain neutral in a Russo-German war, we would not attack the French. I assured him that I could take the responsibility for such a guaranty, and he is to use this assurance at today's Cabinet session.
>
> (P.S.: Sir W. Tyrrell urgently begged me to use my influence to ensure that our troops did not cross the French border. Everything would depend upon that.) [675]

Was this for real? Was Grey saying that if Germany left France alone, Paris and London would remain neutral, thus giving the Central Powers a free hand to crush Russia? Wilhelm, Bethmann-Hollweg, and Jagow thought so. In fact, Wilhelm was so ecstatic that he called for champagne to celebrate! [676] Germany, it appeared, could now hurl her entire strength against Russia. Rather than facing three Great Powers, the Austro-German pact would only face one!

---

[675] G.D. 562, Lichnowsky to German Foreign Office.
[676] Geiss, *July 1914*, 336.

But Berlin's excitement was woefully premature. First off, Lichnowsky's telegram did not say that London was *formally offering* British and French neutrality. It merely indicated that Grey had raised the issue. [677] Though Lichnowsky could have made this distinction clearer, his superiors had read too much into his words. Second, the Schlieffen Plan was based in part on the view that hostilities with one Franco-Russian pact member would bring in the other. How, therefore, could Lichnowsky's less-than-definitive note singlehandedly overturn this longstanding premise? Berlin should have stepped back and examined whether any of this made sense before celebrating.

Finally, even had Grey offered Franco-British neutrality, Germany's mobilization plan posed a serious problem. The Kaiser, we recall, signed the mobilization order at 5 p.m. on the 1st. Moltke and Falkenhayn immediately took it for transmission throughout Germany. [678] Minutes later, Wilhelm, Bethmann-Hollweg, and Jagow learned of Lichnowsky's 4:23 p.m. telegram. [679] Moltke and Falkenhayn were called back and told the good news. [680] The cheerful Kaiser said to Moltke that since Germany need only take on Russia, the whole German army should simply march eastward. [681]

Moltke replied that this was impossible. [682] Germany's mobilization blueprint called for a concentration of forces in the West. To suddenly change this to an eastern-focused mobilization, Moltke explained, would result in an utterly disorganized, unsupplied mass of men. [683] The Kaiser retorted: "Your uncle would have given me a different answer!" [684] This vicious

---

[677] Grey had not even discussed the idea with Paris. See G.D. 631, Lichnowsky to German Foreign Office, August 2.

[678] Albertini, *Origins*, 3:171; Schmitt, *Coming*, 323.

[679] Albertini, *Origins*, 3:172.

[680] Ibid. Moltke believed that Wilhelm would not have signed the mobilization order had Lichnowsky's telegram arrived earlier. Ibid., 3:175.

[681] Ibid., 3:172.

[682] Ibid.

[683] Ibid.

[684] Quoted in ibid. As mentioned earlier, Moltke's uncle had masterminded Prussia's victory over France in 1870-71.

comment hurt Moltke badly. [685] But the general remained adamant: the existing mobilization plan could not be altered. [686] After heated discussion, a compromise was reached. [687] Per Moltke's wishes, Germany's western-focused mobilization would continue. [688] However: (1) German forces would not yet enter France, Belgium, or Luxembourg, and (2) Berlin would respond favorably to Grey's suggestion. [689] Should a neutrality agreement be finalized with London and Paris, Germany would shift her western armies – once they were mobilized - eastward to face Russia. [690]

But Moltke was despondent. [691] What if, he probably thought, Lichnowsky's telegram was a mirage? By delaying her offensive for 48-72 hours and keeping her troops within her borders, Germany could lose her foremost advantage – speed. He recognized the diplomatic dangers of turning Grey down. Yet he felt that military considerations had to take precedence. [692] The Kaiser disagreed. He telegraphed King George at 7:02 p.m. on the 1st:

> I just received the communication from your Government offering French neutrality under the guarantee of Great Britain. Added to this offer was the inquiry whether under these conditions Germany would refrain from attacking France. On technical grounds, my mobilization, which had already been proclaimed this afternoon, must proceed against two fronts east and west as prepared. This cannot be countermanded because I am sorry your telegram came

---

[685] Ibid.

[686] Ibid., 3:173.

[687] Ibid.

[688] Ibid.

[689] Ibid.; Schmitt, *Coming,* 343-45. German forces were to occupy neutral Luxembourg so that the latter's railroads – which were needed for the attack on France - did not fall into French hands. G.D. 640, Bethmann-Hollweg to Buch, August 2; Albertini, *Origins,* 3:175-76. Moltke begged Wilhelm to at least allow the seizure of these railways, but Wilhelm refused. Albertini, *Origins,* 3:176. He did not want to antagonize Grey. See ibid.

[690] Ibid., 3:173.

[691] Ibid., 3:173-74.

[692] Ibid.

too late. But if France offers me neutrality, which must be guaranteed by the British fleet and army, I shall of course refrain from attacking France and employ my troops elsewhere. I hope that France will not become nervous. The troops on my frontier are in the act of being stopped by telegraph and telephone from crossing into France. [693]

At 7:15 p.m., Bethmann-Hollweg telegraphed Lichnowsky:

Germany is willing to agree to the English proposal, provided England will pledge security with all her armed forces for the unconditional neutrality of France in a German-Russian conflict, and, moreover, for a neutrality to last until the final completion of this conflict. Germany alone would have to decide when that completion had been reached.

Germany's mobilization took place today in reply to the Russian challenge before the arrival of (Lichnowsky's telegram). As a consequence, our advance movements, even toward the French border, can no longer be altered. We will guarantee, however, not to cross the French frontier before Monday, August 3, at seven o'clock in the evening, in case England's agreement should be obtained within that time. [694]

And at 8:45 p.m., Jagow wired Schoen about Lichnowsky's telegram. He added: "Please keep the French quiet for the time being. On our part, no hostile action against France is contemplated, despite mobilization, which had already been ordered before the arrival of the London proposal." [695]

So while Germany communicated her acceptance to London, she attached stipulations. First, England had to agree to militarily enforce France's neutrality. Second, said neutrality was to be unconditional and to last as long as Berlin deemed German-Russian hostilities to exist. Third, London had roughly 48 hours to

---

[693] G.D. 575.
[694] G.D. 578.
[695] G.D. 587.

accept Germany's terms. Considering what was at stake, Berlin wanted definite and immediate assurances that France would remain neutral.

A strange sideshow now occurred. As we saw, Jagow sent the declaration of war on Russia to Pourtales at 1 p.m. on the 1ˢᵗ. At 2:05 p.m., this message from Nicholas to Wilhelm arrived:

> (I) understand you are obliged to mobilize, but wish to have the same guaranty from you as I gave you – that these measures do not mean war and that we shall continue negotiating for the benefit of our countries and universal peace dear to all our hearts. Our long proved friendship must succeed, with God's help, in avoiding bloodshed. (I) anxiously, full of confidence, await your answer. [696]

As of that evening, Berlin had not received word from Pourtales confirming his deliverance of the war declaration, though Bethmann-Hollweg probably assumed that it had been done. [697] Asking Nicholas to stop Russia's mobilization would therefore have seemed pointless. Nonetheless, the chancellor encouraged Wilhelm to send this note to the Tsar at 10:30 p.m.:

> Thanks for your telegram. I yesterday pointed out to your Government the way by which, alone, war may be avoided. Although I requested an answer for noon today, no telegram from my Ambassador conveying an answer from your Government has reached me as yet. I therefore have been obliged to mobilize my Army.
>
> Immediate, affirmative, clear and unmistakable answer from your Government is the only way to avoid endless misery. Until I have received this answer, alas, I am unable to discuss the subject of your telegram. As a matter

---

[696] G.D. 546. Nicholas was unaware of Germany's declaration of war when he telegraphed Wilhelm.
[697] Pourtales sent his confirmation at 8 p.m. on the 1ˢᵗ. G.D. 588, Pourtales to German Foreign Office.

of fact, I must request you to immediately order your troops on no account to commit the slightest act of trespassing over our frontiers. [698]

Perhaps Bethmann-Hollweg wanted to offset the diplomatic damage from the war declaration by showing that Germany made one final attempt to avert bloodshed. Or maybe he was growing skeptical of Grey's neutrality suggestion and, faced with a war against the Triple Entente, hoped that Nicholas would back down at the last minute. Whatever Bethmann-Hollweg's thinking, Wilhelm's note understandably befuddled Nicholas, as Germany had already declared war. Sazonov asked Pourtales about it. Pourtales suspected that Wilhelm's telegram had actually been sent on the 31st (before war was declared). [699]

Not surprisingly, Nicholas never replied to Wilhelm. The episode was a weird ending to the ultimately tragic diplomatic discussions between Russia and Germany.

Any doubts Bethmann-Hollweg had about Lichnowsky's 4:23 p.m. telegram were confirmed when this message from George to Wilhelm arrived late on the 1st:

> In answer to your telegram just received, I think there must be some misunderstanding as to a suggestion that passed in friendly conversation between Prince Lichnowsky and Sir Edward Grey this afternoon, when they were discussing how actual fighting between German and French armies might be avoided while there is still a chance of some agreement between Austria and Russia. Sir Edward Grey will arrange to see Prince Lichnowsky early tomorrow morning to ascertain whether there is a misunderstanding on his part. [700]

More than anyone, Wilhelm believed that London had officially offered Franco-British neutrality. But with George

---

[698] G.D. 600. See also Albertini, *Origins,* 3:180.
[699] G.D. 666, Pourtales to German Foreign Office, August 2.
[700] G.D. 612.

having crushed his hopes, he called for Moltke around 11 p.m. [701] He informed the general of the misunderstanding and curtly authorized the Luxembourg invasion - much to Moltke's relief. [702]

H. Germany Invades Luxembourg and Declares War on France

At a meeting with Viviani around 7 p.m. on the 31st, Schoen executed the instructions in Bethmann-Hollweg's 3:30 p.m. telegram to him, which, we remember, read in part:

> We have declared a state of threatening danger of war, which must be followed by mobilization in case Russia does not suspend every war measure against Austria and ourselves within 12 hours. Mobilization will inevitably mean war. Please ask the French Government if it intends to remain neutral in a Russo-German war. Answer must be given within 18 hours. Utmost haste necessary. [703]

While stating that he "was not willing quite yet to give up hope of avoiding the extreme event," Viviani promised to give France's response by 1 p.m. the next day. [704] Around midday on the 1st, Schoen again saw Viviani. [705] Shortly thereafter, he wired Berlin: "To the definite and repeated question whether France would remain neutral in case of a Russo-German war, (Viviani) stated to me hesitatingly that France would act in accordance with her interests." [706] That settled it for Berlin. A draft declaration of war against France was finalized that evening. [707]

But it was not immediately sent. One reason, naturally, was Lichnowsky's telegram regarding Franco-British neutrality. [708] A bigger reason was that Falkenhayn, Moltke, and Tirpitz did not

---

[701] Albertini, *Origins,* 3:176.
[702] Ibid.
[703] G.D. 491; G.D. 528, Schoen to German Foreign Office, July 31.
[704] G.D. 528.
[705] Albertini, *Origins,* 3:100.
[706] G.D. 571, Schoen to German Foreign Office.
[707] Albertini, *Origins,* 3:193.
[708] Ibid., 3:194.

believe that a war declaration was yet necessary. [709] Falkenhayn felt that war with France was essentially a fact; thus, why bother with a war declaration that would only make Germany look bad? [710] Moltke, meanwhile, wanted France to open hostilities, ostensibly so she could be painted as the aggressor. He told the German Foreign Office on the 2nd:

> I do not consider it necessary yet to deliver the declaration of war to France; on the other hand, I am counting on the likelihood that, if it is held back for the present, France, on her part, will be forced by public opinion to organize warlike measures against Germany, even if a formal declaration of war has not been presented. Presumably, France will move into Belgium in the role of the protector of Belgian neutrality...............On our side, arrangements have been made so that the crossing of the French frontier will be avoided until activities on the part of France render it necessary. [711]

Bethmann-Hollweg felt differently. He again seemed focused on complying with international law. Tirpitz later recalled:

> I represented again and again (to Bethmann-Hollweg) that I could not understand why a declaration of war had to be sent to France at all, for it would always have an aggressive flavor.............The chancellor declared that he could not hand over our terms to Belgium without a declaration of war on France. I have never been able to understand this reasoning. [712]

Though Bethmann-Hollweg insisted on the war declaration, the military prevailed after stormy debate. [713] The chancellor reported to Wilhelm early on the 2nd:

---

[709] See ibid., 3:195-98.
[710] See ibid., 3:195.
[711] G.D. 662.
[712] Tirpitz, *My Memoirs*, 368-69.
[713] Schmitt, *Coming*, 362.

In accordance with the understanding with the Ministry of War and the General Staff, presentation of the declaration of war to France is not necessary today for any military reasons. Consequently, it will not be done, in the hope that the French will attack us. [714]

Of course, France was not about to attack Germany lest she alienate England. The Germans and French thus stood face-to-face on the 2nd, each hoping the other would commence hostilities. Neither did, but things were still active in the West on this day. Two campaigns were being waged – one military and one diplomatic.

The former was Germany's invasion of Luxembourg. The goal was to ensure that Luxembourg's railroads – which were needed for the attack on France – did not fall into French hands. [715] The tiny country was easily occupied. There was no resistance. Yet the Germans were hardly welcomed with open arms. On the 31st, Luxembourg's prime minister, Paul Eyschen, fearing a possible Franco-German war, had asked both countries to honor his nation's neutrality. [716] Paris agreed, provided that Germany also respected Luxembourg's neutrality. [717] Berlin, however, gave no response. [718] So when the Germans entered his country, Eyschen protested vigorously. [719] The Grand Duchess of Luxembourg, in fact, wired Wilhelm directly:

At this moment, the Grand Duchy is being occupied by German troops. My Government has lodged a protest in the proper quarter and has demanded an explanation of the occurrence. I beg Your Majesty to hasten this explanation and to respect the country's rights. [720]

Bethmann-Hollweg instructed Berlin's ambassador to Luxembourg to tell Luxembourg's government that Germany had

---

[714] G.D. 629.

[715] G.D. 640.

[716] Schmitt, *Coming,* 363-64.

[717] Ibid., 364.

[718] Ibid.

[719] See G.D. 637, Eyschen to Jagow, August 2.

[720] G.D. 638, August 2.

no hostile intentions but simply needed to secure the railways. [721]
He added that Luxembourg would be compensated for any
damages. [722] Jagow, however, sent a more deceitful explanation to
Eyschen:

> The military measures were, to our great regret, made
> unavoidable by the fact that we have received reliable
> information according to which French armed forces are
> advancing on Luxembourg. We were forced to take the
> measures for the protection of our Army and for the
> security of the railroads.............There was unfortunately
> no time for previous arrangement with the Luxembourg
> Government, as the danger was imminent. [723]

This was absurd. French forces were *not* threatening Luxembourg.
Furthermore, in implying (in his last sentence) that the invasion
was a spur-of-the-moment decision, Jagow conveniently ignored
the fact that it had been part of Germany's war strategy for some
time. Berlin forwarded similar explanations to London, though
they had little effect. [724] If anything, England's dismay over the
Luxembourg operation was compounded by Germany's pitiful
excuses for it. [725]

Berlin's diplomatic dishonesty was equally evident in the
other campaign in the West – the Franco-German mudslinging
contest. Both countries hurled accusations of border violations and
other hostile acts. [726] A number of France's charges, to be sure,
were exaggerations. Some of what came from the Germans,
however, was unbelievable. To illustrate, Jagow telegraphed
Flotow:

> Metz reports on the 2nd: Yesterday, a French physician,
> with the aid of two disguised officers, attempted to infect
> the wells of Montigny, a suburb of Metz, with cholera

---

[721] G.D. 640.

[722] Ibid.

[723] G.D. 649, August 2.

[724] See G.D. 643, Bethmann-Hollweg to Lichnowsky, August 2.

[725] See footnote 835.

[726] Each country's forces had been ordered not to cross the Franco-German
frontier. See Albertini, *Origins,* 3:206.

bacilli. He was shot according to martial law. A French flour dealer poisoned his flour. I beg Your Excellency (Flotow) to make a point of spreading through the press there (in Rome) these acts of the French, perpetrated before any declaration of war – yes, even before the German mobilization. [727]

He told Flotow in a separate note: "French aviators are dropping bombs in the distant neighborhood of Nuremburg." [728] And he wired Lichnowsky and Berlin's ambassadors to Belgium and Holland: "Please inform the local Government that early this morning, 80 French officers in Prussian officers' uniforms made an attempt to cross the German frontier at Walbeck west of Geldern in 12 automobiles." [729]

These flat-out lies were followed by another whopper, this time from the German 8th Army Corps commander. Eyschen informed Jagow:

> At this moment, there is being distributed through the city of Luxembourg a proclamation by the general commanding the 8th Army Corps............
>
> 'Since France, without regard to the neutrality of Luxembourg, has opened hostilities against Germany from Luxembourg territory, as has been unmistakably ascertained, His Majesty has ordered that German troops should move into Luxembourg, also.'
>
> This statement is founded on error. There is absolutely not a single French soldier in Luxembourg territory, nor is there the least indication of a threat to her neutrality on the part of France. [730]

Even the German high command seemed embarrassed by some of these tales. With respect to the well-poisoning and flour-poisoning accusations, it asked the government "not to publish or

---

[727] G.D. 690, August 2.

[728] G.D. 664, August 2.

[729] G.D. 677, August 2.

[730] G.D. 730, August 3.

to make use of any such stories until the General Staff has investigated and confirmed them." [731] Nevertheless, Berlin continued its efforts to portray Germany as the victim. Bethmann-Hollweg telegraphed Lichnowsky about several alleged French misdeeds, including (1) French forces crossing into Alsace and (2) two Frenchmen attempting to blow up the Cochem tunnel on the Moselle railroad. [732] He concluded:

> These transgressions have occurred, although the French Premier stated officially to the (German) Ambassador at Paris that the mobilization of the French army represented no aggressive intentions of any kind towards Germany, and that French troops were obliged to maintain a zone of ten kilometers between themselves and the German border. Kindly notify the English Government of this matter at once, and present seriously to Sir Edward Grey the dangerous position in which Germany is placed by such provocation, made against all good faith and honor, as well as the very serious decisions to which she may be driven. I hope Your Serene Highness may be successful in convincing England that Germany, although she has been advocating the maintenance of peace to the utmost limit, is being driven by her opponent to adopt the role of an injured party who must take to arms for the preservation of her very existence. [733]

Britain was not swayed. Indeed, Paris seemingly won the Franco-German war of words. Late on the 2nd, Lichnowsky wired Berlin that London had received a report about German forces entering France near Nancy. [734] He said that Crowe told him: "(T)his news would make a bad impression upon the Cabinet Council..............and might not be without its influence, perhaps,

---

[731] Albertini, *Origins,* 3:208; Carnegie Endowment, *German Documents Collected by Karl Kautsky,* 508, footnote 7.

[732] G.D. 693, August 2.

[733] Ibid.

[734] G.D. 689, Lichnowsky to German Foreign Office. Berlin called France's accusations of border violations "wholly imaginary." G.D. 713, Jagow to Lichnowsky and Flotow, August 3.

on the eventual decision to be made." [735] Lichnowsky similarly warned Berlin the next morning: "Advance into France without war has had an ominous effect here and has seriously offended the English sense of justice. Urgently request explanation I can use. Morning papers condemn our procedure and characterize us as the actual wreckers of peace." [736]

By midday on the 3rd, Berlin felt it could no longer delay Germany's offensive in the West. Accordingly, around 1 p.m., Bethmann-Hollweg sent to Schoen a declaration of war against France. [737] It was based not on her vague response to Berlin's July 31 note but on her supposed aggressive acts:

> Up to the present time, German troops have been ordered to absolutely respect the French frontier and have implicitly obeyed this order everywhere. On the other hand, yesterday, in spite of the assurance of the ten-kilometer zone, French troops had already crossed the German frontier at Altmunsterol and by the mountain road in the Vosges, and are still on German territory. A French aviator, who must have flown across Belgian territory, was shot down yesterday in an attempt to wreck the railroad at Wesel. Several other French airplanes were unquestionably placed over the Eifel district yesterday. These, also, must have flown over Belgian territory. Yesterday, French airmen dropped bombs on the railroads near Karlsruhe and Nuremberg.

---

[735] Ibid.

[736] G.D. 731, Lichnowsky to German Foreign Office. After Paris protested to Schoen about an alleged German border incursion, Schoen alerted Berlin: "Feeling very much excited here (in Paris) as a result of this and other reports." G.D. 705, Schoen to German Foreign Office, August 2.

[737] Bethmann-Hollweg later wrote: "We had no choice but to declare war on France. And thereby we made ourselves appear as the aggressor..............I do not think that we could have avoided being forced into this position. The rapidity of the military decisions to which we were constrained by the Russian mobilization neither allowed us to adopt a passive strategy with respect to France, nor admitted of time for diplomatic transactions for the improvement of our political position." Bethmann-Hollweg, *Reflections*, 145-46.

Thus, France has forced us into a state of war. I request Your Excellency to communicate the foregoing to the French Government at six o'clock this afternoon, to demand your passports, and to leave, after turning over affairs to the American Embassy. [738]

The long-feared Franco-Russian war against the Central Powers - one that would kill millions - was now a terrible fact. The only remaining question was whether any other countries would enter it.

---

[738] G.D. 734.

X

THE ITALIAN WILD CARD

A. A Deal between Vienna and Rome?

In Chapter VII, we examined the Central Powers' efforts to secure Italy's support. Berlin had pressured Berchtold to offer Rome concessions. The furthest Berchtold would go was his half-baked proposal of the 28th to consider compensation if (1) Austria permanently occupied Serbian territory and (2) Rome had maintained a "friendly attitude" towards Austria during the crisis. Italy declined it.

Rome's rebuff did not surprise Bethmann-Hollweg. He told Tschirschky that Vienna's offer "can scarcely satisfy Italy." [739] Desperate for Rome's backing, Berlin again implored Austria to act. Szogyeny telegraphed Berchtold on the 30th that Germany wanted Vienna to

> interpret most liberally Article VII.............and to meet Italy's wishes as concerns the question of compensation as much as possible, and to declare as soon as possible our readiness at once to enter upon negotiations regarding the interpretation of Article VII (with a view to the most far-reaching concessions), admitting at the same time our liability to grant compensation. [740]

Berlin believed that Italian support was still attainable for the right price. After all, while San Giuliano was irritated with

---

[739] G.D. 361.

[740] Quoted in Geiss, *July 1914*, 303 (parentheses in original).

Vienna, he had not ruled out intervention. As Flotow told Berlin on the 30th:

> Marquis di San Giuliano makes no concealment of the fact that he considers Austria's procedure against Serbia a war of aggression, and that therefore Italy is not bound by the Triple Alliance compact to take part in a general world war resulting from this war. Even the violation of Article 7 of the treaty, he says, frees Italy of any obligation to go in. To my contentions against this point of view, he always stubbornly replies: *'I am not saying that Italy will not finally take part.* I am only stating that she is not *obliged* to take part.' [741]

Merey urged Berchtold to make no further concessions. He felt that Rome was simply blackmailing Austria. [742] Berchtold agreed. He had no interest in sweetening his July 28 offer. And the detachment of any part of the Habsburg Empire (e.g., the Trentino) was absolutely out of the question. The Austrian embassy in Berlin told the Germans:

> Count Berchtold............is under the impression that among many in authority in Italy, compensation at the expense of our territories with Italian populations, especially the Trentino, is what is in mind. Count Berchtold states most emphatically, in regard to this, that the question of the separation of any part whatsoever of the Monarchy must not even be placed in discussion. [743]

Yet Berlin kept hounding Vienna. Tschirschky stressed to Berchtold on the 31st that "it was Austria's duty at this moment to

---

[741] G.D. 419, Flotow to German Foreign Office (emphasis added in next-to-last sentence; emphasis in original in last sentence).
[742] Merey to Berchtold, July 31, in D.D., A.R.B. II, Document No. 18. Flotow informed Berlin that Merey "is violently opposed to any concession to Italy, and had yesterday a sharp verbal clash with Marquis di San Giuliano." G.D. 419.
[743] G.D. 428, Austro-Hungarian embassy in Berlin to German Foreign Office, July 30.

bind Italy unconditionally to us by the greatest concessions." [744] Whether he finally recognized the serious consequences for the Central Powers if Rome remained neutral or he simply wanted to quiet Berlin, Berchtold reconsidered his prior proposal. He told the Cabinet Council on the 31st that he had previously instructed Merey "to reply to (Italy's) demands..............(with) vague phrases and to continue insisting..........(that) territorial aggrandizement was quite beyond our intentions; if, however, we............(had) to undertake a non-temporary occupation, there would then still be time to approach the question of compensation." [745] Since Berlin obviously wanted Vienna to do better, the Council authorized Berchtold "on principle to promise Italy a compensation in the eventuality of a lasting occupation of Serbian territories on our part, and to speak of the relinquishment of Valona (in Albania) to Italy, if circumstances should demand it and Italy actually fulfills its duties as an ally." [746]

That same day, Berchtold met with the Duke of Avarna. With Tschirschky's assistance, the two arrived at the following understanding regarding compensation:

> If...........Austria-Hungary should be compelled by the force of circumstances to make territorial acquisitions in the Balkan Peninsula, especially in Serbia and Montenegro, the (Austrian) Government stands ready to come to an agreement with Italy upon the compensation to be awarded the latter, whether Italy lends her assistance to Austria in case of the occurrence of the *casus foederis* as provided by the treaty, or whether she grants her assistance without the occurrence of the *casus foederis*. This declaration contains the very substance of the interpretation which Italy gives to Article 7 and which I (Berchtold) am prepared to concede to Italy, even though I myself do not agree with that interpretation. [747]

---

[744] G.D. 510, Tschirschky to German Foreign Office, July 31.

[745] Quoted in Geiss, *July 1914*, 322.

[746] Quoted in ibid. San Giuliano told Flotow that Italy was not interested in Valona. G.D. 566, Flotow to German Foreign Office, August 1.

[747] G.D. 573, Tschirschky to German Foreign Office, August 1.

Tschirschky notified Berlin of his apparent diplomatic coup:

> Count Berchtold will immediately notify Rome that, in view of existing conditions, he accepts Article 7 according to the Italian interpretation. (Berchtold), to whose attention I sharply called the fact that I had for weeks been pointing out to him in the most urgent manner the importance of this matter, and that I had requested him, again and again, to bring it to a conclusion, as there was danger in delay, argued that it was yesterday that the Duke d'Avarna had for the first time discussed the question with him. It was also yesterday that, with my cooperation, Count Berchtold's declaration was drafted............Italy would have, in consequence, no right to claim that her wishes were being disregarded. [748]

He also crowed to his superiors that after he secured Avarna's written statement that the planned declaration was acceptable, "a complete understanding has been reached here within 24 hours." [749] Berchtold thought so, too. He wired Merey: "I hope that this question may now be considered as settled............Please inform (San Giuliano) immediately of the foregoing (agreement) and point out to him that we now confidently expect Italy to carry out her obligations as an ally." [750]

But Tschirschky and Berchtold were mistaken for several reasons. First, the understanding was between Vienna and *Avarna*, not the Italian government as a whole. The Central Powers should have realized that Rome's approval was needed. Second, Berchtold's latest proposal was not much better than his first. True, he now *promised* compensation as opposed to merely

---

[748] G.D. 577, Tschirschky to German Foreign Office, August 1.

[749] G.D. 573.

[750] D.D., A.R.B. II, Document No. 19, July 31. In a message to Italy's King Victor Emmanuel III, Franz Josef praised the apparent compensation agreement: "We owe 30 years of peace and prosperity to the treaty which unites us, and I am gratified that our Governments fully agree on its interpretation. At this solemn hour, I am happy to be able to count upon the support of my Allies and their gallant armies, and I cherish the heartiest wishes for the success of our arms and for a glorious future of our countries." D.D., A.R.B. II, Document No. 21, August 1.

agreeing to consider it. And he no longer restricted compensation to *permanent* occupations of Serbian territory. However, Vienna (1) did not explicitly agree to immediate negotiations regarding compensation and (2) did not offer specific concessions. This may have been acceptable to Avarna but not San Giuliano.

B. Italy Declares Her Neutrality

The biggest reason, though, was that unbeknownst to Tschirschky and Berchtold, Italy planned to announce her neutrality! Flotow wired the devastating news to Berlin at 11:45 p.m. on the 31st:

> The local Government has discussed, at the Ministerial Council held today, the question of Italy's attitude in the war. Marquis San Giuliano told me that the Italian Government had considered the question thoroughly, and had again come to the conclusion that Austria's procedure against Serbia must be regarded as an act of aggression, and that consequently a *casus foederis*, according to the terms of the Triple Alliance treaty, did not exist. Therefore, Italy would have to declare herself neutral.

> Upon my violently opposing this point of view, the Minister went on to state that since Italy had not been informed in advance of Austria's procedure against Serbia, she could with less reason be expected to take part in the war, as Italian interests were being directly injured by the Austrian proceeding. All that he could say to me now was that the local Government reserved the right to determine whether it might be possible for Italy to intervene later on behalf of the allies, if, at the time of doing so, Italian interests should be satisfactorily protected.

> The Minister, who was in a state of great excitement, said in explanation that the entire Ministerial Council, with the exception of himself, had shown a distinct dislike for Austria. It had been all the more difficult for him to

contest this feeling because Austria, as I myself knew, was continuing so persistently with a recognized injury to Italian interests as to violate Article 7 of the Triple Alliance treaty, and because she was declining to give a guaranty for the independence and integrity of Serbia. He regretted that the (German) Government had not done more to intervene in this connection to persuade Austria to a timely compliance.

I have the impression that it is not yet necessary to give up all hope for the future here if the Italians should be met halfway with regard to the demands mentioned above or, in other words, if compensation should be offered them.............In the meanwhile, I pointed out to the Minister in the plainest manner possible the extremely regrettable impression which such an attitude would make on us, and then called to his attention the consequences which might develop for Italy in the future as a result. [751]

Along with the compensation issue, factors in Italy's decision thus included (1) the aggressive nature of Austria's action, (2) the threat to Italy's Balkan interests, and (3) Vienna's failure to forewarn Rome of its plans. Another factor, though, was Italy's lack of desire for war. Italian officials had serious concerns about the country's internal and external security should Rome fight alongside the Central Powers. Knowing the Italian population had no interest in shedding blood for Austria, the government feared a revolution. [752] Militarily, Italy's long coastline and weak navy

---

[751] G.D. 534, Flotow to German Foreign Office.

[752] G.D. 566; Z.A.B. Zeman, *The Gentleman Negotiators: A Diplomatic History of the First World War* (New York: The Macmillan Company, 1971), 7. Flotow told Berlin that San Giuliano's concerns about Italy's internal situation had some basis: "(San Giuliano) said in reply to my reproaches that he would tell me in strict confidence that, according to consistent and well-founded reports, the Italian Government would have a revolution on its hands if it took part in the war. It must be admitted that the danger cannot be entirely denied. Conditions here during the past year have become very serious." G.D. 675, Flotow to German Foreign Office, August 2. On the 3rd, Flotow forwarded to Berlin a note from Germany's special envoy to Victor Emmanuel outlining the latter's concerns about Italian public opinion: "The King replied to me (the envoy) that personally he was

would leave her seaside cities exposed to British naval bombardment should England intervene. [753] And an Entente naval blockade would cut her off from most seaborne trade and from Libya, her prize colony. [754] Simply put, the terrible price Italy might pay was hardly worth what little Vienna was offering.

Of course, Italy made her decision reluctantly. Her leaders had desperately wanted the crisis to end peacefully so they would not be faced with two very bad options – going to war or infuriating their allies. And the Central Powers were indeed livid. The Kaiser labeled Italy's King Victor Emmanuel III a "scoundrel." [755] He told Franz Josef that Victor Emmanuel "shamefully betrayed our trust and has failed to fulfill the obligations of his alliance." [756] Merey said that if Italy remained neutral throughout the war, Vienna and Berlin should kick her out of the Triple Alliance once hostilities ended. [757]

---

wholeheartedly with us, and a few weeks ago had not doubted for a moment that Italy would lend her allies her faithful assistance in the event of war. The incredible awkwardness of Austria during the past few weeks, however, had acted upon Italian sensibilities and so turned public opinion against Austria that to take the part of Austria at the present time would precipitate a storm. The Ministry did not want to risk a rebellion. He, the King, had, unfortunately, merely influence, but no power............Italy's refusal (to enter the war) on account of Austria's stupidity was also a refusal as far as regarded Germany, a fact that pained him, the King, deeply." G.D. 771, Flotow to German Foreign Office.

[753] See Zeman, *Gentleman Negotiators*, 4; G.D. 614, Flotow to German Foreign Office, August 1.

[754] G.D. 614; Mark Thompson, *The White War: Life and Death on the Italian Front, 1915-1919* (New York: Basic Books, 2009), 23.

[755] Marginal comment of Wilhelm on G.D. 614.

[756] G.D. 766, August 2. At least one Italian official feared that Italy's decision would tarnish her image. Hans von Wangenheim, Germany's ambassador to Turkey, had the following conversation with his Italian counterpart in Constantinople: "When I (Wangenheim) took Marquis Garroni sharply to task today on account of Italy's attitude, my colleague attempted at first, as its ambassador, to make excuses for his Government, but then told me in his private capacity that he most strongly disapproved of San Giuliano's conduct and had already told him so by telegraph. Italy's refusal, he said, might become a blot on Italy's national honor that could never be wiped out." G.D. 815, Wangenheim to German Foreign Office, August 3.

[757] G.D. 760, Austro-Hungarian embassy in Berlin to German Foreign Office, August 3.

Still, despite their anger, the Central Powers continued discussions with Rome. Bethmann-Hollweg, for instance, forwarded reports of French border violations to Flotow. He instructed him to "convince (San Giuliano) that these provocations.............(constitute) an aggression by our enemies," thereby triggering Rome's alliance obligations. [758] Vienna and Berlin also retained hope that Rome would eventually accept Berchtold's revised offer, though San Giuliano told Merey on the 2nd:

> His (San Giuliano's) first impression was not favorable because (Austria) had laid down conditions; (the offer) would be nothing more than one link in the chain, and the question of Italy's participation in the war or of her neutrality would not be decided solely by a satisfactory settlement of this matter. [759]

The next day, San Giuliano was blunter. In an ugly conversation with Flotow, he actually predicted the Habsburg Empire's annihilation:

> Marquis di San Giuliano takes the position that these acts of France do not constitute a *casus foederis*, since they are nothing but the consequences of Austria's first aggressive act. My (Flotow's) discussion of the subject with him reached a point of such acrimony that its continuance seems doubtful. He accuses us of having planned the whole matter with Austria in advance, in order to place Italy before a *fait accompli*. But it is impossible to involve a Great Power in such a conflict without consulting with it in advance. We should now have to bear the consequences of Italy's unwillingness to allow herself to be caught napping. She was not even allowed the time, he says, to make the necessary military preparations. The country could not allow itself to be exposed to the attacks of England and France in such manner. And then there was also the great peril of the internal situation. We should see,

---

[758] G.D. 694, August 2.
[759] Merey to Berchtold, August 2, in D.D., A.R.B. II, Document No. 25.

he said, what would become of Austria in this struggle; she would emerge from it a corpse, incapable of further existence. She would be utterly destroyed..........

Mr. von Kleist (German special envoy to Victor Emmanuel) reports that His Majesty the King expressed the best of intentions, but stated that he could not act in opposition to his ministers. Austria's chief mistake was, he said, that she did not make an offer of compensation in time.

(San Giuliano) replied to the Austrian Ambassador with reference to the communication concerning Article 7, that Austria-Hungary's conditional declaration about Article 7 was insufficient, and did not actually contain any offer of compensation at all...............In his discussions with Marquis di San Giuliano, the arguments of the Austrian Ambassador, with whom I am cooperating throughout, have already reached a point of extreme sharpness. It is his opinion also that the internal situation, England, and the compensation question are the causes of the determination arrived at here. [760]

Tensions were now so high that Flotow believed the Central Powers should step back, hold their tongues, and try to stay on decent terms with Italy. Otherwise, they might kill any chance of ultimately securing her support. They even risked driving her into the Entente camp. Flotow told Berlin:

(I)t might be better to avoid an open break here (in Rome) for a while............and (I) will adapt my attitude, which has now reached a point of extreme bluntness, towards this end. To judge from some of Marquis di San Giuliano's hints, it must also be considered that in the final event it is not impossible that Italy might align herself *against* Austria. [761]

---

[760] G.D. 745, Flotow to German Foreign Office, August 3.
[761] G.D. 748, Flotow to German Foreign Office, August 3 (emphasis added).

The Central Powers' failure to resolve the Italian question prior to the ultimatum was a wretched blunder. If, well before the 23rd, Vienna had notified Rome of its plans and offered large-scale concessions, the Austro-German pact could have confirmed Italy's attitude early on. Had Rome declined the offer, Austria – knowing that Italy's support was not forthcoming - could have taken a more moderate line towards Serbia rather than one destined to ignite a European war. Conversely, a pre-ultimatum compensation agreement would have put Austria in a powerful position. She could have faced Russia with Germany *and* Italy firmly at her side. This might have made St. Petersburg more reluctant to intervene. Yet by keeping Italy in the dark for weeks, the Central Powers lacked her support when the crisis escalated on and after the 28th. The Kaiser wrote on August 5: "Vienna must under all circumstances make binding promises and offer big compensation, which will be so alluring that they will work. This should have been done long ago." [762]

He was right.

---

[762] Marginal comment of Wilhelm on G.D. 850, Flotow to German Foreign Office, August 4.

XI

ANGUISHED MONARCH

A. Old King Carol of Romania

Romania had been secretly allied with the Central Powers since 1883. Like the situation between Vienna and Rome, however, the Austro-Romanian relationship had tensions. They stemmed largely from the Hungarian government's oppression of its minority Romanian population in Transylvania, a Habsburg territory bordering Romania. [763]

Franz Ferdinand's death had upset many Romanians. [764] Not only had he shared their antipathy towards Hungary, but also his suggestion of a multi-state Habsburg Empire could have resulted in greater autonomy for the Transylvanian Romanians. [765] This, in turn, might have led to Transylvania's eventual incorporation into Romania. [766] The union of all Romanians (the "Greater Romania" concept) was the country's dream. [767] But with the Archduke gone, the dream appeared dead. The Transylvanian issue was so important to Romania that Vienna's ambassador to Bucharest, Ottokar von Czernin, viewed the Austro-Romanian alliance as "nothing but a scrap of paper." [768]

---

[763] Bucharest's pact with the Central Powers was kept secret because the Romanian people would never have accepted an alliance with the Hungarians. Albertini, *Origins,* 3:549.

[764] Czernin, *In the World War*, 91.

[765] Ibid.

[766] See ibid.

[767] Ibid.

[768] Ibid., 86.

Still, Vienna in 1914 was arguably on better terms with Bucharest than with Rome. This was primarily because of Romania's King Carol I. Carol staunchly supported the pact with the Central Powers, for he (1) had blood ties to Germany, (2) admired her military might, and (3) believed that the Triple Alliance would win any war against Russia and France. [769] Berlin and Vienna, in return, greatly respected Carol. Nonetheless, as with Italy, they did not alert him of Vienna's plans regarding Serbia. [770] The ultimatum therefore stunned Carol. Czernin later wrote:

> Like a rock standing in the angry sea of hatred, poor old King Carol was alone with his German sympathies. I had been instructed to read the ultimatum to him the moment it was sent to Belgrade, and never shall I forget the impression it made on the old King when he heard it. He, wise old politician that he was, recognized at once the immeasurable possibilities of such a step, and before I had finished reading the document he interrupted me, exclaiming, 'It will be a world war.' It was long before he could collect himself.......... [771]

Carol was in a quandary. Though dismayed at having been blindsided like this, he wanted to support his allies. Yet how could he, considering the Romanian populace's anti-Hungarian sentiments and its anger over the ultimatum? Indeed, Czernin recalled:

> Genuine and simulated indignation (in Romania) at the tone of the ultimatum was the order of the day, and the universal conclusion arrived at was: Austria has gone mad. Men and women with whom I had been on a perfectly friendly footing for the last year suddenly became bitter enemies. [772]

---

[769] See Albertini, *Origins,* 3:570, 572.
[770] This was undoubtedly to avoid leaking Austria's intentions.
[771] Czernin, *In the World War,* 92.
[772] Ibid.

Romanian public opinion was not Carol's only problem. As a constitutional monarch, he could not compel his government to side with the Central Powers. And Prime Minister Joan Bratianu and other top officials were disinclined to militarily support Austria for several reasons. First, the Austro-Romanian treaty (1913 version) stated:

> Should Romania, without any kind of provocation on her part, be attacked, Austria-Hungary is bound to render her timely assistance and support against the aggressor. If Austria-Hungary should under similar circumstances be attacked in any part of her territories bordering on Romania, then that fact shall at once constitute a *casus foederis* for the latter. [773]

By the 31st, Russia, through her mobilization, was clearly threatening Austria. However, some Romanian officials felt that Vienna's actions against Serbia had provoked Russia; therefore, Romania's treaty obligations were not triggered. [774] Second, aligning with the Austro-German pact would expose Romania to a massive Russian attack. [775] This danger was made worse because Romania would simultaneously need to maintain forces along her southern border to guard against a possible assault from Bulgaria, her foe from the Second Balkan War. Only part of Romania's army would thus be free to face Russia. Third, it would obviously be very hard to convince the Romanian people to fight alongside the Hungarians.

Carol recognized the obstacles he faced. He discussed his dilemma with Heinrich von Waldburg, Berlin's *charge d'affaires* at Bucharest. Waldburg wired Berlin on the 30th that Carol "was trying to prepare public opinion here for a possible war on Russia,

---

[773] Carnegie Endowment, *German Documents Collected by Karl Kautsky,* 613. See also Schmitt, *Coming,* 418-19.

[774] Albertini, *Origins,* 3:573-75; Gerard Silberstein, *The Troubled Alliance: German-Austrian Relations, 1914 to 1917* (Lexington, KY: University Press of Kentucky, 1970), 39.

[775] Bucharest also feared that Russia's navy would bombard Romania's port city of Constanta. Schmitt, *Coming,* 422.

but kept constantly referring to the great difficulties in the way of his living up to the obligations of his alliance." [776]

In attempting to secure Bucharest's support, the Central Powers used several approaches. One involved Bulgaria. Romania remained nervous about a potential Bulgarian attack. [777] To calm Bucharest, Jagow telegraphed Waldburg on the 28th:

> Kindly inform King Carol and Mr. Bratianu that the Bulgarian Government has given Count Berchtold the most binding assurances that it will remain strictly neutral. Neither, according to the reports of the Imperial Minister at Sofia, are there any plans in existence in Bulgaria directed against Romania. Thus, in this matter, there should be no occasion for worry. [778]

Another approach involved arguing that the Central Powers were acting in self-defense. On the 2nd, Bethmann-Hollweg instructed Berlin's ambassador to Romania, Julius von Waldthausen, to tell Bucharest: "We have been forced into war with Russia by the behavior of Russia...............We request the immediate mobilization of the Romanian army and its advance against Russia." [779] In a similar vein, Wilhelm told Carol:

> Since the ruthless deed at Sarajevo, our venerable friend and ally, the Emperor Franz Josef, has demanded atonement from Serbia. Russia, which lays claim to the hegemony of the Balkans, by defending Serbia, adopts as her own the latter's efforts towards the undermining of the Austrian Monarchy. Nor can I shut my eyes to the fact that the Pan-Slavist tendencies have for their purpose, with the destruction of the Danube Monarchy, the dissolution of

---

[776] G.D. 463, Waldburg to German Foreign Office.
[777] See Albertini, *Origins,* 3:559-60.
[778] G.D. 316. Some Habsburg officials had considered bringing Bulgaria into the Triple Alliance to offset the sinking Austro-Romanian relationship. Czernin, *In the World War,* 83, 88; Schmitt, *Coming,* 419. But the idea floundered; Vienna feared that such a move would alienate Romania and drive her into Russia's arms. Czernin, *In the World War,* 88.
[779] G.D. 646, August 2.

the Triple Alliance and the isolation and enfeeblement of Germany, in order to stabilize the domination of Russia over all of southeastern Europe. Fidelity to the alliance, honor and self-preservation force me to the side of Austria.

At this grave hour, my thoughts hasten to you, who have created a civilized nation in Europe's Eastern Marches and thereby erected a dam against the Slavic flood. I trust that.............you will stand faithfully by your friend and unconditionally fulfill the obligations of your alliance. [780]

Yet another approach consisted of enticements. Bessarabia, a Russian territory bordering Romania, contained a predominantly Romanian population. [781] Jagow wired Waldburg on the 31st: "Should war with Russia prove unavoidable, the (German) Government would, in the event of a favorable outcome, guarantee that Romania should receive Bessarabia as a reward for the fulfillment of her alliance obligations and for active participation in the war on our side." [782]

But Bratianu still did not favor Romanian intervention. Waldburg telegraphed Berlin:

(Bratianu) referred to the difficulties in connection with popular sentiment, which was absolutely hostile to Austria. He insisted, however, that he would do everything possible to carry out the obligations of the alliance. Bratianu desires that the Romanians in Transylvania should be given certain assurances on the part of Hungary to the effect that after the war they would be granted greater rights. With regard to Bessarabia, Bratianu stated that it would only be of value to Romania in the event that Russia had to surrender further territories also to Austria and to Germany, and should become so

---

[780] G.D. 472, July 31.
[781] Schmitt, *Coming*, 418.
[782] G.D. 506.

weakened that that province would actually remain a possession of Romania permanently. [783]

Now, Bratianu does state that Romania would try to fulfill her treaty obligations. Yet considering his desire to maintain decent relations with Germany, what else was he going to say? Moreover, he greatly qualified his remark by effectively stating that (1) Romanian public opinion would make intervention difficult and (2) Bessarabia was an insufficient inducement. In short, none of Berlin's assurances, pleas, or offers had changed Bratianu's mind.

Things were obviously working against Carol. But he would have one more chance to convince his ministers that Romania should back the Central Powers.

B. Romania Decides Not to Intervene

The August 3 Crown Council meeting was contentious. Speaking first, Carol outlined Romania's options: (1) alignment with Russia, (2) alignment with the Austro-German pact, or (3) neutrality. [784] Regarding the first alternative, Sazonov had agreed to support Romania's acquisition of Transylvania should she side with Russia. [785] Yet Carol would never go for this. He would rather abdicate than turn against the Central Powers. Even Bratianu recognized that such a sudden and complete break with Berlin and Vienna would be too drastic a step. It could also lead to a crushing Austro-German military strike on Romania. [786] Alignment with St. Petersburg was therefore ruled out.

Concerning the other options, Carol contended that Romania's honor dictated that she uphold her alliance

---

[783] G.D. 582, Waldburg to German Foreign Office, August 1. Tisza refused to consider concessions regarding Transylvania. Schmitt, *Coming,* 423. He was determined to maintain the Magyars' stranglehold on Hungary's minorities. He also felt that appeasing Romania would make Austria look weak: "Everything we have won in prestige by our firm attitude towards Serbia will be lost if we let ourselves be intimidated by Romania." Quoted in ibid.

[784] Ibid., 427.

[785] Albertini, *Origins,* 3:569.

[786] Ibid., 3:573-74; Silberstein, *Troubled Alliance,* 180-81.

obligations. [787] He added that remaining neutral would shut Romania out of the post-war division of spoils; since the Central Powers would likely win the war, Bucharest should side with them. [788] Peter Carp, a former prime minister, seconded Carol's pleas, arguing vehemently for intervention. [789]

No one else did.

Bratianu and the others favoring non-intervention remained worried about Romanian public opinion and the country's vulnerability to a Russian attack. [790] They also argued that Austria's provocation of Russia and failure to consult Bucharest before the 23rd negated any obligation to aid her. [791] One minister, John Lahovary, questioned whether the Central Powers would defeat Russia and France, especially considering Italy's probable neutrality. [792] Carp grew testy, accusing Bratianu of using public opinion as an excuse to avoid backing Austria and Germany. [793] But Bratianu and his supporters held firm.

What was Carol to do? Bulow later described the monarch's agonizing plight:

> King Carol, who, throughout his whole reign, had considered it the first of his duties to give Germany and Austria his support in the event of any general conflagration, was put in such a position that this was impossible.............Without ever having been duly warned or given any reasoned line of argument, the old, wise, and dignified King Carol was brusquely required to aid us in a war which looked as though it would spread all over the world.............The king's dilemma was as follows: after nearly 50 years on the throne, he must

---

[787] Schmitt, *Coming*, 427.

[788] Ibid.; Albertini, *Origins,* 3:572. Carol liked the Central Powers' chances even without Italy's armed support. Albertini, *Origins,* 3:572-73. However, he did not believe that England would intervene. Ibid., 3:572. This no doubt influenced his opinion that the Austro-German pact would win.

[789] Ibid., 3:573.

[790] Ibid., 3:573-75; Silberstein, *Troubled Alliance,* 38.

[791] Albertini, *Origins,* 3:573-75; Silberstein, *Troubled Alliance,* 39.

[792] Albertini, *Origins,* 3:573.

[793] Ibid., 3:574.

abdicate and leave his adopted country, or else…………betray the country of his birth. [794]

After asking the group to vote and finding sentiment nearly unanimous for non-intervention, Carol brokenheartedly acceded to his ministers' wishes. [795] He warned them, however, that they would regret their decision. [796]

The next day, Waldthausen wired Berlin:

> After a heated appeal from the King to put the treaty into effect, the Crown Council declared by a unanimous vote, with one exception, that no party could take the responsibility for such action. The Crown Council decided that since Romania had neither been advised nor taken into consultation concerning the Austro-Hungarian *demarche* at Belgrade, no *casus foederis* existed. [797]

Reading this, the Kaiser vented: "Our allies (Romania and Italy) are already before the war falling away from us like rotten apples! A total collapse of both German and Austrian foreign diplomacy. This should and could have been avoided." [798]

As a whole, though, the Central Powers did not view Bucharest's decision with the same bitterness that they did Rome's. [799] They knew that the alliance was more with Carol than with Romania. The situation was not a total loss, either. Romania would still serve as a partial buffer state between eastern Austria-Hungary and Russia. More importantly, the Austro-German pact

---

[794] Bulow, *Memoirs,* 189-90.
[795] Albertini, *Origins,* 3:574.
[796] Ibid.
[797] G.D. 811, Waldthausen to German Foreign Office, August 4. At Carol's insistence, Romania did not formally proclaim her neutrality. Albertini, *Origins,* 3:575-76. He likely feared that a neutrality declaration would imply that Romania was abandoning her alliance with the Central Powers. Bucharest simply said that there was no *casus foederis.* G.D. 811.
[798] Marginal comment of Wilhelm on G.D. 811.
[799] Indeed, Jagow wired Waldthausen on the 4th: "Please tell Mr. Bratianu, while thanking him for the information, that we regard (Bucharest's) attitude there as in agreement with our friendly relations, and hope for Romania's active cooperation later." G.D. 847.

could rest assured in August 1914 that Romania would never side with Russia so long as Carol was alive.

Two months later, he would be dead.

XII

NIGHTMARE

A. England Gives France an Assurance of Naval Support

Having learned of Austria's willingness to hold discussions with St. Petersburg, Grey retained hope that war could be avoided. On the 1st, the British embassy in Berlin told German officials: "Sir Edward Grey still believes that it might be possible to secure peace if only a little respite in time could be gained before war is begun by one of the Great Powers……………Whilst Russia and Austria are ready to converse, he says, matters ought not to be hopeless." [800] Similarly, Grey instructed Buchanan to "inform (Sazonov)…………that, if in the consideration of the acceptance of mediation by Austria, Russia can agree to stop mobilization, it appears still to be possible to preserve peace." [801] Although his chances of success seemed slim, Grey was determined to see his peacekeeping efforts through to the end.

He also continued to rebuff Paris's pleas for England to side with the Franco-Russian alliance. Talking with Paul Cambon on the 1st, Grey disputed the ambassador's assertion that London was obligated to aid France:

> M. Cambon today…………urged upon me (Grey) very strongly our obligation to help France if she was attacked by Germany. He even said that, for the sake of public opinion in England, France had drawn her forces back

---

[800] G.D. 595, British embassy to German Foreign Office.
[801] B.D. 422, August 1.

from her German frontier, so that she was now in a position to take only the defensive, and not the offensive, against Germany. She had concentrated her fleet in the Mediterranean and had left her northern and western coasts exposed. I said that as long as we did not give Germany any promise of our neutrality - and as a matter of fact we had hitherto definitely refused to give such a promise - the French might be sure that the German fleet would not pass through the Channel, for fear that we should take the opportunity of intervening when the German fleet would be at our mercy............

As to the question of our obligation to help France, I pointed out that we had no obligation. France did not wish to join in the war that seemed about to break out, but she was obliged to join in it because of her alliance. We had purposely kept clear of all alliances in order that we might not be involved in difficulties in this way. I had assured Parliament again and again that our hands were free. It was most unreasonable to say that because France had an obligation under an alliance of which we did not even know the terms, therefore we were bound equally with her - by the obligation in that alliance - to be involved in war.

M. Cambon admitted that there was no obligation of this kind, but he urged very strongly the obligation of British interests. If we did not help France, the Entente would disappear; and, whether victory came to Germany or to France and Russia, our situation at the end of the war would be very uncomfortable. I admitted the force of this, but I said that it was for us to consider the point of what British interests required, and to deal with it in Parliament. [802]

---

[802] B.D. 447, Grey to Bertie, August 1. Lloyd George later wrote of France's alliance obligations: "Had Germany without any provocation attacked France, I have no doubt that public sentiment in this country would have demanded that the Government should go to the aid of the victim of such wanton aggression. But it was thoroughly understood that on this occasion

Grey did, however, agree to ask the Cabinet whether it would authorize Britain's defense of France's Channel coast against the German navy. [803] This was vitally important to France because, as Cambon mentioned, her fleet was concentrated in the Mediterranean.

The following day, Grey wired Bertie:

> After the Cabinet (meeting) this morning, I gave M. Cambon the following *aide-mémoire*:
>
> 'I am authorized to give an assurance that if the German fleet comes into the Channel or through the North Sea to undertake hostile operations against French coasts or shipping, the British fleet will give all the protection in its power. This assurance is, of course, subject to the policy of His Majesty's Government receiving the support of Parliament and must not be taken as binding His Majesty's Government to take any action until the above contingency of action by the German fleet takes place.'
>
> I pointed out that we had very large questions and most difficult issues to consider, and that the Government felt that they could not bind themselves to declare war upon Germany necessarily if war broke out between France and Germany tomorrow. But it was essential to the French Government, whose fleet had long been concentrated in the Mediterranean, to know how to make their dispositions with their north coast entirely undefended. We therefore thought it necessary to give them this assurance. It did not bind us to go to war with Germany unless the German fleet took the action indicated, but it did give a security to France that would enable her to settle the disposition of her own Mediterranean fleet. [804]

As Grey indicated, Britain was not promising to fight alongside France and Russia. Still, as Winston Churchill later

---

France was drawn into the quarrel by her treaty obligations with Russia." Lloyd George, *War Memoirs,* 40.

[803] B.D. 447; B.D. 426.

[804] B.D. 487, August 2.

explained: "Could we, when it came to the point, honorably stand by and see the naked French coasts ravaged and bombarded by German dreadnoughts under the eyes and within gunshot of our main fleet?" The Cabinet had answered "no." [805]

There remained, to be sure, some division within Britain's leadership. Asquith wrote in his diary on the 1st: "I am still not quite hopeless about peace, though far from hopeful, but if it comes to war I feel sure that we shall have a split in the Cabinet." [806] The next day, he penned:

> We had a long Cabinet (meeting) from 11 till nearly 2, which very soon revealed that we are on the brink of a split. We agreed at last with some difficulty that Grey should be authorized to tell Cambon that our fleet would not allow the German fleet to make the Channel a base of hostile operations. John Burns at once resigned, but was persuaded to hold on at any rate till the evening when we meet again. There is a strong party against any kind of intervention in any event..............I suppose a good number of our own party in the House of Commons are for absolute non-interference. [807]

Notwithstanding this anti-intervention faction, however, England's naval guarantee to Paris signified a weakening in her heretofore non-committal stance.

B. Lichnowsky Remains Guardedly Optimistic about British Neutrality

We saw earlier how Jagow refused to promise London that Germany would respect Belgium's neutrality. Lichnowsky reported Grey's reaction in this August 1 note, on which the Kaiser scribbled a number of insulting comments:

---

[805] Jagow wired Lichnowsky on the 3rd: "There will be no threatening of the northern coast of France on our part so long as England remains neutral." G.D. 714.

[806] Quoted in Asquith, *Memories*, 11.

[807] Quoted in ibid., 12.

Sir E. Grey has just read to me (Lichnowsky) the following statement, which was unanimously drawn up by the Cabinet: 'The reply of the German Government with regard to the neutrality of Belgium is a matter of very great regret, because the neutrality of Belgium does affect feeling in this country. If Germany could see her way to give the same positive reply as that which has been given by France, it would materially contribute to relieve anxiety and tension here, while on the other hand, if there were a violation of the neutrality of Belgium by one combatant while the other respected it, it would be extremely difficult to restrain public feeling in this country.' *(Kaiser: "This drivel of Grey's shows that he absolutely does not know what he is to do.")*

To my question whether he could give me a definite declaration on the neutrality of Great Britain on the condition that we respected Belgian neutrality, the Minister replied that that would not be possible for him, though this question would play an important role in connection with public feeling here. Should we violate Belgian neutrality in a war with France, a reversal of public feeling would take place that would make it difficult for the Government here to adopt an attitude of friendly neutrality. For the present, there was not the slightest intention of proceeding to hostilities against us. *(Kaiser: "He lies! He told Lichnowsky so himself four days ago!")* But it would be difficult to draw a line beyond which we might not go without causing them on this side to step in.

He kept returning to the question of Belgian neutrality and stated that in any case this question would play an important role. He had also been wondering whether it would not be possible for us and France to remain facing each other under arms, without attacking each other, in the event of a Russian war. *(Kaiser: "The rascal is crazy or an idiot!")*................

My impression as a whole is that if it is possible in any way, they want here to keep out of the war, but that (Berlin's reply) concerning Belgian neutrality has caused an unfavorable impression. *(Kaiser: "My impression is that Mr. Grey is a false dog who is afraid of his own cheapness and false policy, but who will not come out into the open against us, preferring to let himself be forced by us to do it.")* [808]

Putting aside Wilhelm's habit of using terms such as "liar," "idiot," and "dog" to describe his perceived adversaries ("swine" was another of his favorites), the crux of Lichnowsky's telegram was that the Belgian issue was of monumental importance to London. In case Berlin failed to grasp this, Lichnowsky dispatched a stronger note at 9:10 a.m. on the 2nd:

Should we violate the neutrality of Belgium and a war with the Belgians were to result from it, I believe that the (British) Government would be unable to remain neutral much longer in the face of the storm that could then be expected from aroused local public opinion...........Since it is beginning to be believed here that a violation of Belgian neutrality is to be reckoned with, I think it not impossible that England will take a stand against us within a very short time. [809]

Yet Lichnowsky still did not view British intervention as a given. For days, he had strived to keep Germany on decent terms with London and felt that he was having success. After speaking with Asquith and Grey around midday on the 2nd, he sent the following message to Berlin at 1:23 p.m.; it sounded somewhat more upbeat than his 9:10 a.m. note:

I have succeeded so far in maintaining for us here a feeling that is friendly in the extreme, and I should like to utter an urgent warning against endangering this feeling by any sort of provocative measures. Among such I should

---

[808] G.D. 596, Lichnowsky to German Foreign Office.
[809] G.D. 641, Lichnowsky to German Foreign Office.

count first an attack by the German fleet on the northern coast of France, as well as any approach of our fleet into British waters. I am convinced that for the present, there is not the slightest intention of declaring war on us; that, to the contrary, they prefer first to await the course of events............

I have just called on the Premier (Asquith) and discussed our point of view with him exhaustively. Tears repeatedly stood in the eyes of the old gentleman, and he said to me: 'A war between our two countries is quite unthinkable.' I pointed out to him the great unity of our mutual interests, which had of late undergone so material an extension and development, and the impossibility of ever again knitting such confidential ties once the two countries had been at war. In order to weaken the chief argument of the English – that of having to protect France – I called his attention to the fact that it was really we who most needed protection, since we had to deal with two opponents and the French with only one. Should Great Britain remain out of the strife, she would be in a much stronger position to mediate as a neutral at the rehabilitation of peace than if she took part in a war which would then become a war of annihilation for the entire civilization of Europe.

Asquith replied that a war between England and Germany, in the present state of English public feeling, would be very unpopular, but that a neutral attitude on the part of the local Government would be greatly hindered by two things:

1. By the violation of the neutrality of Belgium, of which England was one of the guarantors. Gladstone had said in the year 1870 that the violation of the neutrality of Belgium would be for Great Britain a cause of war. In any case, there would then occur a serious reversal of public feeling.
2. By any attack by German warships on the totally unprotected northern coast of France, which the French, with a firm faith in British support, had

261

exposed for the benefit of their Mediterranean fleet. He would not say that even in such an event Great Britain would have to take a hand, but it would be made very difficult for the British Government to maintain the neutral attitude as planned for the present.

I have the distinct impression that England is holding back for the present out of regard for us, but I would urgently advise bearing in mind so far as possible the state of feeling here.

I have just talked again with Sir E. Grey before the session, and once more called most urgently to his attention the importance of not destroying for all time to come, our mutual cooperation, of late so fruitful. The Minister repeated that he could give me no definite assurances. But it was plain from his words that he would prefer to refrain from any intervention. We cannot conceal from ourselves, however, that the good intentions of the (British) Government, which undoubtedly exist, and the general pro-German feeling would, in the violation of Belgian neutrality, be put to a severe test - the outcome of which, as a matter of fact, should we win brilliant victories in France, or even press forward as far as Paris, would be a very doubtful one for us. [810]

So despite London's naval commitment to France, Lichnowsky continued to believe that English neutrality was attainable. [811] It was imperative, though, that Germany leave Belgium alone.

---

[810] G.D. 676.

[811] He even told Berlin that Britain's mobilization of her naval reserves "must not be taken as the final decision of the English Government to take an immediate part in the war. I believe that the attitude will be one of waiting for the present." G.D. 707, Lichnowsky to German Foreign Office, August 2.

C. Germany Gives Belgium an Ultimatum

Unfortunately for Lichnowsky, he had no control over Germany's military strategy. He could urge Berlin a thousand times to spare Belgium. But the plan of campaign in the West could not be so altered at this late stage. And this simple fact would wreck his diplomatic efforts.

On July 29, Jagow had sent the following message to Berlin's ambassador to Brussels, Klaus von Below-Saleske: "I respectfully request Your Excellency to keep the enclosure accompanying this dispatch safely locked up, and not to open it until you are so instructed by telegram from here (Berlin)." [812] The enclosure - the first two sentences of which were absolutely false - read:

'The Imperial Government is in receipt of reliable information relating to the proposed advance of French troops along the Meuse, route Givet-Namur. They leave no doubt as to France's intention to advance against Germany through Belgian territory. The (German) Government cannot help being concerned over the probability that Belgium, despite the best of intentions, will be unable to resist without assistance a French advance with a prospect of success so great that sufficient security against the menace to Germany may be found therein. It is for Germany a dictate of self-preservation that she anticipate the hostile attack. It would therefore fill the German Government with the deepest regret, should Belgium view as an act of hostility to herself the entrance of Germany upon Belgium soil, should she be forced by the measures of her opponents to do so in self-protection.

In order to avoid any misunderstanding, the (German) Government makes the following statement:

1. Germany contemplates no hostile activities against Belgium. If Belgium should be willing to adopt an attitude of benevolent neutrality toward Germany in

---

[812] G.D. 375.

the prospective war, the German Government will bind itself to guarantee at the conclusion of peace, not only the sovereign rights and independence of the (Belgian) Kingdom in their full extent, but it will even be prepared to favor with the best of good will any possible claims of the Kingdom for territorial compensation at the expense of France.

2. Germany binds herself, under the above conditions, to evacuate the territory of the Kingdom as soon as peace shall have been concluded.

3. In case of the friendly attitude of Belgium, Germany will be willing, under an arrangement with the Royal Belgian authorities, to buy for cash all the necessities required by her troops, and to make good every damage that may possibly be occasioned by German troops.

Should Belgium oppose as an enemy the German troops, and in particular throw obstacles in their way by the resistance of the Meuse fortifications or by the destruction of railroads, roads, tunnels or other artificial structures, Germany would be obliged, to her regret, to regard the Kingdom as an enemy. In such an event, Germany would be unable to undertake any obligations to the benefit of the Kingdom, but would have to leave the future regulation of the relations of the two nations to each other to the decision of arms.

The (German) Government ventures to feel definitely hopeful that this eventuality may not occur, and that the Royal Belgian Government will be able to take appropriate measures to prevent any such occurrences as those hereinbefore mentioned. In such an event, the friendly ties that bind the two neighboring nations would be subject to a further and a lasting consolidation.'

Your Excellency (Below-Saleske) will communicate this matter to the Royal Belgian Government in detail and in the strictest confidence, and will request the transmission of an unequivocal reply within 24 hours. [813]

This disgraceful note, which Moltke had originally drafted on the 26th, was to be communicated to the Belgians only when war with France became inevitable. [814] With London's suggestion of French neutrality having proved an illusion, Berlin concluded that such time had arrived. On the 2nd, Jagow directed Below-Saleske to open the July 29 dispatch and execute its instructions (though he reduced the 24-hour response time to 12 hours). [815] Jagow also told him (1) to inform Brussels that Berlin's information regarding a French advance against Belgium was accurate (a lie, of course), (2) to make sure Brussels was "left under the impression that all of the instructions relating to this affair had reached you for the first time today" (another lie), and (3) not to mention the passage about territorial compensation at France's expense. [816]

In Brussels, Albert I - Belgium's king and a cousin of Wilhelm – had been understandably worried about a potential Franco-German war. He wanted assurances from Berlin and Paris that Belgium's neutrality would be respected. He wrote the Kaiser on the 1st:

Your Majesty and Dear Cousin:

The war which threatens to break out between the two Powers who are my neighbors gives me, as you can easily understand, cause for great uneasiness. For more than 80 years, during which Belgium has been independent, our country has conscientiously observed its international obligations, often under the most difficult circumstances, and the (German) Chancellor admitted in terms of glowing recognition Belgium's correct and non-partisan attitude in the year 1870. Your Majesty and your Government have repeatedly given us valuable proofs of your friendship and

---

[813] G.D. 376.
[814] Albertini, *Origins,* 3:454.
[815] G.D. 648.
[816] Ibid.

sympathy, and fully authorized personages have assured us that in the event of a new war, Belgium's neutrality would be respected.

We fully understand the reasons which, from a political standpoint, prohibit at this time the publication of this declaration, but we do not doubt that the feelings for and the intentions toward us of that mighty imperial realm whose destinies are guided by Your Majesty, have remained unchanged. The ties of relationship and friendship which so closely bind our families have decided me to write you today and to request you to be gracious enough to repeat to me at so serious a moment as the present the expression of these sentiments toward my country. I should be heartily grateful to you for such kindly beneficence.

In this confidence, I remain as always,

Your faithfully devoted Cousin,

Albert. [817]

Albert's warm sentiments towards Wilhelm and Germany were genuine. Francis Villiers, England's ambassador to Brussels, told Grey that "in official and purely Conservative circles (in Belgium), the proclivities were decidedly German." [818] As late as August 2, Belgium's foreign minister, Julien Davignon, believed there was "no reason whatever to suspect that Germany intended to violate (Belgian neutrality)." [819] Thus, when Below-Saleske presented Germany's ultimatum to Davignon that evening, the latter, according to Below-Saleske, "could not conceal his pained surprise at the unexpected communication............(and) only answered that he would immediately inform (Albert) and the Cabinet of the communication, and would see that I received an answer within 12 hours." [820]

---

[817] G.D. 765.
[818] B.D. 670, August 12.
[819] Ibid.
[820] G.D. 695, Below-Saleske to German Foreign Office, August 2.

If Berlin thought that Belgium would capitulate like Luxembourg, however, it was mistaken. The Belgians' feelings of betrayal quickly turned to rage and determination. [821] They resolved to defend their country, notwithstanding the overwhelming military odds against them. Below-Saleske transmitted Belgium's reply to Berlin on the 3rd. In it, Brussels said that Germany's note "has made a deep and painful impression upon the (Belgian) Government." [822] Berlin was then warned:

> The attack upon (Belgium's) independence with which the German Government threatens her would constitute a flagrant violation of international law. No strategic interest justifies such a violation of law. The Belgian Government, if it were to accept the proposals submitted to it, would sacrifice the honor of the nation and at the same time betray its duty towards Europe...............(T)he Belgian Government is firmly resolved to repel, by all the means in its power, every attack upon its rights. [823]

Berlin's reaction was predictable. Late on the 3rd, Moltke wrote Jagow:

---

[821] Villiers wrote Nicolson on August 12: "Belgian authorities were really convinced that there was nothing to fear from Germany..................They are bitterly incensed at being so deceived." G.P. Gooch and Harold Temperley, eds., *British Documents on the Origins of the War: 1898-1914*, vol. 11 (London: His Majesty's Stationary Office, 1926), 350.

[822] G.D. 779, Below-Saleske to German Foreign Office. Brussels also questioned Germany's allegation that France intended to violate Belgian neutrality. Ibid.

[823] Ibid. Also on the 3rd, Wilhelm responded to Albert's August 1 message. While thanking Albert for his note, he threateningly added: "It is still in the power of Your Majesty to shape the relations between us in the friendly manner offered and under the conditions as communicated." G.D. 783. Albert replied the next day: "The feelings of friendship which I have expressed to Your Majesty and those of which you have so often assured me, the most cordial relations between our two Governments, (and) the constantly correct attitude of Belgium against which Germany has never been able to formulate the least reproach, did not permit me to assume for a single moment that Your Majesty would force us, in the face of all Europe, to the cruel choice between war and dishonor, (and) between fidelity to treaties and faithlessness to our international obligations." G.D. 837.

The Belgian Government must be informed on Tuesday, August 4, at 6 a.m., that, to our regret, we shall be forced by the Royal Belgian Government's attitude of refusal towards our well-meant proposals, to put into execution the measures of self-protection against the French menace which we have already described as unavoidably necessary, even if we have to do it by force of arms. This communication is a necessity, inasmuch as our troops will already be entering upon Belgian territory early tomorrow morning. [824]

Accordingly, Jagow directed Below-Saleske to deliver Moltke's requested communication to the Belgians. [825] Yet Moltke still hoped that Belgium's government would fold after - in his words - it "realize(d) the seriousness of the situation." [826] Again at Moltke's behest, Jagow sent the following message to Below-Saleske:

Even after the invasion has taken place, Your Excellency will continue to maintain the stand that Germany is ready at any time to hold out to Belgium the hand of a brother and to negotiate concerning an acceptable *modus vivendi*. The basis of the negotiations would have to be, however, the opening of Liege (a Belgian fortress) to the passage of German troops and cessation of the destruction of railroads, bridges and artificial structures. [827]

The Belgians were unmoved. They remained perfectly willing to fight. [828]

---

[824] G.D. 788, Moltke to German Foreign Office.

[825] G.D. 791, August 3.

[826] G.D. 788.

[827] G.D. 805, August 4.

[828] Britain's *charge d'affaires* in Holland, H.G. Chilton, wired Grey that the "Belgian Minister..............tells me that there is no question that Belgians will fire on Germans immediately" should the latter invade Belgium. B.D. 547, August 3.

D. British-German Tensions Skyrocket

The cautious optimism in Lichnowsky's 1:23 p.m. telegram of the 2nd was less evident in the following note he sent to Berlin at 1 p.m. on the 3rd. Summarizing his latest talk with Grey, he said:

> The Minister seemed to be very much disturbed, and pointed out that England would not be able to take so calmly the violation of Belgian neutrality, which she had expressly guaranteed..............The Minister told me that he intended to make a statement (before the House of Commons) this afternoon in which he would lay down the conditions upon which his country would remain neutral. He spoke of a conditional rupture (with Germany). I urgently requested him not to bring in Belgium's neutrality as a condition *sine qua non*, as that would lead to disastrous consequences. He gave me no assurance, but I have the distinct impression that, if it should be at all possible, he would like to continue to remain neutral. I bound myself to him in the terms of the following declaration: (1) that even in the event of an armed conflict with Belgium, we would maintain the inviolability of the Belgian domain; and (2) that in the event of England's remaining neutral, we would not approach the Channel or the northern coast of France with our fleet..............Whether (a German-British war) can be avoided depends in great measure upon the feeling in the Cabinet as well as upon local public opinion, which might, perhaps, be roused into too stormy an excitement by our proceedings in Belgium.[829]

---

[829] G.D. 764, Lichnowsky to German Foreign Office. Grey recalled his conversation with Lichnowsky on the afternoon of the 3rd as follows: "When I entered the room at the Foreign Office, a private secretary came in to tell me that the German Ambassador was waiting and most anxious to see me. It was hardly possible that he had come with anything from the German Government, for surely they had nothing more to say to us; but if he had, it was my business to hear it, and essential for me to know what it was before I spoke (to the House of Commons)..............He asked, what had the Cabinet decided? What was I going to say in the House of Commons? Was it a declaration of war? I answered that it was not a declaration of war, but a

We will examine Grey's statement to the House of Commons shortly. The point is that British-German relations on the 3rd were deteriorating fast. Lichnowsky, we saw, alerted Berlin that the alleged movement of German forces into France had angered the British. [830] But there was more. British newspapers reported that (1) an English steamer had been seized in Germany's Kaiser Wilhelm Canal and (2) Germany's fleet was advancing westward. [831] Notifying Berlin of this, Lichnowsky "urgently request(ed) an explanation, so that I may set matters right." [832] He warned that "local public opinion has taken a decided turn against us." [833] The Kaiser, meanwhile, raged about England's naval guarantee to France:

> The English fleet protects France's northern coast by tying up our Fleet. That is the cooperation of an ally, instead of the attitude of a neutral. For England prevents the cooperation of my Fleet with my army against the opponent with whom I am already at war. The latter commenced the war without declaring it, in violation of international law. Things can't be left this way! England must absolutely show her colors! Immediately! One way or another! [834]

---

statement of conditions. He asked very earnestly what were the conditions..............(but) the German Government, of all people, must not know an hour in advance of others abroad what was to be said. I replied that in an hour's time the whole world would know, and I could say nothing in advance. He asked, was the neutrality of Belgium one of the conditions? I could only repeat that I could say nothing before I spoke. He then implored me that we should not make Belgian neutrality one of the conditions; he knew nothing, he said, of the plans of the German General Staff. He could not suppose that a serious violation (of Belgium) was one of them, but it might be that it was part of the plan for German troops to go through one small corner perhaps of Belgium.............I was sure that what he said of his own want of knowledge of German military plans was true................It was the last time that I saw him in the Foreign Office." Grey, *Twenty-Five Years,* 2:13-14.

[830] G.D. 731.

[831] G.D. 732, Lichnowsky to German Foreign Office, August 3.

[832] Ibid.

[833] Ibid.

[834] Marginal comment of Wilhelm on G.D. 661.

He need not have worried. England would show them very soon. But before discussing the final hours of peace between Britain and Germany, let us review why London was moving towards intervention.

A big factor, obviously, was the Belgian question. Its importance to Britain can, to some extent, be seen in London's view of Germany's Luxembourg invasion. In his memoirs, Grey explained that while an 1867 treaty had guaranteed Luxembourg's neutrality, its context was different from the 1839 Belgium agreement:

> What Luxembourg had was a collective guarantee; that no one of the signatory Powers had an obligation to defend Luxembourg unless all the signatory Powers did so; that no other Power had an obligation to act separately and without the others. This made our position quite clear: the violation of Luxembourg entailed no obligation upon us to take action. We could, if we wished, make the German invasion of Luxembourg a *reason* for going to war, but it was not an *obligation*. It was a question of whether the interest of Britain, not its honor, required us to act. The question was further simplified by the fact that Luxembourg itself made no resistance to the German invasion, though it lodged a notification of it with the signatory Powers. The question of Luxembourg was therefore laid aside. [835]

With Luxembourg, consequently, the Powers had *collectively* agreed to uphold her neutrality. Yet with Belgium, each Power (including Prussia) had *separately* and *individually* promised to do

---

[835] Grey, *Twenty-Five Years,* 2:6-7 (emphasis in original). However, Grey added: "It must not be supposed that the violation of Luxembourg was altogether without effect. In the first place, it was the breaking of a treaty and a breach of Germany's pledged word. That was clear; and the wrongdoing of it was not affected by the obligation, or absence of obligation, on our part to resist it. Nor did Luxembourg's submission affect this aspect of the matter. Luxembourg was helpless and had not the means to resist. There was a perceptible hardening of British feeling against Germany." Ibid., 2:7.

so. [836] London thus believed it had a legal obligation to protect Belgium's neutrality. Another difference between Luxembourg and Belgium was strategic. Luxembourg was irrelevant to Britain's security. Belgium, however, was relatively close to England's southeastern coast. Britain did not want Germany's fleet stationed in Belgian ports so near her shores.

France was the other main factor. She served as a partial buffer state between England and Germany. Her defeat could thus place German forces right across the Channel from Britain. [837] Free from any threat to her western frontiers, Germany could then turn east and smash Russia. Victory here would establish Germany's hegemony over the continent and leave England isolated and alone. London feared that a failure to support France could trigger this terrible chain of events. And suppose France and Russia won the war without England's assistance. Would they forget her refusal to stand with them? London thought not. Indeed, Crowe had written of the risks of neutrality on the 25th:

> Should the war come and England stand aside, one of two things must happen. Either Germany and Austria win, crush France, and humiliate Russia. With the French fleet gone, Germany in occupation of the Channel, with the willing or unwilling cooperation (with Germany) of Holland and Belgium, what will be the position of a friendless England? Or France and Russia win. What would then be their attitude towards England?..............Our interests are tied up with those of France and Russia in this struggle. [838]

Buchanan expressed similar sentiments in two separate notes on August 2 and 3:

> If we do not respond to (the Tsar's) appeal for our support, we shall at the end of the war, whatever its issue, find ourselves without a friend in Europe, while our Indian

---

[836] Ibid., 2:3-9.

[837] Asquith wrote on August 2: "It is against British interests that France should be wiped out as a Great Power..............We cannot allow Germany to use the Channel as a hostile base." Quoted in Asquith, *Memories,* 12.

[838] Comment of Crowe on B.D. 101.

Empire will no longer be secure from attack by Russia. If we defer intervention until France is in danger of being crushed, sacrifices we shall then be called upon to make will be much greater. [839]

I only pray that England will prove true to herself and to her friends, as if she deserts them in their hour of need, she will find herself isolated after the war - and the hours of our Empire will be numbered. [840]

And Grey later wrote:

(I)f we did not stand by France and stand up for Belgium against this aggression, we should be isolated, discredited, and hated, and there would be before us nothing but a miserable and ignoble future...............We should have had no friends in the world; no one would have hoped or feared anything from us, or thought our friendship worth having..............Every neutral country would have held that we had turned our back on a clear obligation to Belgium..............France and Russia would not have loved Germany after the war, but in one thing they would have been ready to join with her, and this would have been in a policy directed against Britain, who had stood aside while they suffered..............Germany would have wielded the whole diplomatic strength of the Continent..............Finally, when the German Fleet was ready, war would have been forced on us, and we should have been found dispirited, half-beaten before the war began..............The French shores would have been in unfriendly hands, and the Channel would have been closed to us. Can anyone say that this picture is remote from probability? [841]

Several Cabinet members continued to favor neutrality as of midday on the 3rd. But the Belgian treaty obligation, the strategic

---

[839] B.D. 490, Buchanan to Grey, August 2.

[840] B.D. 665, Buchanan to Nicolson, August 3.

[841] Grey, *Twenty-Five Years,* 2:15-16, 37-39.

danger to Britain should France and Belgium fall, and the prospect of post-war isolation were pushing the government as a whole towards intercession. [842]

E. London and Berlin at War

On the afternoon of the 3rd, Grey spoke before the House of Commons. After discussing the naval guarantee to France, he revealed that uncorroborated information had arrived that Germany had given Belgium an ultimatum. [843] He then outlined the consequences of standing aside:

> If it be the case that there has been anything in the nature of an ultimatum to Belgium asking her to compromise or violate her neutrality, whatever may have been offered to her in return, her independence is gone if that holds. If her independence goes, the independence of Holland will follow. I ask the House, from the point of view of British interests, to consider what may be at stake. If France is beaten in a struggle of life and death, beaten to her knees, loses her position as a Great Power, becomes subordinate to the will and power of one greater than herself – consequences which I do not anticipate, because I am sure that France has the power to defend herself with all the energy and ability and patriotism which she has shown so often – still, if that were to happen, and if Belgium fell under the same dominating influence, and then Holland, and then Denmark..............would (there not) be a common interest against the unmeasured aggrandizement of any Power? [844]

> It may be said, I suppose, that we might stand aside, husband our strength, and that, whatever happened in the course of this war, at the end of it intervene with effect to

---

[842] Grey believed that Cabinet officials were growing uneasy "at the prospect of Britain sitting still and immovable, while great events fraught with incalculable consequences were happening at her very doors." Ibid., 2:1.

[843] Ibid., 2:319-20.

[844] Quoted in ibid., 2:321.

put things right and to adjust them to our own point of view. If, in a crisis like this, we run away from those obligations of honor and interest as regards the Belgian treaty, I doubt whether, whatever material force we might have at the end, it would be of very much value in face of the respect that we should have lost. And do not believe, whether a Great Power stands outside this war or not, it is going to be in a position at the end of it to exert its superior strength. For us, with a powerful fleet, which we believe able to protect our commerce, to protect our shores, and to protect our interests, if we are engaged in war, we shall suffer but little more than we shall suffer even if we stand aside.

We are going to suffer, I am afraid, terribly in this war whether we are in it or whether we stand aside. Foreign trade is going to stop, not because the trade routes are closed, but because there is no trade at the other end. Continental nations engaged in war – all their populations, all their energies, all their wealth, engaged in a desperate struggle – they cannot carry on the trade with us that they are carrying on in times of peace, whether we are parties to the war or whether we are not. I do not believe for a moment that at the end of this war, even if we stood aside and remained aside, we should be in a position, a material position, to use our force decisively to undo what had happened in the course of the war, to prevent the whole of the West of Europe opposite to us – if that had been the result of the war – falling under the domination of a single Power, and I am quite sure that our moral position would be such as to have us lost all respect.........

What other policy is there before the House? There is but one way in which the Government could make certain at the present moment of keeping outside this war, and that would be that it should immediately issue a proclamation of unconditional neutrality. We cannot do that. We have made the commitment to France that I have read to the House which prevents us from doing that. We have got the consideration of Belgium, which prevents us also from any unconditional neutrality, and, without these conditions absolutely satisfied and satisfactory, we are bound not to shrink from proceeding to the use of all the forces in our power. If we did take that line by saying, 'We will have nothing whatever to do with this matter' under no conditions -- the Belgian treaty obligations, the possible position in the Mediterranean, with damage to British interests, and what may happen to France from our failure to support France -- we were to say that all those things mattered nothing, were as nothing, and to say we would stand aside, we should, I believe, sacrifice our respect and good name and reputation before the world, and should not escape the most serious and grave economic consequences. [845]

---

[845] Quoted in ibid., 2:321-24. Churchill and Lloyd George held different opinions of Grey's diplomacy during the crisis. Churchill defended him: "Sir Edward Grey was plunged in his immense double struggle to prevent war, and not to desert France should it come. I watched with admiration his activities at the Foreign Office and cool skill in the Council.......……...He had to try to make the Germans realize that we were to be reckoned with, without making the French or Russians feel they had us in their pockets. He had to carry the Cabinet with him in all he did...............Suppose (that) after the Austrian ultimatum to Serbia, (Grey) had proposed to the Cabinet that if matters were so handled that Germany attacked France or violated Belgian territory, Great Britain would declare war upon her. Would the Cabinet have assented to such a communication? I cannot believe it...............I am certain that if Sir Edward Grey had sent (to Germany) the kind of ultimatum suggested, the Cabinet would have broken up...............(It) would have led to an exposure of division worse than the guarded attitude which we maintained, which brought our country into the war united." Churchill, *World Crisis*, 100, 102-03. Lloyd George, however, was highly critical. He argued that Grey's lack of boldness "explains why he did not take his stand on Belgium in time to give those who dreaded war in Germany a chance of reconsidering their plans in time. He would not take the risk involved in making such a bold declaration. He was still hoping that war could be averted by quieter and more conventional methods. He altogether lacked that quality of audacity which makes a great Minister." Lloyd George, *War Memoirs*, 59.

Grey's underlying message was that as painful as intervention would be for England, remaining neutral might prove even worse. [846]

Oddly enough, after Grey's address Lichnowsky seemed as optimistic as ever about British neutrality! He wired Berlin:

> Even if a decided depression is voiced in Sir E. Grey's speech of today, and if it is not free from a deep distrust of our political intentions, nevertheless, one can certainly gather from it that the local Government has no immediate intention of taking part in the struggle or of deserting its previous neutral stand. So far as concerns Sir E. Grey's statement about England's undertaking the protection of the northern coast of France, this obligation, assumed on behalf of my French colleague, is rendered unnecessary by the assurances which I was in a position to give him.

> With regard to the neutrality of Belgium, the Minister says that if the facts which have so far become public are found to be correct, it would be England's duty to do her utmost to prevent the consequences of such action. This statement is not very clear, but he probably means that England would absolutely oppose any delimitation of Belgian territory or sovereignty.

> According to my views, we can regard the speech as satisfactory, and can consider it to be a great victory that England does not at once enter the fight at the side of her Entente allies. I should like to repeat on this occasion that I am convinced that the local Government will strive to

---

[846] Grey also discussed Germany's potential domination of Western Europe in a note to C.A. Barclay, Britain's *charge d'affaires* at Washington: "(T)he issue for us was that if Germany won, she would dominate France; the independence of Belgium, Holland, Denmark, and perhaps of Norway and Sweden, would be a mere shadow: their separate existence as nations would really be a fiction; all their harbors would be at Germany's disposal; she would dominate the whole of Western Europe, and this would make our position quite impossible. We could not exist as a first-class State under such circumstances." B.D. 638, August 4.

remain neutral. The maintenance of this attitude would be greatly facilitated if the territory of Belgium could be evacuated within a short time and without any great engagements. It is not surprising, moreover, that our policy has had an extremely irritating effect here, and that Sir E. Grey found himself compelled to give expression to this irritation. For here in England, the belief is growing more and more that we wished the war for some unknown reason, and urged our neighbor on to it, and that it would have been easy, had our intentions been of the right sort, to avoid it. Furthermore, the sense of justice of the English has been offended by the double breach of treaty obligations, and I believe that we should feel well satisfied if the local Government will confine itself to a platonic protest and remain in the main content with the two conditions named – the protection of the French coast and the integrity and independence of Belgium. Whether this will prove a possibility will, of course, depend on the attitude of Parliament and, likewise, on public opinion not becoming too excited. [847]

Lichnowsky was clearly underestimating how precarious British-German relations were, partly because he had not read the entire text of Grey's speech. [848] Perhaps Lichnowsky's most striking statement concerned the evacuation of Belgium "within a short time and without any great engagements." Either this represented wishful thinking or, more likely, he was unaware of Belgium's crucial role in Germany's military strategy.

Though Grey's address was well-received by Parliament, four Cabinet members submitted their resignations in protest; two of the four withdrew them, but the other two departed as planned. [849] Once confirmation arrived of Berlin's ultimatum to Brussels, however, the Cabinet united. [850] So did the British

---

[847] G.D. 801, Lichnowsky to German Foreign Office, August 3.

[848] Albertini, *Origins,* 3:489.

[849] Ibid.; Asquith, *Memories,* 13.

[850] Grey recalled: "As it became more and more certain that the German army was going to invade Belgium, the Cabinet began all to face the same way, for we had our backs to the same straight wall." Grey, *Twenty-Five Years,* 2:9.

people. Germany's bullying of Belgium outraged them. As Lloyd George put it: "The threatened invasion of Belgium had set the nation on fire from sea to sea." [851]

Such was the situation late on the 3rd. How serious was it? At 7 p.m., London sent this message to the governors of Britain's dominions and colonies:

> In view of the strained relations with Germany, you should be on your guard against the possibility of attack in advance of any formal declaration of war. This is not the war telegram - please clearly understand. [852]

In Berlin, the Germans realized that Britain would not tolerate their advance into Belgium. [853] During the crisis, Germany had made repeated efforts - bumbling though they sometimes were – to remain in London's good graces. Bethmann-Hollweg now made another attempt, this time arguing that (1) Germany was acting in self-defense and (2) everything was Russia's fault. He telegraphed Lichnowsky at 10:25 p.m. on the 3rd:

> Please state to Sir Edward Grey that if we should take the step of violating Belgian neutrality, we would do so compelled by the duty of self-preservation. We found ourselves in a position of military constraint. While France had also before that time made strong military preparations and while we had up until then confined ourselves in a military way to only the most urgent

---

[851] Lloyd George, *War Memoirs,* 40.

[852] B.D. 555, Colonial Office to the governors of all British dominions and colonies, August 3.

[853] According to Bethmann-Hollweg, Moltke recognized the diplomatic dangers of invading Belgium but believed the operation was necessary in order to defeat France quickly. Bethmann-Hollweg, *Reflections,* 147. Bethmann-Hollweg refused to compel Moltke to spare Belgium, later writing: "It would have been too heavy a burden of responsibility for a civilian authority to have thwarted a military plan that had been elaborated in every detail and declared to be essential." Ibid. The world's outrage over the Belgian invasion irked Bethmann-Hollweg for years. He vented: "(We) were branded as criminals because we had insisted on marching through Belgium in our struggle for life, and no attention was paid to our assurances as to the integrity of and indemnity to Belgium." Ibid., 150.

measures of military preparation for self-defense, the unfortunate Russian mobilization had suddenly exposed us to the danger of being swallowed up by the floods from east and west..............Then, wedged in between east and west, we had to make use of every means to save ourselves. It is not by any means a case of intentional violation of international law, but the act of a man fighting for his life.

I had devoted all my efforts as Imperial Chancellor toward gradually bringing about, in partnership with England, a state of affairs which would make the madness of self-destruction on the part of Europe's civilized nations impossible. Russia, by treacherously playing with fire, has brought these intentions to naught. Say that I firmly hope that England, by her attitude in this world crisis, will lay a foundation on which, after it has come to an end, we may bring to realization all that Russia's policy has for the present destroyed. [854]

This plea for Britain's sympathy was followed by a less melodramatic but more dishonest one. Rather than blaming Russia, Jagow - wiring Lichnowsky early on the 4th – repeated the tiresome line that France had planned to attack Germany through Belgium:

Please dispel any mistrust that may subsist on the part of the British Government with regard to our intentions by repeating most positively the formal assurance that, even in the case of armed conflict with Belgium, Germany will, under no pretense whatever, annex Belgian territory................Please impress upon Sir E. Grey that the German army could not be exposed to a French attack across Belgium, which was planned according to absolutely unimpeachable information. Germany had consequently to disregard Belgian neutrality, it being for

---

[854] G.D. 790.

her a question of life or death to prevent a French advance. [855]

But the game was up. Even Lichnowsky now realized it. By 10 a.m. on the 4th - after he read Grey's full speech - he had lost all hope of British neutrality. He telegraphed Berlin:

> Yesterday, I was not yet acquainted with the complete text of Sir E. Grey's speech, of which only a short parliamentary report was available. Since today's publication of its contents in full, however, I must correct my impressions of yesterday by saying that I do not believe that we shall be able to count much longer on England's neutrality. As I have repeatedly reported to Your Excellency, the question of the violation of Belgian neutrality constituted one of the most important factors in England's self-restraint. Mr. Asquith, as well as Sir E. Grey, had called this to my attention and, as reported, I was able to convince myself before the session that Sir E. Grey was in a state of intense excitement as the result of the violation of Belgian territory by our army.
>
> What form British intervention will take, and whether it will take place at once, I am not able to judge. But I do not anticipate that, as I thought yesterday from my knowledge gained only from extracts of the speech, the local government will keep out, unless we are in a position to evacuate Belgian territory in the very shortest possible time. Hence, we shall probably have to reckon on England's early hostility. The reception which met Sir E. Grey's speech in the House can be interpreted to mean that, outside of the left wing of its own party, the Government will have behind it the overwhelming majority of Parliament in any active policy the purpose of which is the protection of France and Belgium. The news that reached here yesterday concerning the invasion of

---

[855] G.D. 810.

Belgium by German troops brought about a complete reversal of public opinion to our disadvantage. [856]

The coming break in British-German relations was also evident in several messages Grey dispatched on the morning of the 4th. At 9:30 a.m., he formally protested Germany's violation of the 1839 treaty. [857] He requested, through Goschen, "an assurance that the demand made upon Belgium will not be proceeded with, and that her neutrality will be respected by Germany." [858] At 10:45 a.m., he instructed his ambassadors to Belgium, Holland, and Norway to inform those governments that if Germany pressured them to abandon their neutrality, London expected them to resist and promised to "support them in offering such resistance." [859] He added that England was prepared to join France and Russia in helping Belgium, Holland, and Norway resist "(the) use of force by Germany against them." [860] And at 11:30 a.m., he telegraphed Goschen about the reported detention of several British vessels in German ports. [861] In perhaps his strongest note to date, he said: "This action on the part of the German authorities is totally unjustifiable. It is in direct contravention of international law..............You should demand the immediate release of all British ships if such release has not yet been given." [862]

By early afternoon, London learned that German forces had entered Belgium. With both Parliament and the British people

---

[856] G.D. 820, Lichnowsky to German Foreign Office, August 4. Lichnowsky also wired Berlin that a conversation he had with Tyrrell "confirms my impression that after receiving news of serious German-Belgian clashes, continuance of English neutrality can no longer be counted on and that a rupture of relations is imminent." G.D. 835, Lichnowsky to German Foreign Office, August 4. Reading this, the Kaiser wrote: "So now he is willing to believe it at last! Poor Lichnowsky." Marginal comment of Wilhelm on ibid. Wilhelm's remark is astounding, considering how he, Bethmann-Hollweg, and Jagow had ignored Lichnowsky's earlier warnings about England's likely intervention.
[857] B.D. 573, Grey to Goschen.
[858] Ibid.
[859] B.D. 580.
[860] Ibid.
[861] B.D. 585.
[862] Ibid.

livid over Germany's actions, Grey made his move. At 2 p.m., he wired Goschen:

> We hear that Germany has addressed a note to the Belgian Minister for Foreign Affairs stating that the German Government will be compelled to carry out, if necessary by force of arms, the measures considered indispensable. We are also informed that Belgian territory has been violated at Gemmenich.
>
> In these circumstances, and in view of the fact that Germany declined to give the same assurance respecting Belgium as France gave last week in reply to our request made simultaneously at Berlin and Paris, we must repeat that request, and ask that a satisfactory reply to it and to my telegram of this morning (protesting Germany's violation of the 1839 treaty) be received here by 12 o'clock tonight. If not, you are instructed to ask for your passports and to say that His Majesty's Government feel bound to take all steps in their power to uphold the neutrality of Belgium and the observance of a treaty to which Germany is as much a party as ourselves. [863]

Goschen communicated this ultimatum to Bethmann-Hollweg and Jagow that evening. [864] Earlier in the day, when

---

[863] B.D. 594.

[864] Prior to receiving Grey's demand, Bethmann-Hollweg spoke before the Reichstag. He conceded that the Luxembourg and Belgium operations violated international law. Yet he again used the self-defense argument: "Our troops have occupied Luxembourg and perhaps have already entered Belgian territory. This is an infraction of international law. Though the French Government had declared in Brussels to be willing to respect Belgium's neutrality as long as the adversary would respect it, we knew that France was ready for invasion. France was able to wait; we were not. A French aggression into our flank on the lower Rhine would have been disastrous. We were therefore compelled to overrule the legitimate protests of the Luxembourg and Belgian Governments. We shall repair the wrong which we are doing, as soon as our military aims have been reached. Anybody threatened as we are and fighting for his most sacred goods must only think of pulling through. As to the attitude of England, the statement made by Sir Edward Grey in the House of Commons has clearly laid down the point of

Goschen delivered Grey's 9:30 a.m. protest, Jagow replied that he could give no assurances regarding Belgium's neutrality. [865] He and Bethmann-Hollweg responded likewise to the ultimatum; Goschen notified Grey that the two "regretted that they could give no other answer than that which they gave me this afternoon." [866]

The next morning, Goschen asked for his passports. [867]

It was war.

Germany's nightmare of a life-and-death struggle with the entire Triple Entente had come true.

---

view taken by the British Government that as long as England will keep neutral, our fleet would not attack the northern coast of France and that we would not touch the territorial integrity and the independence of Belgium. I herewith repeat this declaration publicly before the whole world and I may add that as long as England keeps neutral, we would be willing in case of reciprocity not to undertake any hostile operations against the French commercial navigation." G.D. 829, Jagow to Lichnowsky, August 4.

[865] B.D. 666, Goschen to Grey, August 4. Jagow added that the invasion of Belgium was a "matter of life and death for (Germany); every other line of attack would have taken too long and enabled Russia to concentrate." Ibid.

[866] B.D. 667, August 4. See Appendix B for Goschen's description of his last hours in Germany.

[867] G.D. 671, Goschen to Grey, August 6.

XIII

CONCLUSION

The "what ifs" of the July Crisis and the years leading up to it are many: if the Russian-German Reinsurance Treaty had been renewed; if the Germans had avoided the Moroccan Crises by using quieter diplomacy; if the 1908 Straits-Bosnia deal had not been made; if Belgrade had stopped its Pan-Serb agitation; if Austria's ultimatum had contained more moderate demands; if Germany and France had restrained their respective allies; if Berlin had correctly predicted whether Russia, France, and Britain would go to war; if Grey had announced well before July 29 that London would side with Paris and St. Petersburg; if Italy had told the Central Powers in mid-July that she would remain neutral should a European conflagration arise from an Austro-Serbian conflict. Had any of these what-ifs actually happened, the war might never have erupted. World War I was not inevitable. A lot of things needed to fall in place for it to occur. In previous European crises, they had not. In 1914, they did.

The main reason that war was not inevitable was that no Great Power wanted one to happen. True, some militant, nationalistic elements within certain Great Power countries favored war for purposes of territorial expansion. And a few military chiefs, especially Moltke, believed that the sooner war came for their countries, the better. Yet no one can really say that Wilhelm, Bethmann-Hollweg, Jagow, Nicholas, Sazonov, Poincare, Viviani, Asquith, Grey, Franz Josef, Tisza, or even Berchtold desired an all-out war. And while Austria certainly wanted a showdown with Serbia, she did not want one with Russia.

Not *wanting* a European war, however, is very different from being unwilling to fight one. The notion that the Powers "slid" into war against their will or by accident is nonsense. Although, considering the speed of events, they had only weeks – even days - in which to do it, the combatant Powers weighed their respective strategic interests and, based on that, made conscious decisions to pursue the diplomatic and military courses they did. While Grey believed in July 1914 that war's horrors "would be so obvious to all the Great Powers that, when on the edge of the abyss, they would call a halt and recoil from it," none of them did because they felt they could not afford to. [868] They knew that a European conflagration would be devastating. But they felt that the alternative could prove worse.

Consider the Entente countries. St. Petersburg believed that imposing the entire ultimatum on Serbia would make her an Austrian vassal state, thereby damaging Russia's Balkan status. This scenario was deemed so disastrous that Russia was prepared to take up arms to prevent it. France, meanwhile, had to choose between (1) fidelity to Russia, which would likely mean war with Germany, and (2) neutrality, which could destroy the Paris-St. Petersburg alliance and enable Germany to vanquish Russia. Concluding that near-isolation in the face of an all-powerful Germany would be more dangerous than fighting the Germans *now* with Russia's assistance, France elected to stand alongside her ally. England, we know, considered neutrality. Yet she decided that the invasion of Belgium – combined with the prospects of complete friendlessness and Germany's domination of Europe - made intervention necessary. As for the Central Powers, Austria felt she had to take extraordinary measures against Serbia, even if a world war resulted. And Berlin was so leery of alienating Austria that it refused to compel her to accept a negotiated solution, regardless of the consequences.

Recognizing that no combatant Great Power wanted a European war but that each chose to fight one, the obvious question is this: which country was responsible for its outbreak? There is blame to go around. One could argue that England's and Italy's failures to announce their intentions earlier in the crisis increased the Central Powers' intransigence. France certainly

---

[868] Grey, *Twenty-Five Years*, 2:19-20.

could have tried to restrain St. Petersburg. Russia's inflexible mobilization blueprint, meanwhile, forced her to eschew partial mobilization and to implement general mobilization, which was destined to trigger extreme German countermeasures. Indeed, St. Petersburg's general mobilization helped transform the crisis from an Austro-Russian diplomatic dispute over the ultimatum into a Russian-German military confrontation. And, while not a Great Power, Serbia deserves substantial blame. Her continued Pan-Serb troublemaking threatened to ignite the already explosive Belgrade-Vienna relationship.

Austria, however, bears the primary responsibility for the war.

The diplomatic realignment of Europe in the quarter-century before 1914 resulted in the Central Powers' isolation and increasing paranoia. Austria believed that several neighboring countries sought to dismember her. Germany suspected that the Triple Entente was trying to squeeze her to death. Fearful, Vienna and Berlin clung tighter and tighter to each other. They viewed their alliance as a matter of national survival, and the Habsburg Empire's fragility and instability only enhanced Germany's determination to sustain her at all costs. So when Franz Ferdinand was murdered, the two saw an opportunity to reinvigorate the Empire. With Berlin's support, Vienna undertook what was akin to a carefully planned robbery by making brutal demands on Serbia backed by the implicit threat of force. When Russian intervention loomed, Austria could have resolved the matter peacefully. She instead chose to shoot it out. Her responsibility for the ensuing four-year firefight is greater than any other country's, for she (1) was the affair's main planner and (2) declined virtually every proposal to settle the crisis.

Austria's obstinance was particularly striking considering that Sazonov had offered to work with her in resolving the Serbian problem. He would not let her go so far as to impose the entire ultimatum; but he was willing to let her go a good portion of the way. He even agreed to the temporary occupation of Serbian territory. Austria had utterly humiliated Serbia and shelled her capital. She had effectively won. Yet rather than cave in an inch regarding her demands, Austria knowingly dragged Europe into war. [869] As Berchtold told Szapary on July 25: "We shall............go to the limit to enforce our demands and shall not draw back before the possibility of European complications." [870]

What about Berlin's culpability?

It has been argued that Germany essentially started the war so as to expand her influence in Europe. [871] Throughout most of July, it is true, Germany advised Vienna to deal firmly with Serbia; in that sense, her policy was tactically *offensive*. *Strategically,* however, it was *defensive*. She saw her security as intertwined with Austria's. A weaker Austria meant a more vulnerable Germany. Berlin therefore wanted a strong Austrian response not as a pretext for a German war of aggression but solely in order to sustain the Habsburg Empire. Had Germany wanted war with Russia and France, she would not have (1) implemented her localization strategy, (2) suggested the pledge plan to Vienna on the 28th, and (3) urged Austria on the 30th to accept a diplomatic solution. [872] Germany's efforts to diffuse the

---

[869] Tirpitz later criticized Vienna's brusque dismissal of Belgrade's reply: "It cannot be denied that the Serbian reply showed an unexpected compliance, and I do not think that the Austrian Government showed a right sense of proportion when it declared this reply to be unacceptable as a basis for further negotiations. But Bethmann-Hollweg and Count Berchtold did not grasp the tangibility of the diplomatic success which had already been achieved. As Austria's honor had been saved.............the danger of war could probably have been regarded as averted if Austria had been satisfied with her success. She could have given the Serbs a short space of time for the immediate fulfillment of the desired concessions as a condition for negotiations regarding the other demands. Even if international supervision had then been imposed for the other demands, the high value to Austria of the accomplished humiliation of Serbia with England's consent would not have been diminished...............Although the reply offered a possibility for future negotiations, this was passed over." Tirpitz, *My Memoirs,* 324-25. Having Austria loosely interpret a few of the ultimatum's demands might also have resolved the crisis. It could have eased Russia's concerns about Serbian sovereignty without forcing Vienna to change the ultimatum's text.

[870] Quoted in Schmitt, *Coming,* 2.

[871] See most notably Fischer, *Germany's Aims.*

[872] Bethmann-Hollweg's strongest efforts to restrain Vienna occurred after Berlin received Grey's veiled threat of the 29th. Yet Telegram 174 – wherein the chancellor recommended the pledge plan in order to "(cut) the vital cord of the Greater Serbia propaganda, *without at the same time bringing on a world war*" - was sent *prior to* Grey's warning. G.D. 323, July 28 (emphasis

crisis in July's final days are why her war guilt is less than Vienna's.

Nevertheless, her responsibility exceeds that of everyone else. The fact remains that she recommended tough Austrian action that she knew could lead to a European war (even though she doubted one would erupt). [873] Furthermore, despite her July 28-30 peace moves, she was not firm enough in getting Austria to accept a negotiated settlement. Having helped perpetuate the crisis, Berlin failed to do what was necessary to stop it.

Perhaps the greatest mystery of the July Crisis is how Germany could have so foolishly gambled her existence when she realized by the 30th that (1) she faced war with the entire Triple Entente and (2) Italy and Romania would probably remain neutral. Indeed, she had all of the 30th and part of the 31st to threaten Vienna with abandonment unless it agreed to the "Halt in Belgrade" formula. Again, though, she declined to take this step lest it wreck their alliance. Amazingly, the prospect of being alone – a unrealistic fear, for Austria would not have ditched Berlin in favor of the Triple Entente countries – seemed more frightening to Germany than fighting three other Great Powers with only the rickety Habsburg realm at her side. [874] Berlin essentially allowed Vienna to determine whether Germany entered a war in which she and Austria would be outnumbered and at a decided disadvantage in manpower and resources. Few governments could have acted more irresponsibly – especially

---

added). The point is that Berlin's interest in a diplomatic settlement was evident even before it concluded that British intervention was likely.

[873] Bethmann-Hollweg later admitted that he underestimated the likelihood of a wider war: "(O)ne confession I must make. And that is that when the crisis came on I assumed that even a Russian mind would shrink from taking that fearful plunge except under extreme necessity, and that I believed also that England, when faced with the final decision, would study the peace of the world before its own friendships." Bethmann-Hollweg, *Reflections*, 126. Tirpitz put it this way: "(Bethmann-Hollweg) drew...............from the assumption that the Entente did not want a war, the short-sighted conclusion that Austria could probably force an entry into Serbia regardless of the Entente, without endangering the peace of the world." Tirpitz, *My Memoirs,* 320.

[874] Berlin did sign a pact with the Ottoman Empire – a state even weaker than Austria - on August 3. But the Turks did not enter the war on the Austro-German side until late October 1914.

considering how much Germany had to lose. She was already a world power and getting only stronger. She had no need for war. But she chose to risk absolutely everything so as not to alienate Vienna. Germany's actions in July 1914, simply put, were incredibly reckless and self-destructive. [875]

Prominent figures later commented on this aspect of the crisis. Bulow maintained: "No other country had so much to gain from peace as Germany...............It was in our interests to keep the peace; in a war, above all in any general war, we had all to lose and little to gain." [876] He likened Bethmann-Hollweg's and Jagow's post-June 28 diplomacy to "a pair of willful little urchins playing with what seems an empty shell case, which is liable to explode at any minute." [877] Lloyd George wrote of Berlin's provocation of England:

> There were many of us who could hardly believe that those responsible for guiding the destiny of Germany would be so fatuous as to deliberately provoke the hostility of the British Empire with its inexhaustible reserves and with its grim tenacity of purpose once it engaged in a struggle. [878]

Of Berlin's failure to stop Vienna, Grey penned:

> (Bethmann-Hollweg and Jagow), after the (Austrian) ultimatum was sent and the Serbian reply received, expressed some criticism of the former and thought the latter went further in the direction of conciliation than could have been expected; (but) who yet let things drift or

---

[875] This is hardly to say that *Austria's* actions were wise. Frail and ethnically fractured, she might not withstand the strains of a world war. But she at least could argue – rightly or wrongly - that drastic action against Serbia was needed to save the Empire, notwithstanding the risks. Germany had no such excuse; her existence was not at all at stake.

[876] Bulow, *Memoirs*, 175.

[877] Ibid., 174-76.

[878] Lloyd George, *War Memoirs,* 44.

spoke only in whispers at Vienna when a decisive word was wanted. [879]

Sazonov similarly wrote:

> Bethmann-Hollweg was a peace-loving man by nature, free from chauvinism or vanity. He did not seek pretexts for war, and probably did not wish it, but when, through the folly of his allies, he was faced with it, he did nothing to drive away the terrible phantom.............(H)e obediently followed the path into which he had been pushed by the Austro-Hungarian Government without realizing clearly whither it led him..............While admitting that the Berlin dispatches to Vienna (in July's final days) did strike a conciliatory note – though rather late in the day – it is to be regretted that (they were) so weak and uncertain as to be completely drowned by the noise and clatter of the Austrian drums and trumpets. [880]

And the Austro-German relationship, in the end, was the core of it all. The crisis and the war stemmed not from an attempted Austro-German power grab but from an almost paranoiac determination to sustain the Habsburg Empire and, in turn, the Berlin-Vienna alliance. [881] While the period of July 23-30

---

[879] Grey, *Twenty-Five Years*, 2:26.

[880] Sazonov, *Fateful Years*, 191, 207.

[881] Two events that have been cited as evidence that Germany started the war for aggressive purposes are (1) the German "War Council" of December 8, 1912, and (2) the development of Berlin's "September Programme." The December 8 meeting between the Kaiser and his military chiefs involved frank discussions about the inevitability of war with Russia; Moltke and even Wilhelm believed that Germany needed to fight such a war sooner rather than later. See David Fromkin, *Europe's Last Summer: Who Started the Great War in 1914?* (New York: Vintage Books, 2005), 91-92. The September Programme, meanwhile, was an outline of Germany's war aims. Drafted shortly after war erupted, it included, among other things: (1) the annexation of Luxembourg and (2) transforming Belgium and Holland into virtual German satellite states. Fischer, *Germany's Aims*, 104-05. To this writer, however, it is an extreme leap to suggest that either event indicates that Germany schemed for a European war in mid-1914. First off, no firm decisions were reached at the War Council (which, significantly, Bethmann-

could be described as "The Crisis over the Terms of the Ultimatum to Serbia," the entire affair (June 28-August 1) can definitely be labeled, "The Crisis over the Preservation of the Habsburg Monarchy."

Within a two-week span, Austria's seemingly simple police action against Serbia had turned into an absolute nightmare for Germany, a near worst-case scenario from a military standpoint. As Tirpitz later wrote: "In order to put a complete stop to the undermining of Austria by the Serbs, the (Berlin-Vienna pact) plunged into a far greater danger, and jumped out of the frying pan into the fire." [882]

And the odds were not good that the outnumbered Central Powers would survive the inferno.

Hollweg, Jagow, and other political leaders did not even attend). Fromkin, *Europe's Last Summer*, 92. There certainly was no implicit agreement to orchestrate a conflict. Second, Germany was hardly the only Great Power to have territorial aims. Russia, for instance, coveted the Straits, while France wanted Alsace and Lorraine. Each Power's establishment of war goals (expansionist though some of them were) was entirely predictable and in no way shows that Germany sought to use Sarajevo as a pretext for territorial aggrandizement. Third, and most importantly, in gauging Germany's war guilt, one must look primarily at her actions *during the crisis itself* rather than at an inconclusive conference held 19 months earlier or a diplomatic blueprint developed several weeks after hostilities erupted. And the evidence indicates that Berlin's main goal in July 1914 was not the expansion of German influence but the preservation of Austria.
[882] Tirpitz, *My Memoirs*, 325.

APPENDIX A

THE SERBIAN REPLY

Below is Serbia's response to the Austrian ultimatum. Vienna's comments are in italics:

The Royal Government (Serbia) has received the communication of the Imperial and Royal Government (Austria) of the 23rd inst. and is convinced that its reply will dissipate any misunderstanding which threatens to destroy the friendly and neighborly relations between the Austrian monarchy and the kingdom of Serbia.

The Royal Government is conscious that nowhere there have been renewed protests against the great neighborly monarchy like those which at one time were expressed in the Skuptschina, as well as in the declaration and actions of the responsible representatives of the state at that time, and which were terminated by the Serbian declaration of March 31, 1909; furthermore, that since that time neither the different corporations of the kingdom, nor the officials have made an attempt to alter the political and judicial condition created in Bosnia and the Herzegovina. The Royal Government states that the (Austrian) Government has made no protestation in this sense excepting in the case of a textbook, in regard to which the (Austrian) Government has received an entirely satisfactory explanation. Serbia has given during the time of the Balkan crisis in numerous cases evidence of her pacific and moderate policy, and it is only owing to Serbia and the sacrifices which she has brought in the interest of the peace of Europe that this peace has been preserved.

The Royal Serbian Government limits itself to establishing that since the declaration of March 31, 1909, there has been no attempt on the part of the Serbian Government to alter the position of Bosnia and the Herzegovina. With this, she deliberately shifts the foundation of our note, as we have not insisted that she and her officials have undertaken anything official in this direction. Our gravamen is that in spite of the obligation assumed in the cited note, she has omitted to suppress the movement directed against the territorial integrity of the Monarchy. Her obligation consisted in changing her attitude and the entire direction of her policies, and in entering into friendly and neighborly relations with the Austro-Hungarian Monarchy, and not only not to interfere with the possession of Bosnia.

The Royal Government cannot be made responsible for expressions of a private character, as for instance newspaper articles and the peaceable work of societies, expressions which are of very common appearance in other countries, and which ordinarily are not under the control of the state. This, all the less, as the Royal Government has shown great courtesy in the solution of a whole series of questions which have arisen between Serbia and Austria-Hungary, whereby it has succeeded to solve the greater number thereof, in favor of the progress of both countries.

The assertion of the Royal Serbian Government that the expressions of the press and the activity of Serbian associations possess a private character and thus escape governmental control, stands in full contrast with the institutions of modern states and even the most liberal of press and society laws, which nearly everywhere subject the press and the societies to a certain control of the state. This is also provided for by the Serbian institutions. The rebuke against the Serbian Government consists in the fact that it has totally omitted to supervise its press and its societies, in so far as it knew their direction to be hostile to the Monarchy.

The Royal Government was therefore painfully surprised by the assertions that citizens of Serbia had participated in the preparations of the outrage in Sarajevo. The Government expected to be invited to cooperate in the investigation of the crime, and it was ready, in order to prove its complete correctness, to proceed against all persons in regard to whom it would receive information.

This assertion is incorrect. The Serbian Government was accurately informed about the suspicion resting upon quite definite personalities and not only in the position, but also obliged by its own laws to institute investigations spontaneously. The Serbian Government has done nothing in this direction.

According to the wishes of the (Austrian) Government, the Royal Government is prepared to surrender to the court, without regard to position and rank, every Serbian citizen for whose participation in the crime of Sarajevo it should have received proof. It binds itself particularly on the first page of the official organ of the 26th of July to publish the following enunciation: 'The Royal Serbian Government condemns every propaganda which should be directed against Austria-Hungary, i.e., the entirety of such activities as aim towards the separation of certain territories from the Austro-Hungarian Monarchy, and it regrets sincerely the lamentable consequences of these criminal machinations.'

The Austrian demand reads: 'The Royal Serbian Government condemns the propaganda against Austria-Hungary........' The alteration of the declaration as demanded by us, which has been made by the Royal Serbian Government, is meant to imply that a propaganda directed against Austria-Hungary does not exist, and that it is not aware of such. This formula is insincere, and the Serbian Government reserves itself the subterfuge for later occasions that it had not disavowed by this declaration the existing propaganda, nor recognized the same as hostile to the Monarchy, whence it could deduce further that it is not obliged to suppress in the future a propaganda similar to the present one.

The Royal Government regrets that according to a communication of the (Austrian) Government, certain Serbian officers and functionaries have participated in the propaganda just referred to, and that these have therefore endangered the amicable relations for the observation of which the Royal Government had solemnly obliged itself through the declaration of March 31, 1909.

The formula as demanded by Austria reads: 'The Royal Government regrets that Serbian officers and functionaries...............have participated............' Also with this formula and the further addition "according to the declaration of the (Austrian) Government," the Serbian Government pursues the object, already indicated above, to preserve a free hand for the future.

The Royal Government binds itself further:

1. During the next regular meeting of the Skuptschina, to embody in the press laws a clause, to wit, that the incitement to hatred of, and contempt for, the Monarchy is to be most severely punished, as well as every publication whose general tendency is directed against the territorial integrity of Austria-Hungary. It binds itself in view of the coming revision of the constitution to embody an amendment into Art. 22 of the constitutional law which permits the confiscation of such publications as is at present impossible according to the clear definition of Art. 22 of the constitution.

Austria had demanded:
1. 'To suppress every publication which incites to hatred and contempt for the Monarchy, and whose tendency is directed against the territorial integrity of the Monarchy.'
We wanted to bring about the obligation for Serbia to take care that such attacks of the press would cease in the future. Instead, Serbia offers to pass certain laws which are meant as means towards this end, viz.:
(a) A law according to which the expressions of the press hostile to the Monarchy can be individually punished, a matter which is immaterial to us, all the more so as the individual prosecution of press intrigues is very rarely possible and as, with a lax enforcement of such laws, the few cases of this nature would not be punished. The proposition, therefore, does not meet our demand in any way, and it offers not the least guarantee for the desired success.

(b) An amendment to Art. 22 of the constitution, which would permit confiscation, a proposal which does not satisfy us, as the existence of such a law in Serbia is of no use to us; for we want the <u>obligation</u> of the Government to <u>enforce</u> it and that has not been promised us.

These proposals are therefore entirely unsatisfactory and evasive, as we are not told within what time these laws will be passed, and as in the event of the not passing of these laws by the Skuptschina, everything would remain as it is, excepting the event of a possible resignation of the Government.

2. The Government possesses no proofs, and the note of the (Austrian) Government does not submit them, that the society Narodna Odbrana and other similar societies have committed, up to the present, any criminal actions of this manner through any one of their members. Notwithstanding this, the Royal Government will accept the demand of the (Austrian) Government and dissolve the society Narodna Odbrana, as well as every society which should act against Austria-Hungary.

The propaganda of the Narodna Odbrana and affiliated societies hostile to the Monarchy fills the entire public life of Serbia; it is therefore an entirely inacceptable reserve if the Serbian Government asserts that it knows nothing about it. Aside from this, our demand is not completely fulfilled, as we have asked besides: 'To confiscate the means of propaganda of these societies to prevent the reformation of the dissolved societies under another name and in another form.' In these two directions, the Belgrade Cabinet is perfectly silent, so that through this semi-concession there is offered us no guarantee for putting an end to the agitation of the associations hostile to the Monarchy, especially the Narodna Odbrana.

3. The Royal Serbian Government binds itself without delay to eliminate from the public instruction in Serbia anything which might further the propaganda directed against Austria-Hungary, provided the (Austrian) Government furnishes actual proofs.

Also in this case, the Serbian Government first demands proofs for a propaganda hostile to the Monarchy in the public instruction of Serbia while it must know that the textbooks introduced in the Serbian schools contain objectionable matter in this direction and that a large portion of the teachers are in the camp of the Narodna Odbrana and affiliated societies. Furthermore, the Serbian Government has not fulfilled a part of our demands as we have requested, as it omitted in its text the addition desired by us: 'as far as the body of instructors is concerned, as well as the means of instruction' – a sentence which shows clearly where the propaganda hostile to the Monarchy is to be found in the Serbian schools.

4. The Royal Government is also ready to dismiss those officers and officials from the military and civil services in regard to whom it has been proved by judicial investigation that they have been guilty of actions against the territorial integrity of the Monarchy; it expects that the (Austrian) Government communicate to it for the purpose of starting the investigation the names of these officers and officials, and the facts with which they have been charged.

By promising the dismissal from the military and civil services of those officers and officials who are found guilty by judicial procedure, the Serbian Government limits its assent to those cases in which these persons have been charged with a crime according to the statutory code. As, however, we demand the removal of such officers and officials as indulge in a propaganda hostile to the Monarchy, which is generally not punishable in Serbia, our demands have not been fulfilled in this point.

5. The Royal Serbian Government confesses that it is not clear about the sense and the scope of that demand of the (Austrian) Government which concerns the obligation on the part of the Royal Serbian Government to permit the co-operation of officials of the (Austrian) Government on Serbian territory, but it declares that it is willing to accept every co-operation which does not run counter to international law and criminal law, as well as to the friendly and neighborly relations.

The international law, as well as the criminal law, has nothing to do with this question; it is purely a matter of the nature of state police, which is to be solved by way of a special agreement. The reserved attitude of Serbia is therefore incomprehensible and on account of its vague general form, it would lead to unbridgeable difficulties.

6. The Royal Government considers it its duty as a matter of course to begin an investigation against all those persons who have participated in the outrage of June 28 and who are in its territory. As far as the cooperation in this investigation of specially delegated officials of the (Austrian) Government is concerned, this cannot be accepted, as this is a violation of the constitution and of criminal procedure. Yet in some cases the result of the investigation might be communicated to the Austro-Hungarian officials.

The Austrian demand was clear and unmistakable:
1. To institute a criminal procedure against the participants in the outrage.
2. Participation by (Austrian) Government officials in the examinations.
3. It did not occur to us to let (Austrian) officials participate in the Serbian court procedure; they were to cooperate only in the police researches which had to furnish and fix the material for the investigation.
If the Serbian Government misunderstands us here, this is done deliberately, for it must be familiar with the difference between 'enquete judiciaire' and simple police researches. As it desired to escape from every control of the investigation which would yield, if correctly carried out, highly undesirable results for it, and as it possesses no means to refuse in a plausible manner the cooperation of our officials (precedents for such police intervention exist in great numbers), it tries to justify its refusal by showing up our demands as impossible.

7. The Royal Government has ordered on the evening of the day on which the note was received the arrest of Major Voislar Tankosic. However, as far as Milan Ciganowic is concerned, who is a citizen of the Austro-Hungarian Monarchy and who has been

employed till June 28 with the Railroad Department, it has as yet been impossible to locate him, wherefore a warrant has been issued against him. The (Austrian) Government is asked to make known, as soon as possible, for the purpose of conducting the investigation, the existing grounds for suspicion and the proofs of guilt obtained in the investigation at Sarajevo.

This reply is disingenuous. According to our investigation, Ciganowic, by order of the police prefect in Belgrade, left three days after the outrage for Ribari, after it had become known that Ciganowic had participated in the outrage. In the first place, it is therefore incorrect that Ciganowic left the Serbian service on June 28. In the second place, we add that the prefect of police at Belgrade, who had himself caused the departure of this Ciganowic and who knew his whereabouts, declared in an interview that a man by the name of Milan Ciganowic did not exist in Belgrade.

8. The Serbian Government will amplify and render more severe the existing measures against the suppression of smuggling of arms and explosives. It is a matter of course that it will proceed at once against, and punish severely, those officials of the frontier service on the line Shabatz-Loznica who violated their duty and who have permitted the perpetrators of the crime to cross the frontier.

9. The Royal Government is ready to give explanations about the expressions which its officials in Serbia and abroad have made in interviews after the outrage and which, according to the assertion of the (Austrian) Government, were hostile to the Monarchy. As soon as the (Austrian) Government points out in detail where those expressions were made and succeeds in proving that those expressions have actually been made by the functionaries concerned, the Royal Government itself will take care that the necessary evidences and proofs are collected therefor.

The Royal Serbian Government must be aware of the interviews in question. If it demands of the (Austrian) Government that it should furnish all kinds of detail about the said interviews and if it reserves for itself the right of a formal investigation, it shows that it is not its intention seriously to fulfill the demand.

10. The Royal Government will notify the (Austrian) Government, so far as this has not been already done by the present note, of the execution of the measures in question as soon as one of those measures has been ordered and put into execution.

The Royal Serbian Government believes it to be to the common interest not to rush the solution of this affair and it is therefore, in case the (Austrian) Government should not consider itself satisfied with this answer, ready, as ever, to accept a peaceable solution, be it by referring the decision of this question to the International Court at the Hague or by leaving it to the decision of the Great Powers who have participated in the working out of the declaration given by the Serbian Government on March 31, 1909.

The Serbian Note, therefore, is entirely a play for time. [883]

---

[883] Quoted in C.D.D., 417-23. According to Rodd, San Giuliano labeled some of Austria's "grounds on which Serbia's reply was considered inadequate.............such as (the) slight verbal difference in (the) sentence regarding renunciation of propaganda.............(as) quite childish." B.D. 231, Rodd to Grey, July 28. Still, notwithstanding its heavy responsibility for the war, Vienna was right about one thing: Belgrade's reply, with its numerous (though subtle) qualifications, was further from an acceptance than San Giuliano and the rest of Europe believed.

APPENDIX B

GOSCHEN'S FINAL HOURS IN GERMANY

The following letter from Goschen to Grey, dated August 6, 1914, describes the ambassador's last hours in Germany. Particularly interesting is Goschen's tense conversation with Bethmann-Hollweg, who seemingly blamed everyone but himself and his colleagues for Germany's horrible predicament. Note also Bethmann-Hollweg's diplomatically irresponsible reference to the 1839 Belgian treaty as a "scrap of paper." The Entente would cite this as evidence of Germany's aggressive behavior and disregard for international law:

Sir.........
    In accordance with the instructions contained in your telegram...............of (9:30 a.m.) of the 4th instant, I called upon the Secretary of State for Foreign Affairs (Jagow) that afternoon and enquired in the name of His Majesty's Government whether the (German) Government would refrain from violating Belgian neutrality. Herr von Jagow at once replied that he was sorry to say that his answer must be 'No' as, in consequence of the German troops having crossed the frontier that morning, Belgian neutrality had been already violated. Herr von Jagow again went into the reasons why the (German) Government had been obliged to take this step - namely, that they had to advance into France by the quickest and easiest way so as to be able to get well ahead with their operations and endeavor to strike some decisive blow as early as possible. It was a matter of life and death for them, as if they

had gone by the more southern route they could not have hoped, in view of the paucity of roads and the strength of the (French) fortresses, to have gotten through without formidable opposition entailing great loss of time. This loss of time would have meant time gained by the Russians for bringing up their troops to the German frontier. Rapidity of action was the great German asset, while that of Russia was an inexhaustible supply of troops. I pointed out to Herr von Jagow that this *fait accompli* of the violation of the Belgian frontier rendered, as he would readily understand, the situation exceedingly grave and I asked him whether there was not still time to draw back and avoid possible consequences which both he and I would deplore. He replied that for the reasons he had given me, it was now impossible for them to draw back.

During the afternoon, I received your telegram (of 2 p.m.)............and I again proceeded to the (German) Foreign Office and informed the Secretary of State for Foreign Affairs that unless the (German) Government could give the assurance by 12 o'clock that night that they would proceed no further with their violation of the Belgian frontier and stop their advance, I had been instructed to demand my passports and inform the (German) Government that His Majesty's Government would have to take all steps in their power to uphold the neutrality of Belgium and the observance of a treaty to which Germany was as much a party as themselves.

Herr von Jagow replied that to his great regret, he could give no other answer than that which he had given me earlier in the day – namely, that the safety of the Empire rendered it absolutely necessary that (German) troops should advance through Belgium. I gave his Excellency a paraphrase of your telegram and, pointing out that you had mentioned 12 o'clock as the time when His Majesty's Government would expect an answer, asked him whether, in view of the terrible consequences which would necessarily ensue, it was not possible even at the last moment that their answer should be reconsidered. He replied that if the time given were even 24 hours or more, his answer must be the same. I said that in that case I should have to demand my passports. This interview would have taken place at about 7 o'clock. In a short conversation which ensued, Herr von Jagow expressed his poignant regret at the crumbling of his entire policy and that of the

Chancellor, which had been to make friends with Great Britain and then, through Great Britain, to get closer to France. I said that this sudden end to my work in Berlin was to me also a matter of deep regret and disappointment, but that he must understand that under the circumstances and in view of our engagements, His Majesty's Government could not possibly have acted otherwise than it had done.

I then said that I should like to go and see the Chancellor, as it might be perhaps the last time I should have an opportunity of seeing him. He begged me to do so. I found the Chancellor very agitated. His Excellency at once began a harangue which lasted for about 20 minutes. He said that the step taken by His Majesty's Government was terrible to a degree; just for a word 'neutrality,' a word which in war time had so often been disregarded - just for a scrap of paper, Great Britain was going to make war on a kindred nation who desired nothing better than to be friends with her. All his efforts in that direction had been rendered useless by this last terrible step, and the policy to which, as I knew, he had devoted himself since his accession to office, had tumbled down like a house of cards. What we had done was unthinkable; it was like striking a man from behind while he was fighting for his life against two assailants. He held Great Britain responsible for all the terrible events that might happen!

I protested strongly against that statement and said that in the same way as he and Herr von Jagow wished me to understand that for strategic reasons it was a matter of life and death to Germany to advance through Belgium and violate her neutrality, so I would wish him to understand that it was, so to speak, a matter of 'life and death' for the honor of Great Britain that she should keep her solemn engagement to do her utmost to defend Belgium's neutrality if attacked. That solemn compact simply had to be kept, or what confidence could anyone have in engagements given by Great Britain in the future? The Chancellor said, 'But at what price will that compact have been kept? Has the British Government thought of that?' I hinted to his Excellency as plainly as I could that fear of consequences could hardly be regarded as an excuse for breaking solemn engagements, but his Excellency was so excited, so evidently overcome by the news of our action, and so little disposed to hear reason, that I refrained from adding fuel to the flame by further argument.

As I was leaving, he said that the blow of Great Britain joining Germany's enemies was all the greater that almost up to the last moment he and his Government had been working with us and supporting our efforts to maintain peace between Austria and Russia. I admitted that that had been the case and said that it was part of the tragedy which saw the two nations fall apart just at the moment when the relations between them had been more friendly and cordial than they had been for years. Unfortunately, notwithstanding our efforts to maintain peace between Russia and Austria, the war had spread and had brought us face to face with a situation which, if we held to our engagements, we could not possibly avoid, and which unfortunately entailed our separation from our late fellow-workers. He would readily understand that no one regretted this more than I..........

The next morning, I demanded my passports in writing.

In the meantime...............a flying sheet, issued by the 'Berliner Tageblatt,' was circulated stating that Great Britain had declared war against Germany. The immediate result of this news was the assemblage of an exceedingly excited and unruly mob before His Majesty's Embassy. The small force of police which had been sent to guard the embassy was soon overpowered and the attitude of the mob became more threatening. We took no notice of this demonstration as long as it was confined to noise; but when the crash of glass and the landing of cobble stones into the drawing-room where we were all sitting warned us that the situation was getting unpleasant, I telephoned to the Foreign Office an account of what was happening. Herr von Jagow at once informed the Chief of Police, and an adequate force of mounted police, sent with great promptness, very soon cleared the street. From that moment on, we were well-guarded and no more direct unpleasantness occurred.

After order had been restored, Herr von Jagow came to see me and expressed his most heartfelt regrets at what had occurred. He said that the behavior of his countrymen had made him feel more ashamed than he had words to express. It was an indelible stain on the reputation of Berlin. He said that the flying sheet circulated in the streets had not been authorized by the Government; in fact, the Chancellor had asked him by telephone whether he thought that such a statement should be issued and he had replied, 'Certainly not until the morning.' It was in consequence of his decision to that effect that only a small force of police had been sent to the neighborhood of the Embassy, as he had thought that the presence of a large force would inevitably attract attention and perhaps lead to disturbances. It was the 'pestilential 'Tageblatt,'' which had somehow got hold of the news that had upset his calculations. He had heard rumors that the mob had been excited to violence by gestures made and missiles thrown from the Embassy, but he felt sure that that was not true (I was able soon to assure him that the report had no foundation whatever), and even if it was, it was no excuse for the disgraceful scenes which had taken place. He feared that I would take home with me a sorry impression of Berlin's manners in moments of excitement. In fact, no apology could have been more full and complete.

On the following morning, the 5th August, the Emperor sent one of His Majesty's aides-de-camps to me with the following message:

> The Emperor has charged me to express to Your Excellency his regret for the occurrences of last night, but to tell you at the same time that you will gather from those occurrences an idea of the feelings of his people respecting the action of Great Britain...........His Majesty also begs that you will tell the King (George) that he has been proud of the titles of British Field-Marshal and British Admiral but that in consequence of what has occurred he must now, at once, divest himself of those titles.

I would add that the above message lost none of its petulant acerbity by the manner of its delivery.

On the other hand, I should like to state that I received all through this trying time nothing but courtesy at the hands of Herr von Jagow and the officials of the Imperial Foreign Office. At about 11 o'clock on the same morning, Count Wedel handed me my passports and told me that he had been instructed to confer with me as to the route which I should follow for my return to England. He said that he had understood that I preferred the route via the Hook of Holland to that via Copenhagen; they had therefore arranged that I should go by the former route, only I should have to wait till the following morning. I agreed to this and he said that I might be quite assured that there would be no repetition of the disgraceful scenes of the preceding night, as full precautions would be taken. He added that they were doing all in their power to have a restaurant car attached to the train, but it was rather a difficult matter. He also brought me a charming letter from Herr von Jagow couched in the most friendly terms. The day was passed in burning the ciphers and other confidential papers, in sealing up the archives with the help of the secretaries of the United States Embassy, and in packing up such articles as time allowed.

The night passed quietly without any incident. In the morning, a strong force of police was posted along the usual route to the Lehrter Station, while the Embassy was smuggled away in taxi-cabs to the station by side streets. We there suffered no molestation whatever and avoided the treatment meted out by the crowd to my Russian and French colleagues. Count Wedel met us at the station to say goodbye on behalf of Herr von Jagow and to see that all the arrangements ordered for our comfort had been properly carried out. A retired colonel of the Guards accompanied the train to the Dutch frontier and was exceedingly kind in his efforts to prevent the great crowds which thronged the platforms at every station where we stopped from insulting us. But beyond the yelling of patriotic songs, and a few jeers and insulting gestures, we had really nothing to complain of during our tedious journey to the Dutch frontier. [884]

---

[884] B.D. 671.

APPENDIX C

LICHNOWSKY VERSUS JAGOW

In 1916, Lichnowsky crafted a private memorandum blasting German diplomacy before and during the July Crisis. [885] He had two main criticisms. First, Germany's overwhelming reliance on her pact with Austria was destined to lead to disaster. Second, Berlin eschewed every peace proposal made during the crisis and consistently egged Vienna on. His latter reproach was not entirely fair. True, the Germans advised Austria to deal firmly with Serbia. But they honestly tried, though without sufficient vigor, to restrain her once things started to get out of control. Lichnowsky further contended that in July's final days, Berchtold "wanted to give way" and was prepared to "satisfy himself with the Serbian reply." [886] He was wrong. Berchtold never decided to "give way." He continually refused to modify Vienna's demands or to accept Belgrade's reply.

At any rate, Lichnowsky's memorandum made clear that he held his own country responsible for the war. On a more personal level, he accused his pre-war superiors of disregarding his advice, undercutting his efforts as ambassador, and making him the scapegoat for the break in German-British relations in August 1914.

---

[885] Karl Max Lichnowsky and Gottlieb von Jagow, *The Guilt of Germany for the War of German Aggression: Prince Karl Lichnowsky's Memorandum Being the Story of His Ambassadorship at London from 1912 to August 1914, Together with Foreign Minister Von Jagow's Reply* (New York: G.P. Putnam's Sons, 1918), 89.
[886] Ibid., 81.

Lichnowsky's document inadvertently became public. [887] Predictably, Berlin was infuriated by it and had Jagow craft a rebuttal. [888] Jagow essentially painted Lichnowsky as an egomaniac, a crybaby, and excessively pro-British. [889] He also suggested that Lichnowsky did not appreciate the need for alliances, the dangers of isolation, and Austria's strategic importance to Germany. [890] Indeed, in quoting Bismarck, he reemphasized the principle that guided Germany throughout July 1914: the need to preserve Austria at any price.

Excerpts of both treatises follow:

LICHNOWSKY: The rage of certain gentlemen over my success in London and the position I had achieved was indescribable. Schemes were set on foot to impede my carrying out my duties. I was left in complete ignorance of most important things, and I had to confine myself to sending in unimportant and dull reports. Secret reports from agents about things of which I could know nothing without spies and necessary funds were never available for me............

After my arrival (in London), I became convinced that in no circumstances need we fear a British attack or British support of a foreign attack, but that under all conditions England would protect

---

[887] Ibid., 90.

[888] Ibid.

[889] Some in Berlin had long suspected that Lichnowsky was under Grey's thumb. On June 27, 1914, Zimmermann commented on Lichnowsky's discussion with Grey regarding rumors of secret British agreements with France and Russia: "In this conference, as was to be expected, Lichnowsky was once again put completely into swaddling clothes by Grey, and allowed his conviction that he was dealing with an honorable and truth-loving statesman to be strengthened anew. There is nothing left to do but to give Lichnowsky some naturally very cautious hints concerning the secret but absolutely reliable reports we are getting from St. Petersburg, which permit no doubt at all to arise as to the existence of permanent political and military agreements between England and France or concerning the initiation already in progress of transactions between England and Russia directed towards similar results." G.D. 6, Zimmermann to Bethmann-Hollweg.

[890] Berchtold believed that Lichnowsky had an anti-Austrian bias. He told the Cabinet Council for Common Affairs on July 31: "Anything might sooner be expected from Prince Lichnowsky than that he would warmly represent our interests (in London)." Quoted in Geiss, *July 1914*, 320-21.

France. I advanced this opinion in repeated reports with detailed reasoning and insistence, but without gaining credence..............I repeatedly urged that England as a commercial State would suffer greatly in any war between the European great powers, and would therefore prevent such a war by all available means, but, on the other hand, in the interest of the European balance of power and to prevent Germany's overlordship would never tolerate the weakening or destruction of France. Lord Haldane told me this shortly after my arrival. All influential people spoke in the same way...............

I then received instructions (after Sarajevo) that I was to induce the English press to take up a friendly attitude if Austria gave the 'death blow' to the great Serbian movement, and so far as possible I was by my influence to prevent public opinion from opposing Austria...............(I) gave a warning against the whole project, which I described as adventurous and dangerous, and I advised that moderation should be recommended to the Austrians because I did not believe in the localization of the conflict. Herr von Jagow answered me that Russia was not ready; there would doubtless be a certain amount of bluster, but the more firmly we stood by Austria, the more would Russia draw back. He said that Austria was already accusing us of want of spirit, and that we should not squeeze her. On the other hand, feeling in Russia was becoming ever more anti-German, and so we must simply risk it. This attitude, as I learned later, was based upon reports from Count Pourtales to the effect that Russia would not move in any circumstances; these reports caused us to stimulate Count Berchtold to the greatest possible energy. Consequently, I hoped for salvation from an English mediation because I knew Sir Edward Grey's influence in (St. Petersburg) could be turned to use in favor of peace. So I used my friendly relations with Sir Edward Grey, and in confidence begged him to advise moderation in Russia if Austria, as it seemed, demanded satisfaction from the Serbs.

At first, the attitude of the English press was calm and friendly to the Austrians because the murder was condemned. But gradually more and more voices were heard to insist that, however necessary.................an exploitation of the crime for political purposes could not be justified. Austria was strongly urged to show moderation. When the ultimatum appeared, all the newspapers, with the exception of *The Standard,* which was always in low water and apparently was paid by the Austrians, were at one in their condemnation. The whole world, except in Berlin and Vienna, understood that it meant war, and indeed world war. The British fleet, which chanced to be assembled for a review, was not demobilized.

At first, I pressed for as conciliatory an answer as possible on the part of Serbia, since the attitude of the Russian Government left no further doubt of the seriousness of the situation. The Serbian reply was in accordance with British efforts; M. Pashitch had actually accepted everything except two points, about which he declared his readiness to negotiate. If Russia and England had wanted war in order to fall upon us, a hint to Belgrade would have been sufficient, and the unheard-of (ultimatum) would have remained unanswered Sir Edward Grey went through the Serbian reply with me, and pointed to the conciliatory attitude of the Government at Belgrade. We then discussed his mediation proposal, which was to arrange an interpretation of the two points acceptable to both parties.................(I)t would have been easy to find an acceptable form for the disputed points, which in the main concerned the participation of Austrian officials in the investigation at Belgrade. Given goodwill, everything could have been settled in one or two sittings, and the mere acceptance of the British proposal would have relieved the tension and would have further improved our relations with England. I urgently recommended the proposal, saying that otherwise, world war was imminent, in which we had everything to lose and nothing to gain. In vain! I was told that it was against the dignity of Austria, and that we did not want to interfere in the Serbian business, but left it to our ally. I was told to work for 'localization of the conflict.'

Of course, it would only have needed a hint from Berlin to make Count Berchtold satisfy himself with a diplomatic success and put up with the Serbian reply. But this hint was not given. On the contrary, we pressed for war. What a fine success it would have been.

After our refusal, Sir Edward asked us to come forward with a proposal of our own. We insisted upon war. I could get no other answer from Berlin than that it was an enormous 'concession' on the part of Austria to contemplate no annexation of territory. Thereupon Sir Edward justly pointed out that even without annexations of territory, a country can be humiliated and subjected, and that Russia would regard this as a humiliation which she would not stand. The impression became ever stronger that we desired war in all circumstances. Otherwise, our attitude in a question which, after all, did not directly concern us was unintelligible. The urgent appeals and definite declarations of M. Sazonov, later on the positively humble telegrams of the Tsar, the repeated proposals of Sir Edward, the warnings of San Giuliano................my urgent advice - it was all of no use, for Berlin went on insisting that Serbia must be massacred. The more I pressed, the less willing they were to alter their course, if only because I was not to have the success of saving peace in the company of Sir Edward Grey.

So, Grey on July 29 resolved upon his well-known warning. I replied that I had always reported that we should have to reckon upon English hostility if it came to war with France. The Minister said to me repeatedly: 'If war breaks out, it will be the greatest catastrophe the world has ever seen.' After that, events moved rapidly. When Count Berchtold, who hitherto had played the strong man on instructions from Berlin, at last decided to change his course, we answered the Russian mobilization - after Russia had for a whole week negotiated and waited in vain - with our ultimatum and declaration of war............

Up to the last moment, I had hoped for a waiting attitude on the part of England. My French colleague also felt himself by no means secure (about British intervention), as I learned from a private source. As late as August 1, the King (George) replied evasively to the French President. But in the telegram from Berlin which announced the threatening danger of war, England was already mentioned as an opponent. In Berlin, therefore, one already reckoned upon war with England.

Before my departure, Sir Edward Grey received me on August 5 at his house. I had gone there at his desire. He was deeply moved. He said to me that he would always be ready to mediate, and 'We don't want to crush Germany'...............Our departure was thoroughly dignified and calm...............A special train took us to Harwich, where a guard of honor was drawn up for me. I was treated like a departing sovereign. Thus ended my London mission. It was wrecked not by the perfidy of the British, but by the perfidy of our policy................

When now, after two years, I realize everything in retrospect, I say to myself that I realized too late that there was no place for me in a system which for years had lived only on tradition and routine, and which tolerates only representatives who report what one wants to read. Absence of prejudice and an independent judgment are combated, want of ability and of character are extolled and esteemed, but successes arouse hostility and uneasiness.

I had abandoned opposition to our mad Triple Alliance policy because I saw that it was useless and that my warnings were represented as Austrophobia................(A) policy which is based merely upon Austrians, Magyars, and Turks must end in hostility to Russia, and ultimately lead to a catastrophe...............(But) everything was still possible in July 1914................We should have (sent) to (St. Petersburg) a representative who, at any rate, reached the average standard of political ability, and we should have (given) Russia the certainty that we desired neither to dominate the Straits nor to throttle the Serbs............

We needed neither alliances nor wars, but merely treaties which would protect us and others, and which would guarantee us an economic development for which there had been no precedent in history. And if Russia had been relieved of trouble in the west, she would have been able to turn (her attention) to the east................We could also have approached the question of limitation of armaments, and should have had no further need to bother about the confusions of Austria. Austria-Hungary would then become the vassal of the German Empire - without an alliance, and, above all, without sentimental services on our part..............

I had to support in London a policy which I knew to be fallacious. I was punished for it, for it was a sin against the Holy Ghost.

On my arrival in Berlin (after war erupted), I saw at once that I was to be made the scapegoat for the catastrophe of which our Government had made itself guilty in opposition to my advice and my warnings. The report was persistently circulated by official quarters that I had let myself be deceived by Sir Edward Grey, because if he had not wanted war Russia would not have mobilized. Count Pourtales, whose reports could be relied upon, was to be spared, if only because of his family connections. He was said to have behaved 'splendidly,' and he was enthusiastically praised, while I was all the more sharply blamed............It was made out that the whole business was a perfidious British trick which I had not understood............

As appears from all official publications...........

1. We encouraged Count Berchtold to attack Serbia, although no German interest was involved, and the danger of a world war must have been known to us; whether we knew the text of the ultimatum is a question of complete indifference.

2. In the days between July 23 and July 30, 1914, when M. Sazonov emphatically declared that Russia could not tolerate an attack upon Serbia, we rejected the British proposals of mediation, although Serbia, under Russian and British pressure, had accepted almost the whole ultimatum, and although an agreement about the two points in question could easily have been reached, and Count Berchtold was even ready to satisfy himself with the Serbian reply.

3. On July 30, when Count Berchtold wanted to give way, we, without Austria having been attacked, replied to Russia's mere mobilization by sending an ultimatum to (St. Petersburg), and on July 31 we declared war on the Russians, although the Tsar had pledged his word that as long as negotiations continued not a man should march - so that we deliberately destroyed the possibility of a peaceful settlement. (*Note*: Lichnowsky's dates were incorrect. The ultimatum was sent on the 31st, the war declaration on August 1.)

In view of these indisputable facts, it is not surprising that the whole civilized world outside Germany attributes to us the sole guilt for the world war. [891]

JAGOW: Prince Lichnowsky, otherwise so susceptible to public opinion................saw everything only through his London spectacles. His charges against the attitude of the (German) Foreign Office are too untenable to be bothered with. I would only like to point out that Prince Lichnowsky was not left in ignorance regarding the 'most important things,' in so far as they were of value to his mission...........

---

[891] Lichnowsky and Jagow, *The Guilt of Germany*, 64-82.

That Austria-Hungary wished to proceed against the constant provocations stirred up by Russia that reached their climax in the outrage of Sarajevo, we had to recognize as justified. In spite of all the former settlements and avoidances of menacing conflicts, Russia did not abandon her policy, which aimed at the complete exclusion of the Austrian influence..................from the Balkans. The Russian agents, inspired by (St. Petersburg), continued their incitement. It was a question of the prestige and the existence of the Danube Monarchy. It must either put up with the Russo-Serbian machinations, or command a *quos ego,* even at the risk of a war. We could not leave our ally in the lurch. Had the intention been to exclude the *ultima ratio* of the war in general, the alliance should not have been concluded. Besides, it was plain that the Russian military preparations...................for which a France lusting for revenge had lent the money and which would have been completed in a few years, were directed principally against us. But despite all of this, despite the fact that the aggressive tendency of the Russian policy was becoming more evident from day to day, the idea of a preventive war was far removed from us. We only decided to declare war on Russia in the face of the Russian mobilization and to prevent a Russian invasion...............Lichnowsky pleaded for the abandonment of Austria. I replied, so far as I remember, that we, aside from our treaty obligation, could not sacrifice our ally for the uncertain friendship of England. If we abandoned our only reliable ally, later we would stand entirely isolated, face-to-face with the Entente............

We could not agree to the English proposal of a conference of Ambassadors, for it would doubtless have led to a serious diplomatic defeat. For Italy, too, was pro-Serb and, with her Balkan interests, stood rather opposed to Austria...............The best and only feasible way of escape was a localization of the conflict and an understanding between Vienna and (St. Petersburg). We worked toward that end with all our energy. That we 'insisted upon' the war is an unheard-of assertion which is sufficiently invalidated by the telegrams of His Majesty the Kaiser to the Tsar and to King George, published in the White Books; Prince Lichnowsky only cares to tell about 'the really humble telegram of the Tsar'..............

Objectively taken, the statements of Prince Lichnowsky present such an abundance of inaccuracies and distortions that it is hardly a wonder that his conclusions are also entirely wrong. The reproach that we sent an ultimatum on July 30 to (St. Petersburg) merely because of the mobilization of Russia and on July 31 declared war upon the Russians - although the Czar had pledged his word that not a man should march so long as negotiations were under way, thus willfully destroying the possibility of a peaceful adjustment - has really a grotesque effect. In concluding, the statement seems almost to identify itself with the standpoint of our enemies.

When the Ambassador makes the accusation that our policy identified itself 'with Turks and Austro-Magyars' and 'subjected itself to the viewpoints of Vienna and Budapest,' he may be suitably answered that he saw things only through London spectacles and from the narrow point of view of his desired rapprochement with England..............He also appears to have forgotten completely that the Entente was formed much more against us than against Austria.

I, too, pursued a policy which aimed at an understanding with England because I was of the opinion that this was the only way for us to escape from the unfavorable position in which we were placed by the unequal division of strength and the weakness of the Triple Alliance. But Russia and France insisted upon war. We were obligated through our treaty with Austria, and our position as a Great Power was also threatened.............But England, who was not allied in the same way with Russia and who had received far-reaching assurances from us regarding the sparing of France and Belgium, seized the sword.

In saying this, I by no means share the opinion prevalent among us today that England laid all the mines for the outbreak of the war; on the contrary, I believe in Sir Edward Grey's love of peace and in his earnest wish to arrive at an agreement with us. But he had allowed himself to become entangled too far in the net of the Franco-Russian policy; he no longer found the way out and he did not prevent the world war - something that he could have done. Neither was the war popular with the English people; Belgium had to serve as a battlefield.

'Political marriages for life and death' are, as Prince Lichnowsky says, not possible in international unions. But neither is isolation, under the present condition of affairs in Europe. The history of Europe consists of coalitions that sometimes have led to the avoidance of warlike outbreaks and sometimes to violent clashes. A loosening and dissolving of old alliances that no longer correspond to all conditions is only in order when new constellations are attainable. This was the object of the policy of a rapprochement with England. So long as this policy did not offer reliable guarantees, we could not abandon the old guarantees – even with their obligations.............

The personal attacks contained in (Lichnowsky's) work, the unheard-of calumnies and slanders of others condemn themselves. The ever-recurring suspicion that everything happened only because it was not desired to allow him – Lichnowsky – any successes, speaks of wounded self-love, of disappointed hopes for personal successes, and has a painful effect.

In closing, let us draw attention here to what Herman Oncken has also quoted in his work, *The Old and New Central Europe,* the memorandum of Prince Bismarck of the year 1879, in which the idea is developed that the German Empire must never dare allow a situation in which it would remain isolated on the European Continent between Russia and France, side by side with a defeated Austria-Hungary that had been left in the lurch by Germany. [892]

---

[892] Ibid., 114-17, 119-22.

APPENDIX D

BETHMANN-HOLLWEG'S AUGUST 1 STATEMENT

On August 1, Bethmann-Hollweg spoke before the Federal Council (consisting of officials from Germany's federated states) regarding the overall situation and the ultimatums to Russia and France:

"Contrary to our desire and despite all our efforts, unless God performs a miracle at the eleventh-hour, a crisis greater than ever was seen before is breaking upon the peace of Europe and Germany..............The Greater Serbia movement of many years' standing, the object of which is the undermining of the existence of Austria-Hungary, had found its expression in the crime of Sarajevo. It was not only the right, but the duty of Austria-Hungary to take steps against this movement............It is to our own interest that the Austro-Hungarian Monarchy be kept powerful, that it shall not succumb in the struggle with the southern Slavs...............Should the Austrian nation be destroyed, a blow would at the same time be struck at the roots of the German Empire................

The conflict which thereupon broke out between Austria and Serbia, we wished to localize. We supported this intention from the beginning, before all Cabinets. We were in agreement with all of them, with the exception of Russia, which declared from the beginning that it regarded it as impossible that Austria and Serbia should fight their fight out alone...............An understanding (with Russia) was being considered at Vienna yesterday...............(when) Russia mobilized her entire military forces on land and sea. Only two days before, the solemn assurance had been given us that absolutely no measures were being taken against us................A general mobilization we can only accept as a hostile act directed against us. It places us in a position from which we can escape only by action, unless we are willing to sacrifice our honor and our security. It is nothing less than a challenge, when mobilization is directed against us while we are engaged in mediation. Russia is attempting to so represent matters that no hostile action against us will be perceived in this mobilization. Should we commit ourselves to this view, we should be transgressing against the safety of our fatherland.

Germany has been watching with an astonishing, not to say an almost inexcusable, calmness the preparations for war in Russia and France, which, if they did not actually constitute mobilization themselves, were nevertheless calculated to expedite it tremendously. By so doing, we have become subject to the danger of losing the advantage of the start which lies in the possibility of the more rapid mobilization of our troops; we risked the danger of finding both on our eastern and western borders, within a short period of time, an army equipped for war and ready to strike; we no longer dared to remain inactive, unless Prussian territory in the east was to be occupied and, at the same time, the crown lands in the west, imperiled...............We attached to the ultimatum to Russia a very brief respite because our own safety did not permit of allowing a further postponement of military preparations.........

Germany has been working up to the last moment for the maintenance of peace.................But the provocation we have received from Russia is impossible for us to bear, if we are not to abdicate as one of the Great Powers of Europe............

We did not wish the war; it was forced upon us. The war will demand from the German people the most extreme sacrifice that has ever been demanded from them. We rely, however, on the help of God, as we did not bring about the war, but wished to prevent it, and will go bravely and determinedly into the struggle, which we must wage for the honor, the freedom, and the power of the German Empire." [893]

---

[893] G.D. 553.

After the federated governments approved war declarations against Russia and France should they become necessary, the chancellor concluded: "If the iron dice are now to be rolled, may God help us." [894]

For all the times in his address that Bethmann-Hollweg invoked God's name, it is tragic that the Almighty had not given him the strength to tell Austria to either accept the "Halt in Belgrade" formula or lose Germany's support.

[894] Ibid.

WORKS CITED

Albertini, Luigi. *The Origins of the War of 1914.* Vols. 2 and 3. 1952. Reprint. New York: Enigma Books, 2005.

Anderson, Frank Maloy, and Amos Shartle Hershey. *Handbook for the Diplomatic History of Europe, Asia, and Africa: 1870-1914.* Washington, DC: United States Government Printing Office, 1918.

Asquith, Herbert. *Memories and Reflections: 1852-1927.* Vol. 2. Boston: Little, Brown and Company, 1928.

Berghahn, V.R. *Germany and the Approach of War in 1914.* New York: St. Martin's Press, 1973.

Bethmann-Hollweg, Theobald von. *Reflections on the World War, Part 1.* London: Thornton Butterworth, 1920.

Brandenburg, Erich. "Conclusion: The Causes of the War." In *The Outbreak of the First World War: Who Was Responsible?* edited by Dwight Lee. Boston: D.C. Heath, 1963.

Bulow, Bernhard von. *Memoirs of Prince von Bulow.* Vol. 3. Boston: Little, Brown and Company, 1932.

Carnegie Endowment for International Peace. *Diplomatic Documents Relating to the Outbreak of the European War.* New York: Oxford University Press, 1916.

---. *Official German Documents Relating to the World War.* Vol. 1. New York: Oxford University Press, 1923.

---. *Outbreak of the World War: German Documents Collected by Karl Kautsky.* New York: Oxford University Press, 1924.

Churchill, Winston. *The World Crisis: 1911-1918.* 1931. Reprint, New York: Free Press, 2005.

Clark, Alan. *The Eastern Front, 1914-18: Suicide of the Empires.* 1971. Reprint, Gloucestershire: The Windrush Press, 1999.

Collected Diplomatic Documents Relating to the Outbreak of the European War. London: His Majesty's Stationary Office, 1915.

Cowles, Virginia. *The Kaiser.* New York: Harper and Row, 1963.

Czernin, Ottokar von. *In the World War.* 1919. Reprint, Charleston, SC: BiblioBazaar, 2007.

de Bussy, Carvel. *Count Stephen Tisza, Prime Minister of Hungary: Letters (1914–1916).* New York: Peter Lang, 1991.

Eyck, Erich. *Bismarck and the German Empire.* 1950. Reprint, New York: W.W. Norton and Company, 1968.

Fay, Sidney. *The Origins of the World War.* 2 vols. 2nd ed. New York: The Free Press, 1966.

Fischer, Fritz. *Germany's Aims in the First World War.* New York: W.W. Norton and Company, 1967.

Fromkin, David. *Europe's Last Summer: Who Started the Great War in 1914?* New York: Vintage Books, 2005.

Gauss, Christian. *The German Emperor as Shown in His Public Utterances.* New York: Charles Scribner's Sons, 1915.

Geiss, Imanuel, ed. *July 1914, The Outbreak of the First World War: Selected Documents.* New York: Charles Scribner's Sons, 1967.

Glaise-Horstenau, Edmund von. *The Collapse of the Austro-Hungarian Empire.* New York: E.P. Dutton and Co., 1930.

Gooch, G.P., and Harold Temperley, eds. *British Documents on the Origins of the War: 1898-1914*. Vol. 11. London: His Majesty's Stationary Office, 1926.

Grey, Edward. *Twenty-Five Years: 1892-1916*. 2 vols. New York: Frederick A. Stokes Company, 1925.

Hamilton, Richard, and Holger Herwig. *Decisions for War: 1914-1917*. Cambridge: Cambridge University Press, 2004.

Horne, Charles, ed. *Source Records of the Great War*. Vol. 1. 1923. Reprint, Indianapolis: American Legion, 1930.

Jarausch, Konrad. *The Enigmatic Chancellor: Bethmann-Hollweg and the Hubris of Imperial Germany*. New Haven, CT: Yale University Press, 1973.

Joffre, Joseph. *The Memoirs of Marshal Joffre*. Vol. 1. London: Geoffrey Bles, 1932.

Joll, James. *The Origins of the First World War*. 2nd ed. Essex: Pearson Longman, 1992.

Lafore, Laurence. *The Long Fuse: An Interpretation of the Origins of World War I*. Philadelphia: J.B. Lippincott Company, 1965.

Lichnowsky, Karl Max, and Gottlieb von Jagow. *The Guilt of Germany for the War of German Aggression: Prince Karl Lichnowsky's Memorandum Being the Story of His Ambassadorship at London from 1912 to August 1914, Together with Foreign Minister Von Jagow's Reply*. New York: G.P. Putnam's Sons, 1918.

Lloyd George, David. *War Memoirs of David Lloyd George*. Vol. 1. 2nd ed. London: Odhams Press, 1938.

Ludwig, Emil. *Wilhelm Hohenzollern: The Last of the Kaisers*. New York: G.P. Putnam's Sons, 1927.

Martel, Gordon. *The Origins of the First World War*. New York: Longman, 1987.

May, Arthur. *The Passing of the Habsburg Monarchy: 1914-1918.* Philadelphia: University of Pennsylvania Press, 1966.

Morton, Frederic. *Thunder at Twilight: Vienna 1913/1914.* New York: Collier Books, 1989.

Paleologue, Maurice. *An Ambassador's Memoirs: 1914-1917.* 1923. Reprint, London: Hutchinson & Co., 1973.

Ritter, Gerhard. *The Sword and the Scepter: The Problem of Militarism in Germany.* Vol. 2. 1965. Reprint, Coral Gables, FL: University of Miami Press, 1970.

Sazonov, Sergei. *Fateful Years, 1909-1916: The Reminiscences of Serge Sazonov.* 1928. Reprint, New York: Ishi Press International, 2008.

Scheer, Reinhard. *Germany's High Seas Fleet in the World War.* 1920. Reprint, Nashville, TN: Battery Press, 2002.

Schilling, M.F. *How the War Began in 1914, Being the Diary of the Russian Foreign Office.* London: George Allen and Unwin, 1925.

Schmitt, Bernadotte. *The Coming of the War, 1914.* Vol. 2. New York: Charles Scribner's Sons, 1930.

Shanafelt, Gary. *The Secret Enemy: Austria-Hungary and the German Alliance, 1914-1918.* Boulder, CO: East European Monographs, 1985.

Silberstein, Gerard. *The Troubled Alliance: German-Austrian Relations, 1914 to 1917.* Lexington, KY: University Press of Kentucky, 1970.

Snyder, Jack. *The Ideology of the Offensive: Military Decision Making and the Disasters of 1914.* Ithaca, NY: Cornell University Press, 1984.

Stubbs, Kevin. *Race to the Front: The Material Foundations of Coalition Strategy in the Great War*. Westport, CT: Praeger Publishers, 2002.

Thompson, Mark. *The White War: Life and Death on the Italian Front, 1915-1919*. New York: Basic Books, 2009.

Tirpitz, Alfred von. *My Memoirs*. Vol. 1. New York: Dodd, Mead and Company, 1919.

Tuchman, Barbara. *The Guns of August*. 1962. Reprint, New York: Ballantine Books, 1994.

Williamson, Jr., Samuel. "Aggressive and Defensive Aims of Political Elites? Austro-Hungarian Policy in 1914." In *An Improbable War? The Outbreak of World War I and European Political Culture before 1914*, edited by Holger Afflerbach and David Stevenson. New York: Berghahn Books, 2007.

Zeman, Z.A.B. *The Gentlemen Negotiators: A Diplomatic History of the First World War*. New York: The Macmillan Company, 1971.

Made in the USA
Monee, IL
07 July 2026

56551286R00193